Global Healthcare and the Supply Chain

Effective supply chain management (SCM) in healthcare significantly impacts various aspects, including cost reduction, improved patient care, and enhanced efficiency. By optimizing inventory, reducing waste, and streamlining processes, healthcare organizations can improve financial performance, ensure timely access to essential supplies, and ultimately deliver better patient outcomes.

SCM is essential for delivering high-quality care to improve patient experience. There is a large network of systems and processes that guarantee the delivery of medicines and supplies to healthcare institutions and patients. In addition, there are challenges to the supply chains such as disruptions, which force innovative strategies to mitigate negative consequences from these disruptions.

Ensuring that products end up with customers is an important objective for all businesses, but it is completely critical in healthcare. Lives depend on receiving supplies and medications on a timely basis. Collaboration and communications between all involved in the healthcare supply chain—suppliers, manufacturers, distributors, healthcare institutions, clinicians—facilitate this movement of goods, services, and information. Only then will hospitals and other healthcare institutions meet patient needs.

This book addresses many of the disruptors and delays experienced in the supply chain including regulatory compliance, fluctuating demand, systems' complexity, and visibility. The author also addresses how artificial intelligence (AI) is changing the supply chain as well as how digitalization has generated benefits and deliverables. The author shares his experience to examine the operational, regulatory, and strategic aspects in healthcare SCM as well as a look into the future and what is shaping the industry.

Stuart Rosenberg is an accomplished supply chain management professional with a number of years of experience using outstanding communication and leadership skills to coach, mentor, and motivate professionals in challenging environments. As the president and chief consultant of First Choice Supply Chain, his reputation as a savvy supply chain leader is beyond reproach for delivering resourceful business strategies and customer focused solutions. His work with several multi-national corporations—Johnson & Johnson, Cadbury, Reckitt Benckiser, and Linde Gas—and his far-reaching experience in launching, managing, and mentoring new programs and strategies resulted in greater customer confidence and improved business results. Stuart is a Professor of Supply Chain at Middlesex College. He sits on two advisory committees—one at Seton Hall University's Stillman School of Business and the other at Middlesex College's Faculty Development Committee. Stuart is also the author of three supply chain books, with a fourth one to be released in 2026.

Global Healthcare and the Supply Chain

Revolutionizing Healthcare, One Patient at a Time

Stuart Rosenberg

Routledge
Taylor & Francis Group
A PRODUCTIVITY PRESS BOOK

Designed cover image: Shutterstock

First published 2026
by Routledge
605 Third Avenue, New York, NY 10158

and by Routledge
4 Park Square, Milton Park, Abingdon, Oxon, OX14 4RN

Routledge is an imprint of the Taylor & Francis Group, an informa business

ISBN: 978-1-041-13232-5 (hbk)
ISBN: 978-1-041-13230-1 (pbk)
ISBN: 978-1-003-66873-2 (ebk)

DOI: 10.4324/9781003668732

Typeset in Garamond
by Apex CoVantage, LLC

Contents

Prologue: How Medical Innovations of Preceding Centuries Affected Modern Healthcare Supply Chain

In the complex world of modern healthcare, the supply chain often operates behind the scenes—a hidden influence that ensures the seamless delivery of care to millions. Its influence is far-reaching as it is touching upon every aspect of patient treatment—from the availability of critical medical supplies to the competence of surgical procedures to the patient well-being.

This book aims to enlighten its readers on the vital role the supply chain plays in the healthcare industry. It is an exploration of how strategic supply chain management (SCM) can lead to improved patient outcomes, cost savings, and overall operational effectiveness. In an era where healthcare demands are ever-increasing, the need for a robust and resilient supply chain has never been more critical.

The exploration will uncover the complexities and challenges faced by healthcare supply chain professionals and the innovative solutions and strategies they employ. From the use of cutting-edge technology to the importance of ethical and sustainable sourcing, we will delve into the multifaceted world of healthcare SCM.

Whether you are a healthcare professional, a supply chain expert, or simply someone interested in the behind-the-scenes workings of the healthcare system, this book will provide you with valuable insights and practical knowledge.

Introduction

Coordinated, Efficient, Cost-Effective, Goal-Oriented, Accessible, Affordable

A complex network that handles the purchasing, distribution, and management of essential medical supplies, tools, and resources is at the core of healthcare delivery. Healthcare providers may experience disruptions and delays as a result of this complex web's ongoing struggles to ensure the smooth flow of essential commodities. There are a number of significant challenges facing all healthcare providers and their ability to deliver quality healthcare to patients. The following are some of those challenges:

1. Visibility: The healthcare supply chain involves a host of stakeholders, from manufacturers and distributors to healthcare facilities to clinicians, which leads to complex procedures and potential inefficiencies from a lack of coordination. Healthcare supply chains may strengthen their resilience by recognizing and proactively resolving these issues, providing a constant and consistent delivery of medical supplies to patients at the time of greatest need.
2. Regulatory Compliance: Due to the constant shift of government regulations and laws such as Obamacare and Health Insurance Portability and Accountability Act (HIPAA) laws, the nature of patient care, emergency situations. These ever-evolving patterns are unpredictable and increase difficulty in maintaining the best medical practices.
3. Fluctuating Demand: The healthcare industry's attention to strict rules and quality standards adds a layer of complication to the supply chain and careful management of resources and supplies. An overabundance of supplies can lead to obsolescence and waste.
4. Systems Complexity: An unclear picture of inventory levels, poor distribution networks, and supplier inability to deliver provides a broken supply chain line. It can be difficult to coordinate various parties so that supplies flow smoothly, especially in emergency situations where quick access to essential supplies is essential.

The need to improve healthcare supply chain has been highlighted by the rise of pandemics. Personal protective equipment (PPE) supply constraints were the most obvious effect of these pandemics on healthcare supply chains. As hospitals struggled financially as a result of fewer elective surgical procedures and higher clinical staff costs, the pandemic sent supply costs surging. The unexpected increase in medical supply demand and the unforeseen interruptions in global logistics highlighted the importance of adaptable and flexible supply chains. During times of emergencies, the capacity to quickly reallocate resources, adjust inventory levels, and establish partnerships with new supply-chain partners has become crucial.

Control and visibility are two essential elements of a successful healthcare SCM system. In order for any and all healthcare providers or institutions to make informed choices to improve treatment and lower costs, there is a need for reliable and complete data on supply status—from the time of product purchase through its use on a patient. Healthcare firms may accurately estimate future needs, analyze previous demand patterns, and adjust inventory levels by utilizing advanced analytics. Providers are better able to make informed decisions, reduce waste, and guarantee the timely availability of essential resources, thanks to the integration of data-driven insights.

The healthcare industry's supply chain produces a lot of waste materials. According to the American Hospital Association (AHA), the "majority of the materials collected by a hospital end up being waste". The discarded materials are never even used. In today's SCM, taking sustainability and the environment into account is vital, especially when using technological breakthroughs. Eco-friendly methods are incorporated into operations for long-term advantages for enterprises and society at large. They also correspond with ethical and environmental principles.

Challenges in the field of healthcare supply chains are more than just obstacles. They act as drivers for change and expansion. Modern technology such as data analysis and artificial intelligence (AI) is a sign of progress as we set out to overcome healthcare and supply chain obstacles.

It is our hope for a future where supply chains are resilient in the face of upheavals, patient care is unwavering, and healthcare delivery reaches new levels, thanks to the cutting-edge technologies.

Abstract

The healthcare supply chain offers a worldwide view and strategic context for SCM in healthcare. It addresses tangible strategies for risk management, partnerships, logistics, performance assessment, and information technology, just to name a few of many aspects in healthcare. Readers will gain an all-inclusive understanding of the issues facing the global healthcare supply chain and the opportunities we will need to look at for the future. This impactful book exposes the complexities within the supply chain field and the healthcare system.

The healthcare industry is ever-changing, and the role of the supply chain is shifting in response. All types of healthcare institutions and clinicians are collaborating more closely than ever before with supply chain leaders. This swing in focus introduces new opportunities and challenges at the level of healthcare quality delivery. The role of supply chain in protecting the social determinants of health—food, transportation, critical-health-related products—is rapidly expanding. This is true in historically underserved populations. The work will take an approach as to the needs of people and organizations. The following four objectives are the basic guidelines to improve both economic and health outcomes.

1. Gain the understanding you need to work toward building a mature supply chain organization
2. Develop perspectives on how the needs of the healthcare supply chain are shifting in the modern era
3. Holistically assess supply chain performance and improve clinical, financial, and operational outcomes
4. Identify opportunities to generate value, improve alliances, and cut costs

The adaptability and effectiveness of supply chains are essential in the complex world of modern-day healthcare to guarantee timely, efficient, and quality patient treatment. Despite its many difficulties, the field of medical healthcare, which includes logistics within the scope of SCM, offers a blank canvas for creativity and progress. This work will delve into the complexities of medical supply chain issues, including such present-day technological issues of data analysis and artificial intelligence (AI). The fundamental premise guiding us is where healthcare and supply chains are successful interacting, and obstacles are tackled with confidence.

This book will be of interest to graduate students in the health sector and supply chain programs, as well as to working clinicians, health sector managers, and supply chain leaders.

THE EVOLUTION OF THE HEALTHCARE SUPPLY CHAIN

1

This work is not meant to be a history of healthcare. Thus, the title will be limited to the last 15 years of the healthcare industry. Within these last 15 years, as seen in Figure 0.1, we will see the vast changes that have taken place and are more to come.

The healthcare supply chain industry has come a long way in a relatively short time. Just a few decades ago, hospitals managed supplies manually with pen and paper. Today, technology drives healthcare inventory management, providing real-time visibility into medical resources. However, the supply chain industry still faces obstacles. There are shortages, waste, and inefficiencies. However, in spite of new health threats which always introduce uncertainties, there are innovative solutions transforming healthcare supply chain operations. New technologies can optimize the hospital supply chain to improve community health.

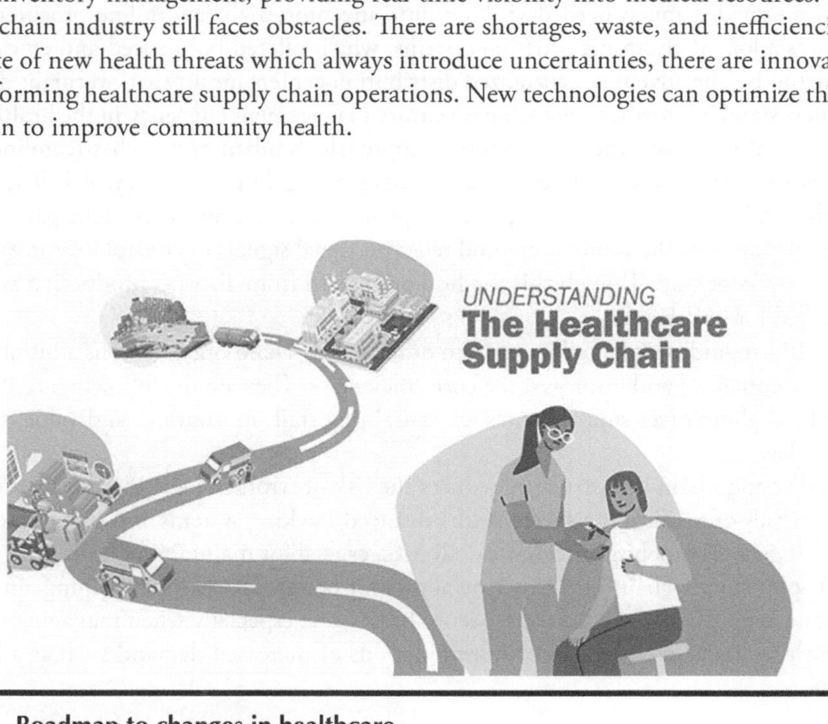

Figure 0.1 Roadmap to changes in healthcare.

DOI: 10.4324/9781003668732-1

Healthcare is a complex and many-sided industry that requires a series of interconnected systems to function efficiently. One of these key systems is the healthcare supply chain industry. It comprises a network of resources and processes that coordinate and manage the transportation of goods and services from manufacturers and suppliers to healthcare providers. These goods range from pharmaceutical products and medical devices to general hospital supplies and provider services. The healthcare supply chain, a critical component of healthcare operations, consists of several closely interlinked elements, each playing a significant role in the delivery of quality care.

In the 1980s and 1990s, supply chain strategy focused on "just-in-time" (JIT) delivery and Lean processes to eliminate waste. Reducing inventory improved efficiency. However, it also increased fragility. Hospitals lacked safeguards when demand increased. Disruptions led to shortages, impacting patient care. The most recent pandemic highlighted these healthcare supply chain vulnerabilities. Since adopting the JIT delivery strategy, healthcare institutions, including hospitals, have continuously pursued optimizing and enhancing this complex process.

In the past, healthcare supply chain management (SCM) was centralized. Manufacturers shipped products to distributors, who supplied to hospitals. This model was inflexible as it relied on paper tracking. Hospitals lacked the information to anticipate and respond to shortages when they arose. With little coordination between the parties involved, inefficiencies rose. Excess and expired supplies were wasted. Staff spent hours on manual inventory counts. Despite the advancements in managing healthcare supply chains, one challenge still remained: *rising costs*. Increasing prices of medical equipment and supplies, along with budget constraints, forced a constant pressure on improving cost-effectiveness in healthcare.

Several new technologies and methodologies created a new way of controlling hospital inventories and thus costs. They were bar-coding, RFID or Radio Frequency Identification Tags, and kanban system. The advent of barcode scanning and Radio Frequency Identification (RFID) tracking technologies provided much-needed visibility into inventories. To streamline procurement, many organizations adopted electronic ordering systems, which offered both speed and efficacy over traditional methods. The advent of centralized distribution centers meant that overnight deliveries became the new standard, further enhancing inventory management efficiency in the healthcare sector.

This methodology uses the JIT inventory approach. Kanban approach streamlines and simplifies ordering and storing supplies, reducing costs and greater efficiency. All of these benefits enhance the healthcare institution's capacity to provide effective and consistent patient care. In a Lean inventory system, the Kanban method relies on visual signals to control inventory movement and prevent overstocking. Though this method originated from Toyota's production system, it has been modified for healthcare.

The healthcare industry has adopted from other supply chain organizations a number of methods that have enhanced and improved the cost-efficiencies. They are the following: resiliency, localizing suppliers, alternatives supply routes, cross-training staff, innovation, and value. Each will be discussed below.

A sound supply chain infrastructure reduces the risk of errors in logistics such as wrong deliveries or late arrivals of medical materials. With advanced tracking systems and streamlined transport operations, it ensures timely and accurate deliveries, crucial for maintaining healthcare service consistency. A solid supply chain infrastructure allows for better forecasting, planning, and managing demand variations. This is an essential aspect of healthcare, especially when managing the distribution of sensitive items like vaccines or during periods of increased demand such as a health crisis or epidemic.

Reducing dependence on international suppliers, healthcare systems are better equipped to maintain operations and patient care standards in the face of geopolitical, economic, or logistical turbulence that might otherwise compromise the availability of supplies from overseas. This type of system significantly reduces risk by concentrating on local suppliers and the production of vital hospital supplies. In addition to localized production of healthcare supplies, *investing in establishing alternate supply routes* contributes to maintaining an uninterrupted supply. This building of infrastructure ensures that the healthcare supply chain has multiple sourcing options to rely on. This "new network" of transportation will increase continuity and advance resiliency in unpredictable situations.

The resourcefulness of a healthcare supply chain is significantly increased when employees are *cross-trained*. The supply chain gains flexibility by arming staff with diverse skills to handle various roles. Even when disruptions impede some procedures, employees can fill in the gaps. Of course, this cross-training is limited to non-clinician roles.

In its enthusiastic effort to improve the quality of care, the healthcare industry is slowly but steadfastly moving away from volume-based approaches toward a more value-centric perspective—responding or reaction to patients' illness to preventative approach.

Over the last 15 years, there have only been five major changes to healthcare. But they have been significant. These five changes will show how healthcare supply chains have evolved, and the industry has changed.

Over the past 15 years, things have evolved. The best indication of this is the title chief supply chain officer from being nearly zero in 2009 to now accounting for 34% of the titles of top leaders in the healthcare supply chain. Another example is the growth beyond sourcing of mostly medical surgical products to an increased focus on clinical alignment, sourcing, logistics, risk, and analytics.

In 2009, the size of the health systems in our ranking was all under $10 billion. Moving to the present, 50% of the 27 health systems are above $10 billion. Many are multistate organizations with $20 billion or more in operating expenses. Governance and span-of-control have taken center stage. Size of the company has grown and so have the areas under supply chain influence to include listening to end users, setting specifications, sourcing, delivering, and holding the organization accountable. Healthcare institutions show that their supply chain represents 36% of the operating expense of a health system.

Back in 2009, risk and resiliency in healthcare were a binder on a shelf providing guidance on a local weather event. By 2018, disruptions primarily caused to manufacturers in Puerto Rico from Hurricane Maria accelerated leaders in the industry, and the pandemic cemented the need for maturation. A recent research project with Healthcare Industry Resilience Collaborative (HIRC) shows that 56% of the health systems polled have independent risk and resiliency teams. Risk management is a major priority for investment for this industry.

Digital supply chain seemed like a distant occurrence in 2009. Of course, that is no longer the case now. The original concepts of "timely accurate data" and "aligned metrics" in 2009 transformed into digitalization and utilization analytics in 2023. These are big ideas to capture in a few phrases. But the progress has been irreversible, with the advent of digital supply chain leaders and control-tower technology all taking on growing importance. Digitalization has become a top-tier area of investment for the Chief Supply Chain Officers.

Environmental, social, and governance (ESG) concerns have become a growing focus in the healthcare industry. The main focus of ESG in this industry is the impact it has on human health and well-being. Providers, payers, and pharmaceutical companies have embraced ESG in caring for

Figure 0.2 Global healthcare and the supply chain.

patients, creating new medications, medical equipment, and vaccines to improve our well-being and save lives.

The healthcare supply chain (see Figure 0.2) has made huge strides, from pen and paper to artificial intelligence (AI)-driven technology. However, there is further opportunity to build strategic resilience, enable care coordination, provide visibility, eliminate waste, and contain costs through healthcare supply chain improvements. Solutions are emerging to strengthen healthcare logistics. With clinicians leading the way, innovative supply chain strategies can deliver better care, thriving communities, and a brighter future for health.

Chapter 1

Understanding the Healthcare Supply Chain System

The healthcare industry supply chain system flows behind the scenes in most healthcare institutions. No one notices it's even there until the flow of needed supplies is interrupted or stalled. The risks in this interruption can be high. For instance, when a clinician does not have the necessary medical or surgical supplies they need to deliver patient care, and treatment is delayed. On top of the clinical impacts, the costs of the healthcare industry supply chain are astounding and show no signs of bottoming out in the near future.

The evolution of the healthcare supply chain over the past 20 years has been substantial, driven by technological advances, regulatory changes, and shifts in healthcare practices. The pace of advancement grows even more rapid in the face of cost and quality pressures resulting in a more complex, technology-driven, and globally interconnected system. This evolution has brought about efficiency improvements and cost savings, but new challenges and dangers have risen.

Some of these developments are the following:

- **Technology Integration**: The integration of information technology systems, including enterprise resource planning (ERP) systems, electronic health records (EHRs), and supply chain management (SCM) software, has revolutionized how inventory is tracked and managed. Automation and digital data capture have greatly increased efficiency and accuracy.
- **Globalization**: The supply chain has become increasingly global, with pharmaceuticals, medical devices, and supplies being sourced from around the world. This has not only led to more diverse supply sources but also introduced complexity and risks related to global logistics and geopolitical factors.
- **Regulatory Changes**: There has been a significant increase in regulatory oversight to ensure the safety and quality of medical products. Both the U.S. Food and Drug Administration (FDA) and European Commission continue to strengthen regulations aimed at MedTech manufacturer quality management (e.g., the FDA's proposed amendment to its Medical Device Quality System (QS) Regulation and the EU's amended Medical Device Regulation (MDR)).

DOI: 10.4324/9781003668732-2

- **JIT Inventory Practices**: The shift from bulk stockpiling to JIT inventory practices has helped reduce costs and minimize waste. However, it has also made the supply chain more vulnerable to disruptions, as seen during the COVID-19 pandemic. Supply chain leaders struggle to find a middle ground that offers resiliency without added expense.
- **Increased Focus on Cost Management**: Cost management in the supply chain has grown more complex in the value-based payment environment. The focus has shifted from purchasing items with the lowest price tags to determining how products impact overall care delivery costs and quality, for example, determining whether a product plays a role in costly infections, longer hospital length of stay (LOS), or readmissions not covered by payers.
- **Advances in Logistics and Distribution**: Innovations in transportation and logistics, including real-time tracking and improved distribution methods, have enhanced the efficiency and reliability of supply deliveries. The growing trend of consolidated service centers (CSCs), where health systems buy items in bulk, store them in their own warehouses, and distribute them to their care sites, contrasts with traditional distribution channels.
- **Risk Management and Resilience**: Ongoing supply chain disruptions and supply shortages have underscored the importance of having resilient supply chains capable of responding to crises. This has led to more emphasis on risk assessment and contingency planning.
- **Sustainability and Ethical Sourcing**: There's been an increasing focus on environmental sustainability and ethical sourcing practices within the supply chain, reflecting broader societal concerns.
- **Personalized Medicine and Specialized Products**: Advances in medical technology, including personalized medicine and biologics, have created new challenges for the supply chain, requiring more specialized handling and distribution processes.
- **Non-Acute Care Expansion**: As health systems and hospitals shift more care from acute to non-acute settings to reduce costs, the healthcare supply chain grows longer and more complex. Healthcare supply chain leaders are increasingly being called upon to equip clinicians and patients with equipment and supplies in areas far beyond the reach of traditional hospital logistics—all the way through to patient homes.

Regulatory agencies, health system leaders, healthcare providers, patients, and other stakeholders recognize the importance of SCM in healthcare and quality patient care, given the recent shortages in critical supplies and the impact on healthcare services. For the leaders of healthcare organizations, increasing pressure to control supply chain costs, eliminate unnecessary spending, and improve efficiency must be balanced with delivering high-quality care for optimal patient outcomes. Our understanding of the healthcare supply chain would be difficult if we did not try to connect all the dots—understanding of the system is tied to several key functions.

SCM in healthcare is of overriding importance as it ensures the seamless flow of medical products and services, ultimately influencing patient care and overall system efficiency. An effective healthcare supply chain facilitates timely access to critical items such as medications, medical devices, and vaccines, preventing shortages and optimizing inventory levels. Efficient supply chain practices contribute to cost containment, enabling healthcare institutions to allocate resources strategically. Strong SCM enhances visibility, enabling quick response to changes in demand or disruptions. In the healthcare sector, where patient outcomes hinge on timely and accurate delivery of products, an optimized supply chain not only improves operational effectiveness but also plays a vital role in enhancing patient safety and well-being. The key functions—sourcing, procurement, inventory management, distribution, logistics, regulatory compliance, technology integration, and quality assurance—are of the utmost importance unto themselves, but we must never forget their interconnected relationship that should not be broken. In this chapter, I have only highlighted the importance of the key functions. However, due to their interconnected relationship to the entire healthcare supply chain, I believe a separate chapter for each is required to fully understand their impact.

Chapter 2

Procurement Strategies in the Healthcare Industry

Healthcare procurement refers to the healthcare supply chain process that allows medical industry professionals to identify, select, and acquire the materials, products, and services required to accommodate their current needs. The process is divided into two categories: direct procurement and indirect procurement. Direct procurement involves sourcing and acquiring what is needed for patient diagnosis and treatment operations, while indirect procurement involves sourcing and acquiring what is needed for administration activities and housekeeping. By establishing and managing a solid supply chain, the procurement team is better able to ensure that they can source and acquire the products and services they need when they need them.

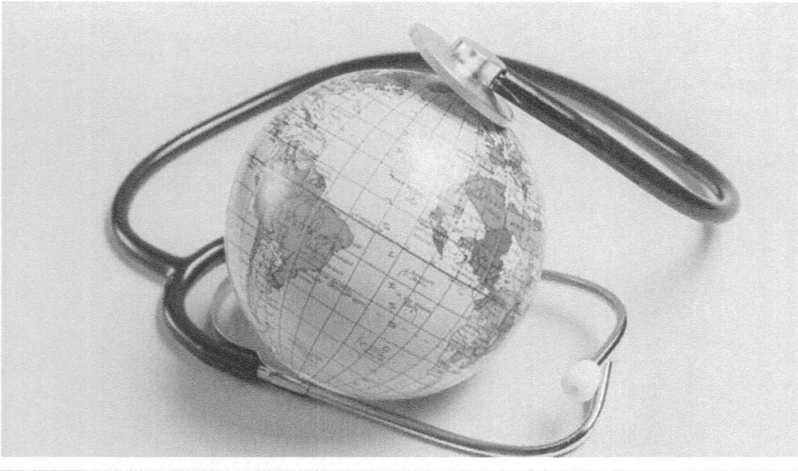

Figure 2.1 This picture of the globe depicts today's global sourcing and procurement of vital medical supplies.

DOI: 10.4324/9781003668732-3

As in Figure 2.1, the complex issues that stand in the way of successful procurement in the medical industry are the following:

- **Outdated technology.** Many healthcare facilities rely on inventory tracking and management systems that are old or outdated, which can lead to significant inefficiencies or errors in procurement operations.
- **Provider/personnel preference bias.** Some healthcare organizations take into account requests and preferences from providers and personnel when managing procurement. As a result, they must contend with unknown product/service costs.
- **Variable product/service costs.** Custom products and services, which are often required for highly specific or unique applications, come at a higher cost than standard solutions.
- **Supply shortages.** Product shortages are common in the medical device industry. When they occur, healthcare organizations are often forced to satisfy themselves with more expensive or less effective alternatives. One method of avoiding them is maintaining a backup product inventory, but this carries a greater risk of products expiring and a larger inventory management cost.
- **Hidden costs.** The total cost of inventory encompasses more than the purchasing price. It also includes the cost of shipping and storage. Additionally, any excess supplies that expire reduce the overall cost-efficiency of the healthcare facility.

By establishing a strategy that helps them navigate the challenges of procurement, medical organizations can better develop and manage their supply chains. The four steps to creating this strategy are:

- **Data Gathering.** When a medical sales representative approaches a healthcare facility, they typically have all of the information they need to close a sale, such as product datasheets, studies and white papers, material safety data sheets (MSDS) documents, pricing plans, and supplier contact information. This gathered information helps the facility's value analysis team (VAT)—that is, the procurement team—evaluate whether the product/service solution fulfills their clinical needs.
- **Negotiating.** The primary goals of healthcare facilities are satisfying their physicians, patients, and bottom lines. As a result, the product/service solutions they invest in must meet the needs of their personnel and patients at a competitive price. Procurement professionals should evaluate how a particular solution stands up to alternative solutions with regard to effectiveness and price point. If needed, they can negotiate with suppliers to achieve a better rate.
- **Testing and Trialing.** Setting up test and trial periods allows healthcare facilities to try out a product or service and see whether personnel and/or patients like it.
- **Resolving.** After evaluating the product/service information presented by a sales representative, pricing plans, and data gathered from the test/trial periods, the healthcare facility's procurement team should be able to determine whether the product/service meets their clinical and financial needs. If it does, they can allocate budget funds toward investing in it.

During and after any health crisis, disruptions within the supply chain have a significant impact on healthcare provisions.

As risk management and resiliency became central components to the survival of supply chains, procurement strategies in healthcare had to be redesigned to meet the needs of suppliers and consumers alike. The unprecedented demand for health crisis equipment, cleaning supplies, tests kits, and vaccines meant the focus of procurement in healthcare could no longer be on cost reduction. Instead, the manufacturing and supply of essential healthcare products had to be about increasing efficiency, reducing waste, and aligning with global healthcare needs.

We explore how healthcare companies altered their procurement strategies in recent years, in order to better serve their customers. The demand for responsible global sourcing in healthcare procurement has increased tenfold.

As with all healthcare crisis, people across the world have become more health conscious. Along with the digital transformation of the supply chain and the development of e-commerce, this meant the healthcare industry had to improve its customer value, as well as maintain profitability. Healthcare companies have made great strides to deliver responsive service to customers. By targeting efficiencies and customer satisfaction as top objectives the commitment to an improved supply chain is indeed noticeable.

With the increasing emphasis on localization as a key aspect of sustainable procurement, companies are aiming to reduce their environmental impact by manufacturing goods locally. This means healthcare products can be distributed and used in the regions where they are needed, rather than being shipped and potentially wasted around the world. Having access to reliable local suppliers also offers consumers better procurement security and product quality, making stakeholders more likely to invest in the development of local healthcare services and products.

This is all part of a new type of procurement in healthcare, which is called value-based procurement. This new type of procurement promises to improve operational productivity and patient experiences as it cuts out wasted time, especially waiting time for medical appointments and products. This reduction of waste also lessens the environmental impact of procurement in healthcare.

Healthcare companies are starting to use their procurement team's know-how and supplier diversity to purchase and provide the highest quality products to consumers around the world. From the standardization of goods to building better relationships between suppliers and consumers, procurement departments in healthcare companies are on the right track to supporting the development of more resilient, sustainable, and ethical supply chains.

Chapter 3

Streamlining Healthcare Supply Chain Inventory

For healthcare providers, whether it is hospitals or clinicians, it is not just about having enough stock on hand but also ensuring that the right items are available when and where they are needed. This is a delicate balancing act of maintaining the correct inventory levels, tied to the urgency and healthcare settings. Supply chain managers must navigate these complexities effectively to prevent detrimental impacts on patient care and institutional budgets.

A solid understanding of supply chain principles serves as the foundation for efficient healthcare inventory management. To cultivate this knowledge, training should be provided in several key areas of the healthcare supply chain. Included in this training should be not only inventory employees but also medical institutions' health equity officers and chief supply chain officers. This training should be required in several important areas:

- **Inventory Control Principles:** Hospital inventory managers must understand inventory control principles such as demand forecasting, safety stock calculations, and reorder point planning.
- **Latest Technology:** The rapidly evolving SCM technology landscape requires constant learning and up-skilling. Training should be allocated to best utilize inventory management software systems, barcoding technologies, and automated storeroom solutions.
- **Regulation Compliance:** The healthcare industry is highly regulated. Staff must be trained in maintaining compliance, from adhering to strict storage rules for certain items to ensuring that paperwork for controlled substances is properly completed and filed.
- **Data Analysis:** In the era of Big Data, proficiency in analyzing and interpreting healthcare supply chain data is essential. Staff should be trained in basic statistical analysis, data visualization, and how to extract actionable insights from large datasets.

After this training is completed, effective supply chain professionals can identify inefficiencies in processes and devise solutions to improve them. An open dialogue about process improvement should be encouraged, and staff should be empowered to suggest and implement changes.

DOI: 10.4324/9781003668732-4

Inventory management holds a crucial role in the field of healthcare. It directly influences the quality of patient care, financial stability, and efficiency of healthcare facilities. A supply chain manager at a hospital will tell you that one can never stress enough the importance of having the right supplies in the right quantities, at the right locations, at the right time. Poor inventory management can lead to critical shortages, waste through expiration, or an increase in costs as a result of overstocking.

An effective inventory management system can radically *reduce costs* for a healthcare facility. According to a report by Paul Walsh, VP of Cardinal Health, hospitals could potentially save up to $25 billion annually just through improved SCM and inventory control and these improvement processes as given below.

- **Reducing Overstock:** Overstocking is a costly mistake. Not only does it tie up capital, but it also leads to waste if items expire before they can be used. Effective inventory management strategies can greatly eliminate overstocking.
- **Minimizing Shortages:** On the other side of the spectrum, product shortages can compromise patient care and lead to financial losses. Accurate forecasting can help hospitals anticipate demand and avoid shortages.
- **Optimizing Ordering:** By strategically scheduling orders, hospitals can minimize delivery costs and avoid emergency purchases, which are usually more expensive.
- **Improving Performance:** A well-managed inventory flows smoothly, increasing operational efficiency and improving patient outcomes.

The healthcare industry, in particular, hospitals and surgi-care institutions, has developed a host of best practices to manage inventory efficiently. These range from utilizing technology like automation and data analytics to adopting Lean management techniques. Here are some methodologies to consider for a more efficient inventory management system in healthcare surroundings:

- Invest in an Advanced Inventory Management System: These systems, often equipped with machine learning capabilities, significantly streamline inventory processes by predicting demand, automating reordering, and providing real-time stock levels.
- Regularly Audit Your Inventory: Regular audits ensure that no inaccuracies go unnoticed. They also help in identifying trends such as frequently out-of-stock items or areas of wastage.
- Implement JIT Purchasing: JIT purchasing means ordering supplies as needed rather than in large quantities ahead of time. This approach minimizes storage costs and reduces the possibility of obsolete or expired items.
- Effective Vendor Relationships: Whether negotiating better prices or asking for expedited delivery, a strong relationship with your vendors is crucial. Maintain open lines of communication to understand how their capabilities can best meet your inventory needs.
- Employee Training: As the backbone of the inventory management process, trained and competent staff are essential. They should understand all aspects of the inventory management process—from procurement to storage, right to the point of usage. Regular training sessions that keep up with the latest best practices can significantly improve inventory management.
- Sustainability Practices: Given the growing emphasis on the environment and responsible use of resources, the importance of sustainability in healthcare supply chain practices has roared to the forefront. Organizations are encouraged to use recycling and minimizing energy consumption in storage areas.

- Data Decision-Making: In an efficient healthcare environment, decisions are not made on guesses or gut feelings. Utilize the power of data analytics to make informed decisions about inventory levels, stock reordering, and supplier performance.

Due to the critical nature of patient healthcare, medical inventory needs to be available upon demand. This requires the hospital to have accurate knowledge of current stock levels, right down to the location of specific items. Gaining such a detailed summary of the hospital's inventory is not as simple as it sounds. It's not just the stock items themselves that need to be visible but all of the associated data too.

Managing inventory is:

- a critical process that underscores the delivery of quality patient care
- one of the largest budget areas for the hospital
- a major contributor to the organization's commercial success

Although hospital inventory management systems need to be vigorous, they also have to be flexible. With lives at stake, inventory management deserves a high-level priority. It is a complex and cross-organizational issue. Inventory may have the operating room at its core, but there are key fringe functions involved in total hospital care.

Chapter 4

Healthcare Distribution: Growth and Challenges

The healthcare industry is constantly evolving, with new technologies, treatments, and regulations being introduced every day. Thus, the demand for efficient and effective healthcare distribution has never been elevated in the eyes of the industry. The healthcare distribution market, which includes healthcare logistics and SCM, plays a crucial role in ensuring that medical products and equipment reach their intended destinations in a timely and cost-effective manner. This focus of this chapter will be the current state of the healthcare distribution market, the key factors driving its growth and the future challenges.

The healthcare distribution segment of the supply chain is a complicated and very regulated industry that involves the storage, transportation, and delivery of medical products and equipment. It is very regulated as the primary method of delivery is through the trucking industry. The products being moved within the trucking industry includes pharmaceuticals, medical devices, medical equipment, and healthcare supplies. This segment of the supply chain is responsible for ensuring that these products reach hospitals, clinics, pharmacies, and other healthcare facilities in a safe and timely manner. It is a critical link between manufacturers and healthcare providers, ensuring that the right products are available at the right time and place.

According to a report by Grand View Research, the global healthcare distribution market size was valued at USD 1.2 trillion in 2020 and is expected to reach USD 1.8 trillion by 2028. This growth can be attributed to the increasing demand for healthcare products, advancements in technology, and the rising prevalence of chronic diseases. The market is also being driven by the growing need for specialized and advanced distribution services due to the increasing complexity of healthcare products and treatments.

Healthcare distribution and logistics is a vital cog in the healthcare supply chain world. It involves the planning, implementation, and control of the flow of medical products and equipment from the point of origin to the point of consumption. This planning includes tactical procurement, warehousing, inventory management, transportation, and tracking of products. It is a critical function that ensures the smooth operation of the healthcare system, enabling healthcare providers to deliver quality care to patients.

The increasing demand for temperature-sensitive products, such as vaccines and biologics, is a major factor driving the growth of the healthcare logistics market. The increased need for efficient

DOI: 10.4324/9781003668732-5

and reliable logistics services due to the increasing complexity of healthcare products and treatments is also contributing to the market growth.

The distribution industry is a crucial element of the healthcare supply chain. It involves the management of the entire process of sourcing, procurement, and delivery of medical products and equipment. The goal of the healthcare supply chain is to ensure that the right products are delivered to the right place at the right time, while also minimizing costs and maintaining quality. It is a complex process that requires careful coordination and management to ensure efficiency and effectiveness. The process often requires the use of modern *medical inventory management* solutions.

The increasing focus on reducing healthcare costs and improving efficiency is a major factor driving the growth of the healthcare supply chain market. The ever-increasing need for transparency and traceability in the supply chain due to increasing regulatory requirements of the trucking industry and patient safety concerns is also contributing to the mounting dangers of breakdowns in the supply chain.

Both drivers for growth and challenges to this section of the healthcare supply chain, growth dynamics and challenging opportunities, are presented below.

Growth Dynamics

Rising Demand for Healthcare Products: The global population is aging, and there is a growing demand for healthcare products and services. This is due to the increasing prevalence of chronic diseases such as diabetes, cancer, and cardiovascular diseases. As a result, the demand for efficient and effective healthcare distribution is also increasing. The growing focus on preventive care and wellness is also driving the demand for healthcare products, thereby enhancing the growth of the healthcare distribution market.

Advancements in Technology: The healthcare industry is constantly evolving with new technologies being introduced to improve the delivery of healthcare products and care. These new technologies include the use of temperature-controlled packaging, real-time tracking systems, and automation in warehouses. These advancements are making the distribution process more efficient and reliable.

Increasing Focus on Patient Safety: Patient safety is a top priority in the healthcare industry, and this extends to the distribution of medical products and equipment. As a result, there is a growing demand for temperature-controlled and tamper-proof packaging, as well as strict regulations for the transportation and handling of medical products. The rising focus on traceability and transparency in the healthcare supply chain to ensure patient safety is also driving the growth of the healthcare communications.

Growing Importance of Supply Chain Visibility: With the increasing complexity of the healthcare supply chain, there is a growing need for visibility and transparency. This includes real-time tracking of products, inventory management, and data analytics to identify areas for improvement and cost-saving opportunities. The increasing adoption of digital technologies for supply chain visibility is also expected to contribute to the growth of the healthcare distribution market.

Challenging Opportunities

Stringent Regulations: The healthcare industry is highly regulated, and this extends to the distribution of medical products. Companies must comply with strict regulations for the transportation, storage, and handling of these products, which can be a costly and time-consuming process. The regulations vary across different countries, regions, and even in the United States, within the fifty states. All of this adds to the complexity and cost of compliance.

Lack of Standardization: The lack of standardization in the healthcare industry can lead to inefficiencies and errors in the distribution process. This includes variations in packaging, labeling, and tracking systems, which can make it difficult to ensure the safety and timely delivery of products. The need for standardization of the entire healthcare supply-chain processes, in this case, specifically the distribution industry, is a major challenge that needs to be addressed.

High Costs: The healthcare distribution market is a capital-intensive industry, with high costs associated with warehousing, transportation, and technology. This can be a barrier for smaller companies looking to enter the market. Moreover, the increasing cost of compliance with regulatory requirements and the need for investment in advanced technologies and systems are also adding to the cost pressures faced by companies in the market.

The healthcare distribution market is a crucial component of the healthcare industry, responsible for ensuring the safe and timely delivery of medical products and equipment. With the increasing demand for healthcare products, advancements in technology, and the focus on patient safety and supply chain visibility, the market is expected to continue its growth path. However, companies must also address the challenges faced by the industry, such as stringent regulations and high costs, to maintain their competitive edge. The impact of these challenges has accentuated the importance of a resilient and efficient healthcare distribution system, and it is expected to drive further innovation and transformation in the market.

Chapter 5

Regulatory Compliance

The healthcare industry is subject to stringent regulations, and compliance is paramount. Changes in regulations, especially those related to pharmaceuticals, can impact the supply chain, necessitating quick adaptations to maintain compliance and avoid legal repercussions.

The supply chain domain continues to transform wildly as more trade requirements are implemented daily. From local to national to even international levels, supply chain regulations have become an absolute maze of compliance agencies.

Healthcare regulatory compliance is the practice of meeting or exceeding the requirements of all applicable federal, state, local, and industry regulations and any voluntary standards a healthcare organization adopts in order to demonstrate a good faith effort to comply with the regulations. Due to the number of regulations and standards, a healthcare organization may have to comply with healthcare regulatory compliance that is complex and has the potential for failure in many different areas, specifically in supply chain adherence.

Most healthcare organizations are required to comply with dozens of federal, state, local, and industry regulations. The regulations can cover subjects as diverse as building safety, data security, codes of conduct, the regulation of controlled substances, sourcing, and the proper storage of medicines and medical equipment.

To understand the importance of regulatory compliance in healthcare and its supply chain, it is necessary to understand the purposes of federal, state, local, and industry regulations and why they exist. The supply chain "world" continues to transform as more trade requirements are implemented daily. From local to national to even international levels, supply chain regulations have become an absolute tangle that poses many challenges to healthcare businesses and institutions.

In addition to the regulations enacted by various governments, companies must also answer to a slew of agencies and adhere to a wide range of industry standards. Restriction of Hazardous Substances (RoHS), Registration, Evaluation, Authorization and Restriction (REACH), the FDA, the U.S. Securities and Exchange Commission, U.S. Customs and Border Protection's Automated Commercial Environment (ACE) system, and OSHA are just a few of the standards and organizations companies must defer to on a regular basis.

Along with these regulations, companies now also have to contend directly with social media and nonstop public opinion. In today's digital society, consumers are more socially and politically aware of the supply chain system that is tied to healthcare.

DOI: 10.4324/9781003668732-6

It's becoming increasingly important for consumers to purchase items that were manufactured under the most ethical standards. Questions about humane labor, safe working conditions, and material sourcing are now normal topics of discussion in public dialogue.

The global community of suppliers is constantly expanding at an ever-increasing rate. While having more than one option for suppliers is a desirable supply chain practice, it can make the process of selecting an ethical supplier a much more drawn-out affair.

As a result, transparency is now increasingly important in supply chain compliance and management. Companies are no longer only accountable for their own actions—they are also being scrutinized for their suppliers' practices.

Prediction of future healthcare supply chain compliance and regulation and risk has become an enormously laborious task. Without a proper plan in place, keeping track of all the requirements can easily result in a torrent of confusion and disorder. This disarray will eventually lead to delayed shipments, inefficiency, and increased waste.

To consistently address supply chain compliance issues, healthcare institutions and organizations are starting to acquire third parties who specialize in this field of endeavor. An analytical expert from one of these healthcare companies works hand in hand with their counterpart to handle all the necessary paperwork, keep up to date with the constant legislative fluctuations, run a multitude of demanding compliance codes required by various agencies, and manage supply chain databases.

Current and technological advancements can also serve as powerful tools for achieving the highest level of supply chain integrity. While the use of automation and robotics is nothing new to supply chains, these practices will become more refined over time. As robots become more sophisticated, they accomplish more and increase productivity. The use of robots puts safety compliance concerns at bay due to the replacement of susceptible human employees with automated alternatives.

To understand the importance of regulatory compliance in healthcare, it is necessary to understand the purposes of federal, state, local, and industry regulations and why they exist. This is not a guide to every healthcare regulation or compliance, and I will provide a synopsis of some of these regulations that healthcare companies and institutions may have to deal with on a daily basis.

Health and Human Services Office of Inspector General (OIG) investigates individuals and organizations suspected of fraud, patient abuse and neglect, or other incidents of misconduct—for example. Individuals and organizations found guilty of fraud, patient abuse, or misconduct are excluded from the Medicare and Medicaid programs in addition to being fined and/or given a custodial sentence.

Healthcare organizations are prohibited from conducting business with, or engaging the services of, an individual or organization that appears on the Health and Human Service Exclusion List. Healthcare organizations that violate this condition of participation can themselves be excluded from the program, fined up to $20,000 per violation, and made to repay up to three times the amount claimed for non-compliant services or items.

The Occupational Safety and Health Act (OSH Act) in 1970 created the Occupational Safety and Health Administration (OSHA). The Administration was authorized to develop standards for workplace safety and health to reduce the number of avoidable accidents, injuries, and workplace illnesses attributable to poor working conditions. The Administration enforces the standards with a program of inspections and investigations in response to accident reports and workforce complaints. This includes inspection of warehouses or any other facility that stores medicine or any medical equipment or medical instruments.

The FDA ensures the safety and purity of drugs, biologics, and medical devices. However, because the Administration is the enforcer of more than 200 laws, regulations, and standards, there is no one-size-fits-all approach to FDA regulatory compliance in healthcare supply chain. It is up to each healthcare organization to determine which FDA laws, regulations, and standards apply to their activities and implement compliance programs for each.

To ensure compliance with healthcare-related laws, the FDA's Office of Regulatory Affairs conducts regulatory assessments, inspects drug facilities and all warehouses, oversees laboratory testing and clinical trials, and investigates fraudulent or other criminal activities that threaten public health. The FDA has the authority to seize illegally procured drugs from the supply chain pipeline.

Without having a solid plan in place, state-of-the-art technologies and industry experts are limited in their supply chain compliance management tactics. Ultimately, the strongest weapons in any company's arsenal will be well-crafted contingency plans and versatile solutions that are based on continual ebb and flow of supply chain regulations.

By recognizing past and current regulatory trends, and then using these insights to identify possible future scenarios, companies can continue to operate seamlessly and boost productivity without being impeded by supply chain regulations and compliance issues.

Chapter 6

Technological Integration into Healthcare Supply Chain

In a world of rapidly changing technology, exceptional healthcare does not depend on clinicians alone. Healthcare organizations need functional, dependable technology to meet patient care needs and optimize processes. From the rapidly expanding world of virtual care and clinical mobility, to patient data security and streamlined vaccine distribution, technology is essential to providing the best care while enhancing experiences.

Management of healthcare supply chain systems is a high-pressure and high-stakes job due to what is at stake—patient well-being.

A hospital's or medical center's senior director of technology for supply chain supports services team that is responsible for everything from the procurement-to-pay process to supply chain technology and innovation. This team collaborates closely with the IT department to ensure that all the systems speak to each other and that transactions are flowing without a glitch across all departments—even nonmedical or administrative areas.

Most of this work takes place behind the scenes, but the results are visible all over the hospital. If we don't get the supplies that are needed to each medical area, it could very well stop necessary medical procedures. The idea of "the right medical supplies, in the right place at the right time" is and must continue to be taken extremely seriously.

Keeping this in mind we must ask: What is the best technology or who is the best partner to help us achieve these goals? The answer is a fully integrated ERP system.

One very important example and a part of the ERP system is the inventory management system or module. This module within the platform allows detailed tracking needs for a wide range of supplies. For high-volume, low-dollar commodities, this module creates a two-bin kanban system. As soon as a bin of items is emptied, a worker scans it to automatically alert the supplier. The order flows from the inventory management system to the ERP, which then creates a purchase order, which is sent to the supplier to replenish the used inventory. As each order is filled, the workers in the storage room—there's one in each of the hospitals' medical departments—take the items from the second bin.

For the high-end dollar supplies, the process is slightly varied. In a hospital's operating rooms or procedural rooms, stents and hip implants are registered in the inventory management system

 DOI: 10.4324/9781003668732-7

with a radio-frequency identification tag. When a product is used, the clinician scans the tag to automatically deduct it from the inventory and capture data for the patient's medical record. Included in this tag is information such as lot information, serial number, and the item's expiration. This data allows a hospital to replenish the item on an as-needed basis.

Gartner, Inc. awarded the Cleveland Clinic the no. 1 position on its annual Healthcare Supply Chain Top 25 list in 2021. The Cleveland Clinic won this award and recognition due to, in the words of Gartner, its exemplary leadership and collaboration with other departments and its use of self-driving vehicles to move materials and supplies. The health system was investing "locally and with diverse suppliers", Gartner notes, and its successful implementation of RFID technology had not only improved patient safety but also was "capturing revenue and reducing loss and expiration".

Cleveland Clinic is not immune to the supply chain challenges all healthcare organizations face.

Another organization that has taken huge steps to improve their healthcare supply chain is BJC Healthcare of Missouri. As of 2025, it is in year 3 of a five-year plan to simplify their supply chain.

In 2022, BJC HealthCare opened a 415,000-square-foot distribution center with a three-level picking system that is equipped with robots and hundreds of photographic sensors. This new system has allowed for more than 40% of the health system's inventory to be processed automatically—efficiently and assisting with labor shortages.

Like the Cleveland Clinic, BJC HealthCare uses a fully integrated ERP system with an up-to-date kanban system and inventory management module to improve the management of low-value items, while RFID technology is used to track high-dollar inventory and enable important patient information to reach patient files on a timely basis.

The reason for the importance of technological innovation is due to the weak links in the current healthcare industry supply chain. Technological innovations can reduce the risk. Healthcare organizations looking to bolster their supply chains look toward emerging technologies that offer the prospect to stabilize supply chains. The public and/or news media cannot just be focused on headline-making technology, such as robotic surgeries or telehealth—supply chain solutions concentration needs to be on real-time tracking of inventory and procurement of those supplies.

This concentration on both healthcare procedures and administrative tasks leads to the implementation of automation and predictive analytics. If organizations can automate key ordering, shipping, and receiving processes, they can reduce the amount of time and resources required to manage incoming supply. The use of automation and analytics sets the stage for more efficient operations.

As with any new innovations or processes, technology itself isn't enough to solve supply chain challenges. Healthcare organizations still require gifted and skilled people to put into practical use. One without the other will not work.

The bottom line is that strengthening supply chains starts with consolidation. Armed with relevant data, organizations can leverage real-time tracking to understand current conditions, apply automation to reduce process complexity, and deploy predictive analytics to anticipate ongoing needs.

The impact of technology on healthcare SCM: No matter where goods are produced and how they're shipped, automation and analytics—paired with intelligent human oversight—are now essential to build stable and sustainable supply chains.

Chapter 7

Quality Assurance and the Healthcare Supply Chain

In the global economy of today, supply chains reaching all ends of the world is the norm. Sourcing materials overseas yields cost efficiencies that often outweigh the risks involved—or so we thought. These risks are highlighted by both man-made and natural disasters when restrictions on travel are put upon moving products along the supply chain. The longer your supply chain, the more severe the ripple effects of the log jam after log jam will be.

As stated in Figure 7.1, the assurance of quality raw materials is not guaranteed. A few years ago, there had been some movement toward a global approach to the sourcing of materials.

Figure 7.1 Assuring quality raw materials.

DOI: 10.4324/9781003668732-8

Due to a recent health crisis, that approach backfired. Domestic manufacturers weren't able to get the raw materials they needed into the United States in order to make products.

Despite the drawbacks—risk exposure, language barriers, unstable exchange rates, and long lead times—global supply chains are still with us. They pose an ongoing challenge to the healthcare industry. The raw materials needed to produce medications, biotechnology or medical devices are often fragile and must meet stringent specifications. With a global supply chain, it's challenging to regularly audit suppliers to meet strict quality requirements. The materials must be transported in a way that keeps them safe and viable over a long journey.

The healthcare supply chain is concerned not just with medications but also with medical equipment and the electronics that go into some of these devices.

If you have component parts manufactured overseas to your specifications, you have to be cautious about who you're choosing to work with to ensure that your product is going to be made according to those specifications. There are concerns with transparency and visibility into long supply chains and new players suddenly emerged to fill any openings in the supply chain shortages.

If these new players continue operating in the healthcare industries, it is hopeful that they will be held to the same standards as every other participant in the industry. The challenge for them is to meet the quality requirements—there's a real concern about the depth of their quality team and their quality operations. Let's remember that many of these "johnnies come lately" to healthcare were not required to meet the regularity processes to meet safety and effectiveness requirements, and now they have come back to haunt the industry.

Thus, we have to ask: How can the healthcare industry and its supply chain ensure that it is receiving high-quality products in the midst of todays' supply chain challenges? There are three possible strategies:

1. Shorten Supply Chains Wherever Feasible: It is simple fact that global supply chains are here to stay, especially for larger manufacturers. Smaller companies should transition to more domestic sourcing. Shorter supply chain means more control. A company can more readily and more frequently audit a supplier if they are in the United States. The logistics disappear. There is more opportunity to build closer relationships with your suppliers, which makes it easier to anticipate backlogs and find solutions. All of these things make domestic supply chains really valuable. There will be cases where companies will have no choice but to source overseas. Where possible, medical health systems and institutions that keep suppliers close gain greater control over quality assurance.
2. Vendor Qualification and Audit Program: Due diligence in the vendor selection process is critical.

   Companies should review a potential vendor's regulatory history. Component part manufacturers will be registered with the FDA, and their history will be readily available. For raw materials suppliers, which aren't required to register with the FDA, a strong vendor qualification program is key. One needs to develop an outline of all of the criteria that are critical for your healthcare institution with the products you're sourcing. Ensure that your supplier partner meets all your required standards. Take a tour of their facility—when and if possible—to see what their quality control methods are. At the same time, review their history for any quality issues, recalls, or any issues their customers may have had with them. Inquire if the vendor has contingency plans if there's a supply chain disruption so that it doesn't end up impacting your lead times.

Frequent audits go together with the qualification process. Site visits with inspections help to ensure that your manufacturing specifications and standards are being met. The tour and frequent audits of your supplier's facility make sure that they are complying with all regulations and with any applicable standards identified in your qualification process.

3. Create Contracts That Transfer Risk: A critical safeguard is a contract that shifts product liability risk to the supplier if an injury is caused by their work. When working with new suppliers, it is always best to ask if the company is underwritten by insurance companies or brokers for any claims that might arise from negligence. One needs to see and read these contracts and what is their share of liability.

   A strong contract will also include language that guarantees regular site visits and a certain level of transparency into the manufacturing or quality control process. Anything that will make you feel comfortable doing business with these suppliers—confident about the quality, effectiveness, and safety of a product—should be specified into a contract.

   Using these three strategies will assist all healthcare institutions identify exposures, review contracts, properly source suppliers, provide guidance on regulatory standards, and build solid supply chains.

   If these three subjects/strategies are not implemented from one overall team effort within every healthcare institution, then hospitals and others are leaving themselves open to failure.

THE HEALTHCARE SUPPLY CHAIN AND HEALTHCARE SYSTEMS

II

The healthcare supply chain is a critical component of the healthcare system. It ensures the timely delivery of healthcare supplies, medical equipment, and medications to healthcare providers. It frequently encounters contemporary challenges that affect its reliability and effectiveness.

The healthcare supply chain is essential for maintaining the quality and accessibility of healthcare services. In recent years, it has encountered a number of challenges such as global disruptions, increased demand for medical supplies, and the need for greater resiliency.

This part of the work will explore these challenges, including supply shortages, logistical inefficiencies, and regulatory changes. It will highlight strategies for improvement in areas like diversification of suppliers, investment in technology, and collaboration among stakeholders. Addressing these issues is vital for ensuring a responsive healthcare supply chain capable of meeting the demands of the modern healthcare systems and delivery of quality care.

DOI: 10.4324/9781003668732-9

Chapter 8

Are Supply Chain Inefficiencies a Threat to Healthcare?

Altering healthcare's inefficient supply chain may eliminate the dangers posed by numerous inefficiencies. *The manufacturing* of healthcare supplies and medical equipment is becoming increasingly complex. Companies are expanding their product selection to meet rapidly changing market demand, emerging economies want more affordable products, quality and compliance issues are rising because products are more complex, regulations are stricter, and the number of drug recalls is increasing. But the supply chain is still split into pieces with weaknesses that put patients at risk, cost billions in value, and lessen the healthcare sector's ability to take on the challenges it faces.

There are models existing that can strengthen and improve the healthcare supply chain. By learning from the fast-moving consumer goods (FMCG) industry, the healthcare sector could cut production lead times and obsolescence. At the same time, manufacturers, distributors, hospitals, and pharmacies could carry significantly smaller inventories. Improving the healthcare supply chain also could give millions of people around the world access to safer and more affordable healthcare, reduce costs, and provide new revenue sources for manufacturers.

Operational inefficiencies are open to huge opportunities.

This table (see Figure 8.1) suggests a number of opportunities that can have a huge impact on mitigating inefficiencies in the healthcare supply chain—better sourcing of products and markets, increasing flexibility, closer alignment with global standards, and collaboration across healthcare chain.

There is recognition that transforming supply chains isn't easy. Limited improvement efforts yield poor results, while inclusive efforts are often complex. The payoff can be significant. Supply chains now account for nearly 25% of healthcare costs. Annual spending of about $230 billion on medical supplies and $122 billion on medical devices are areas where even minor efficiency gains could free up billions for other investments.

The cost of shortages, as depicted in Figure 8.1, are substantial. Since 2005, drug shortages have nearly tripled in the United States and added more than half a billion dollars in costs for hospitals worldwide. Supply issues and the ever-growing list of healthcare manufacturers lend

DOI: 10.4324/9781003668732-10

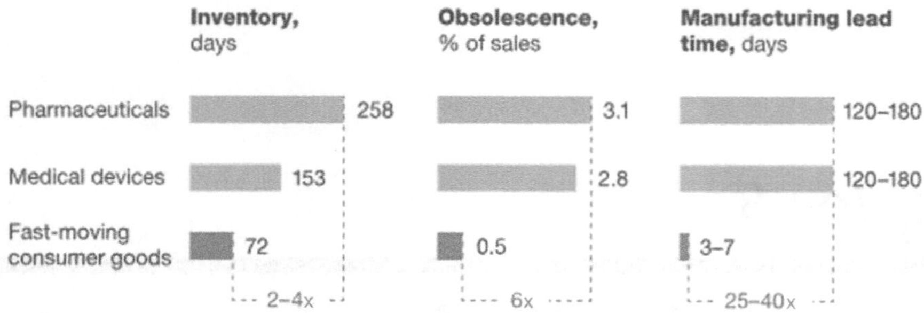

Figure 8.1 Cost of shortages and obsolescence.

themselves to counterfeiters, threatening patient safety and cutting into the revenues of legitimate companies. Supply-chain security breaches are increasing by an average of more than 33% every year, rising not in emerging markets such as China, India, and Brazil alone.

At the same time and sometimes due to counterfeiting, medication errors occur in roughly 10 to 20% of all inpatient hospital admissions. About 1 in 10,000 patients admitted dies from adverse drug events, which can add $20 billion to $90 billion in costs to the healthcare system globally. Better supply-chain processes are central to increasing patient safety. There is a belief, within the legitimate healthcare industry, that adopting a common global data standard and upgrading supply-chain processes could slash counterfeiting in half.

Inefficiencies that have plagued healthcare supply chains have been identified—segmentation, agility, measurement, alignment, and collaboration. All will be discussed below.

- Segmentation: Many healthcare and medical-device companies/manufacturers seem to fit one-size-fits-all supply chains. However, there can be and are major differences in profitability, value per unit of weight, demand, the importance of a drug or device to patients, a customer's cost to serve, and service expectations. Forcing products with such varied characteristics through a single set of supply-chain processes creates inefficiencies, such as overages and/or shortages in inventories, the use of expensive air freight when slower surface modes would do, or reschedule production to meet urgent delivery requirements. Leading companies tackle these problems by intelligently segmenting their supply chains according to the characteristics of products and the requirements of customers. They then develop forecasting, production, and distribution strategies for each category.
- Agility: This means more than just being fast when there's an emergency. It means building an operating model that can better respond to demand shifts and customer wishes. Replenishment lead time from healthcare manufacturing plants to distribution centers usually takes about 75 days. This is in direct contrast to FMCG that take a fraction of that time. Companies must better align the production cycle with the patterns of patient demand and increase the low frequency of their manufacturing processes. In addition, an agile supply-chain model also requires stability in production, replenishment, and visibility. Many healthcare companies need to make deliveries from third parties and in-house plants more reliable and to upgrade their sales—and operations—planning capabilities to the standards of the fast-moving-consumer-goods industry. The necessary improvements include a more disciplined cross-functional process, a better understanding of demand-and-supply scenarios, and more effective communication.

- Measurement: Healthcare companies need to increase the clearness their costs, including manufacturing, transport, warehousing, inventory, staff, and obsolescence of supplies. These measures could cut operational costs and optimize market sourcing and product portfolios. Improvements are also needed in responsiveness, manufacturing frequency, reliability of supply, and stability. These are not systematically measured or managed across the network, but they need to be. Consumer-goods companies are clearly more advanced as they keep under observation metrics such as the manufacturing-frequency index to measure the share of stock-keeping units (SKUs) that are produced with high frequency. Finally, companies must standardize metrics across countries and plants.
- Alignment: Manufacturers of consumer goods use point-of-sale information from retail customers to build efficient production plans. To build an efficient and cost-effective supply chain, the healthcare sector should align around a single set of global standards that support data interchange, processes, and capabilities. Accomplishing this task will enhance patient safety by making it harder for counterfeiters to operate by reducing medication errors and by improving recall processes.
- Collaboration: While the use of common standards is part of the challenge, supply-chain partners must find ways to collaborate more effectively to reap the full benefit. Barriers to improvement are often cultural not technical. There are six essential steps that will make the difference between a productive collaboration or a frustrating collaboration:
  1. Identify: The first step is to identify the organization's clinical service lines.
  2. Evaluate: What products best serve your current and future clinical outcomes?
  3. Coordinate: Coordination means securing 'buy-in' from other key healthcare supply chain participants. The supply chain requirements should be aligned with all organizational goals.
  4. Develop: Strike a balance between the goals of customer satisfaction and operational requirements.
  5. Assess: Determine how the plan is working.
  6. Re-design: Return to the drawing board if necessary, if the new approach does not achieve the expected results.

Transforming the healthcare supply chain into a more robust and efficient system can do much more than improve the bottom line. By embracing the challenge of supply-chain leadership, all healthcare institutions, manufacturers, and medical-device companies can provide safer, more affordable access to products that boost or even save the lives of people across the world.

And now we'll turn to some of the other subjects that may or may not add to the efficiencies of the healthcare system—demand fluctuations, risks, technology, supply shortages, logistical issues, and regulations.

Chapter 9

Healthcare Demand versus Other Demand Models

Before we explore demand fluctuations in healthcare, perhaps it would be prudent to understand the difference between the demand in healthcare and demand in other industries.

When people are asked why health is important, many are unable to answer it. The reason for this may be due to their lack of awareness of the importance of health and the consequent lack of proper self-care. Health can generally be considered an essential basis of life, but many people still do things that show that health is not a priority in their lives. They spend a lot of time on the opportunities they find, but do not spend time learning what is good for them to exercise or stay healthy.

As per the World Health Organization's definition, first stated in 1978 at a United Nations Health Summit, health is a state of complete physical, mental, and social well-being and not just the absence of disease or infirmity. Due to the differences in the level of health in different countries of the world, the members of United Nations provided primary healthcare with a package intended to reduce this health gap. One of the most critical concerns and challenges that different countries have faced in providing primary healthcare to their population has been the lack of resources.

Thus, health is a durable good that provides services. The flow of services produced from the stock of health supplies is continuously used over an individual's lifetime. Over the period of a person's lifespan, these health supplies slowly dwindle due to age and compromised immune systems. Death occurs when their age and compromised immune system lose the "battle" in spite of all medical treatment or supplies available.

To demand a product or service, you must ask for it, afford it, and have a specific plan for purchasing it. Desires are the inclinations that people have for goods and services. Imagine being able to afford something if you could afford it or it was not so expensive. When we make choices, scarcity guarantees that many of our desires will never be met. Demand reflects our plan and vision for the demands that will be met. The amount of goods and services that the consumer plans to buy depends on many factors: commodity prices, related commodity prices, personal income, expected future prices, population, advertising.

The prices of nonmedical goods depend in part on the prices of other goods and services. There are two types of goods: substitute goods and complementary goods. Two substitute goods can be

DOI: 10.4324/9781003668732-11

used instead of each other, and if the price of one of them increases, the demand for that product will decrease, and people will be more likely to demand a substitute product. For example, if beef and chicken are two substitutes, as the price of beef increases, it results in the demand for chicken. The other factors impacting consumer demand are income, population, and consumer preferences.

As people's incomes increase, they buy more goods and services. Demand increases as income increases. And the reverse is true. But, in general, it can be said that the demand for health goods and services has little to do with income. Because medical goods and services provide the basis for health treatments, people's income cannot have a significant impact on demand for these goods. However, rising incomes will increase the demand for luxury medical services.

Demand also depends on the demographics of the population. If the population increases, the demand for all goods and services increases, and if the population decreases, the demand for goods and services decreases. At the same time, assuming other factors remain constant, as the population in a particular age group increases, so does the demand for goods and services used by that age group. As far as consumer preferences are concerned, preferences are predicated on people's tastes and attitudes toward different goods and services.

Conversely, medical care goods maintain, improve, or restore a person's health. For example, a young man may have wrist surgery to repair a torn tendon so he can return to work, an older woman may have cataract surgery to improve her vision, or a parent may have to bring their child to a healthcare center for an annual dental checkup to prevent future problems. Prescription drugs, prescription glasses, and dentures are examples of medical supplies, while surgeries, periodic physical examinations, and visits to medical professionals are examples of medical services. Preventive and medical care are difficult to measure and quantify. Medical care demands have four characteristics that distinguish these from other industries goods and services: intangibility, inseparability, inventory, and inconsistency.

People's five senses are incapable of evaluating medical services. Unlike new shoes, a vegetable salad dinner, or a new cell phone, the consumer cannot see, taste, or touch medical services. The production and consumption of a medical service take place concurrently. Inventory is directly related to inseparability. Because the production and consumption of a medical service occur simultaneously, healthcare providers cannot store or maintain medical services. Finally, inconsistency means that the variety, composition, and quality of medical services are very different. Although different people may see a doctor simultaneously, there are various reasons for visiting a doctor. One person may see a doctor because of a typical physical problem, while another may see a doctor because of a heart attack. The combination of prescribed medical care or the frequency of its use can vary significantly from person to person and at different times.

Demand requires people to seek a service they can afford and are willing to pay for it. The need for healthcare is the care that doctors believe is essential for a person to stay healthy. Sometimes, patients think they need healthcare, but doctors believe they cannot benefit from such care. Sometimes, the doctor believes that there is a medical need, but the patient does not consult his doctor because he prefers not to receive treatment or that he has not recognized the need. Even if patients have as much knowledge as doctors, their demands may be different from their needs.

Demand for healthcare depends on the level of consumption of an individual in case of illness. The amount of consumption differs according to the factors impacting the demand, such as income, service price, education, norms, social traditions, and quality. A person's decision to use services is related to his or her illness/injury status rather than healthcare.

Health is both a consumer good and a capital good. From the consumer's point of view, health is a consumer product because it makes them feel better. As a capital good, it is seen as suitable for people's health because it increases the number of healthy days of life to work. People consume a range of health goods including diet, exercise, and time. These investments help maintain or improve consumers' health. Over time, health demand for health goods may grow, remain constant, or decrease with age due to illness or injury. We will see that the prices of healthcare, the rate of wages of individuals, and their productivity in the production of health determine how resources are allocated between health capital and other goods and services that people buy.

Human beings are at the center of healthcare development. They have long sought to maintain and improve their health by increasing the innovation of health supplies and medical goods. The use of services or the demand for medical services has a vital role in improving the level of health of each person. The demand for healthcare is a challenge derived from the need for well-being and is influenced by several factors, including price, income, and population.

Chapter 10

Healthcare Supply Chain's Response to Demand Fluctuations

Demand fluctuations are a fancy manner of stating supply and demand. The law of supply and demand combines two fundamental economic principles—prices and need for product. As product supply lessens, demand grows as the price drops.

As Figure 10.1 shows, the "demand" for a product or commodity or a service is not the same thing as the "desire" for the product.

Global access to essential medicines is crucial for effective healthcare supply chain systems, yet equitable availability remains a global challenge. Many nations, particularly those in Africa and Asia, struggle with access due to unaffordability and supply chain inefficiencies. Drug shortages are no stranger to modern industrial regions like the United States and Europe, which affect

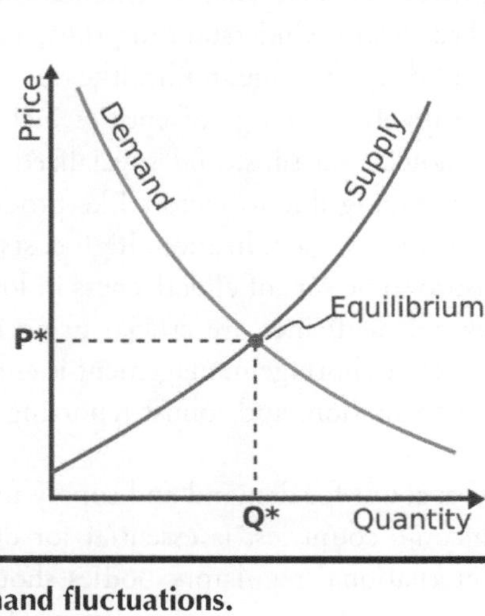

Figure 10.1 Supply and demand fluctuations.

DOI: 10.4324/9781003668732-12

healthcare quality and patient care. These shortages, caused by supply chain disruptions, have financial and patient care consequences.

There are several factors that affect or contribute to medical shortages—globalization, manufacturing issues, natural disasters, and regulatory requirements. Supply chain difficulties introduce additional challenges like demand variations, resource limits, material cost increases, demand variations due to medical crisis, and other supply chain interruptions, which have exposed the weakness of supply chains. All of these challenges display the need for reevaluation of supply chain strategies to enhance these fluctuations. A strong supply chain strategy will join together suppliers, manufacturers, and distributors to optimize resources and service levels. Addressing shortages, especially in low-income countries, involves managing stock use restrictions and efficient redistribution.

An efficient healthcare supply chain is integral to organizational success in all healthcare industries as shortages can have dangerous consequences. Managing supply and demand uncertainty remains a persistent challenge.

As SCM becomes increasingly complex due to changing customer demands, disruptions, and natural disasters, recent global economic turbulence emphasizes the urgency for resilient and sustainable supply chain strategies. Demand fluctuations due to seasonality and uncertain economic conditions necessitate a strong supply chain. Supply chain uncertainty poses challenges such as supplier unreliability, communication issues, and quality concerns. Effective management will aid in the mitigation of transportation delays and production disruptions. These issues highlight the need for strategic supply chain planning. Geopolitical events disrupt international supply chains, highlighting their vulnerability.

There are and have been a number of shortages of different products in all types of industries involved in healthcare supply chain. However, the chapter will focus on drugs or medicines.

Drug shortages occur when the total supply of all clinical versions of a regulated drug does not meet the demand. In spite of increased research, the reliable data to combat medicine shortages globally remains insufficient. The global rise in essential medicine shortages poses a significant threat to demand and resources. Drug shortages drastically impact global healthcare due to patients' lack of control over prescriptions and limitations in manufacturing such as delays, capacity limits, internal business decisions, and shortages in raw materials. Other supply chain risks and factors from environmental, organizational, regulatory demands and market entry barriers further erode consumer confidence in healthcare. Understanding these factors is crucial for developing strategies to mitigate the impact of drug shortages on healthcare.

The pharmaceutical industry involves a range of entities including research-based multinationals, generic manufacturers, biotech startups, and specialized logistics providers. Managing this complex supply chain is challenging due to factors like product diversity, short life cycles, outsourcing, technological advancements, globalization, high costs, prolonged clinical trials, and uncertainties in demand. To ensure some sort of effectiveness in low-income countries, the availability and affordability of essential medicines are crucial using these strategies limiting stock transparent distribution, and proactive shortage management is employed. Effective communication among regulatory bodies, coordination, and robust reporting systems are essential for mitigating drug shortages.

Supply chain strategies must account for demand and supply uncertainties. Global collaboration, particularly among low-income countries, is essential for developing effective mitigation strategies for drug shortages. International regulatory bodies should work together on a global mitigation plan. Countries need to establish proactive systems for drug shortage notification, reporting, and tracking. Policies should promote robust supply chains, encourage quality manufacturing systems, and prioritize the production of high-risk medicines.

In conclusion, addressing demand fluctuations in the entire healthcare industry requires a fine distinction and understanding of product characteristics, supply processes, and effective supply chain strategies. It is clear that collaboration and communication at the national and international levels are critical to mitigating the global issue of medical supply and demand across all economic levels.

Chapter 11

Why Medical Supply Shortages Keep Occurring

Many people trying to fill a routine prescription or treat an ailment during the winter cold and flu season are discovering that it is not as convenient as dropping by their local pharmacy. Amoxicillin, Tamiflu, and Adderall are just some of the drugs in short supply now, forcing people to hunt them down across cities, go without them for days, or search for an alternative treatment. While these shortages may be an annoyance for some, they could be harmful for many—risking the health and lives of people across the country. Why is the country still facing such shortages?

Medical product supply chain disruptions are not new. This has been taking place for decades. While shortages of drugs and medical devices are life-threatening for some, they also have systemic effects. Shortages increase pressure on manufacturers and suppliers to meet these unpredicted demands. Disruptions in medical product supply chains have greater implications than making people wait for a new television set—with the potential to seriously compromise patient care.

It is a complex issue as medical product supply chains vary considerably for different drugs and medical devices. However, all have multiple stages of production, global systems that involve people, production processes, technologies, and policies. Given these variations, the steps that should be taken to increase the resilience of supply chains for medical products vary.

COVID-19 led to an increase in demand for N95 respirator face masks, while at the same time limiting the ability to ramp up supply—due to manufacturing shutdowns across the board. Prior to the pandemic, the United States had been using about 50 million N95s per year, but in 2020, that figure soared to about 560 million. With few N95s made domestically, half of the world's supply came from China.

Early in the pandemic, lockdowns in China limited their ability to ramp up supply, and it banned exports to other countries. The U.S. government tried to stimulate domestic production by ordering 500 million masks and attempted to reduce demand by recommending that N95s be sterilized and reused. However, no such production and recycling were established, leaving hospitals and other parts of the healthcare industry battling for limited resources. Price gouging and restrictions on sales were the results.

In August 2022, the U.S. Food and Drug Administration was able to remove N95s from the agency's medical device shortage list as demand fell and supply rose—partly as a result of increased domestic manufacturing.

DOI: 10.4324/9781003668732-13

Natural disasters or manufacturing process problems can disrupt medical product supply chains in various ways. For example, a surge in consumer needs can drive demand for a product well above the normal levels for an extended period. A power outage or lack of workers could reduce manufacturing output. Political crises, social disruptions, or communication breakdowns during a natural disaster are other possible causes of shortages.

One of these major disruptions occurred with the production of saline solution. Their components are simple, the products are complex to manufacture, expensive to ship, and difficult to stockpile. The production of one batch of saline involves a 10-day, 29-step process that includes 350 regulatory checks.

Saline shortages go as far back as 2013 when several product recalls occurred during a difficult flu season. In 2017, Hurricane Maria hit Puerto Rico and cut off power to a major manufacturer for four months, crippling saline production. The manufacturer was responsible for roughly 43% of IV saline solutions used in the United States, and other companies could not make up the difference. Another bad flu season the same year compounded the shortages. Hospitals were forced to delay elective procedures, and some providers began hoarding IV bags.

To help address the shortage, FDA allowed saline imports from other countries. The U.S. manufacturer invested $1 billion in its manufacturing network and now stores its finished product on the U.S. mainland instead of Puerto Rico.

A supply chain that plans to mitigate shortages should have the capacity to reliably supply medical products under both normal conditions and in public health crisis or emergencies. Achieving these standards means implementing safeguards and multiple layers of protection against disruptions and shortages.

One of the first steps is building awareness of risks involved in medical product supply chains. This includes making information on sourcing, quality, volume, and capacity for all medical products publicly available and establishing a public database of medical product supply chain information that health systems could access to make better purchasing decisions.

Additional actions that could be taken to bolster medical product supply chains include resilience contracting by health systems, modernizing and optimizing inventory stockpiling management, and cultivating capacity cushion for medical products critical to the supply chain.

After a crisis or natural disaster, measures could also be taken to minimize harm and resolve the shortage in a timely manner. Major medical product producers could negotiate a treaty prohibiting export bans and restrictions, and a working group of key transportation experts could examine and identify effective last-mile strategies.

In order to make the medical product supply chain more secure and the American public safer, all these measures and more will have to be integrated flawlessly under a sound, cost-effective strategy.

Chapter 12

Supply Chain Transportation Barriers to Healthcare Industry

Shipping challenges and transportation delays are hampering the U.S. supply chain health industry. It is causing disruptions that are negatively impacting the nation's healthcare. Prioritizing critical medical products throughout the nation's transportation system could help healthcare providers get the critical products they need for patient care.

Shipping log jams have persisted since 2021 and rolled into 2025. This traffic jam will delay the delivery of medical supplies to healthcare providers. Ports, railways, and the trucking industry are all suffering from worker shortages, logistics holdups, and other issues such as strikes. Transportation workforces were depleted as employees fell ill to the virus or stayed home to care for loved ones.

For many, the fourth quarter of the year is also the beginning of "cough and cold season". In some regions of the country, the season is ramping up early. In August 2025, Georgia and New Mexico already were experiencing high levels of flu, according to the Centers for Disease Control, which led to increasing demand for flu vaccine products, as well as for medical supplies essential for healthcare. The nation's current transportation woes are intensifying the supply and demand strain. Healthcare providers need to know how many products they are receiving and when to ensure appropriate, clinical patient care.

Figure 12.1 depicts the U.S. healthcare supply chain transportation issues.

Figure 12.1 U.S. healthcare supply chain transportation issues.

DOI: 10.4324/9781003668732-14

These are important issues now facing all aspects of the healthcare transportation supply chain. Some are shipping or ocean-going vessels, and other are more local means of transportation like trucks.

Slowdowns in the Red Sea—attacks on commercial ships carried out by Yemen's Houthis in support of Hamas—have impacted vital sea-based shipping lanes. Six of the top ten container carriers have changed their routes away from the Red Sea to Africa's Cape of Good Hope to bypass the Suez Canal. This alteration in course will add 4,000 nautical miles or 10–14 days to the journey. In addition, the Panama Canal situation of the environmental project initiated by the Panamian Government to combat a drought has delayed shipping through the canal by days. U.S. healthcare and supply chain leaders must find alternative options to get these medical supplies to all healthcare institutions.

These two situations—one a conflict and other environmental—highlight the interrelated nature of global supply chains and how geopolitical unrest in one region can have ripple effects on logistics operations and supply chains around the world.

Healthcare institutions can improve their supply chain dilemma by using these strategies:

1. Monitor the global supply chain landscape and pursue proactive preparedness efforts, including ongoing supplier communications on contingency planning and continuous updates for our members.
2. Healthcare institutions and providers rethink inventory management strategies as manufacturer lead times have increased.
3. Make risk management and contingency plans.
4. Stronger supplier relationships and using the power of group purchasing organizations can position providers for greater resiliency during this period of uncertainty.
5. Healthcare industry should maintain appropriate conservation and stockpiling strategies to help keep supply levels maintained.
6. Disaster Preparedness and Response teams can mitigate clinical disruptions. Examples of medical supply categories for this team are surgical masks, fetal monitors, IV products, surgical gloves, blood products, etc.

In addition to the global tasks, reshoring is growing as a key tool for healthcare industry. Healthcare manufacturing CEOs are evaluating reshoring their operations and have reshored. U.S. healthcare supply chain leaders also say that domestic manufacturing is an "extremely" or "very important" component to their organizations' supply chain resiliency strategies. "Increasingly, U.S. hospitals and health systems are seeking out diverse and domestic suppliers that can reliably provide product without the worry of higher global shipping costs and potential delays that can impact patient care," according to Bruce Radcliff, Senior VP of Supply Chain at Premier.

There is another aspect of healthcare supply chain transportation we need to examine. This aspect is not new, but due to the emphasis on healthcare supply chain equity and to ensure all receive medical quality—"medical care transport".

The principal task of national healthcare systems is to provide health services that are safe, accessible, high-quality, and people-oriented. To ensure the continuity of healthcare, support activities related to patient transfer and logistics are necessary. Effective implementation of transport processes is a factor impacting the possibility of medical intervention, in terms of both planned and life-saving care. The reliability of the healthcare supply chain is a key factor in patient health.

Another term for medical care transport might be patient logistics. Patient logistics as a field in the area of SCM covers all planning and control decisions aimed at matching supply and demand throughout the entire healthcare supply chain, in particular the coordination of activities between healthcare organizations. Patient transfer is carried out in two forms: A primary form, where the patient is transferred from the place of injury or illness to the hospital, and a secondary form, where the patient is transferred to another hospital. Safe patient flow is one aspect of healthcare supply chain that is taken for granted. But it should never be for granted or dismissed as unimportant as it requires efficient logistics based on cooperation within the partner network of entities participating in health services.

The reliability of the healthcare supply chain through which the flow of patients, medical staff, information, and material goods takes place is vital in ensuring the stability of healthcare in the field of medical interventions and in life-saving emergencies. The aim of this section is to identify the factors that affect the reliability of the healthcare supply chain in the case of patients transported by medical air transport between hospitals.

Moving patients by means of medical transport between hospitals requires joint coordination between the receiving and releasing medical facilities, as well as the Medical Air Rescue. Although this transport is planned, in the healthcare supply chain, there is uncertainty related to the patient's state of health. It disrupts patient flows between hospitals and blocks the necessary resources in the form of available means of air transport.

This method of moving patients as close as possible to medical quality begs these two questions, of which the answers are not conclusive.

1. What factors affect the reliability of the supply chain in the case of interhospital medical air transport?
2. To what extent does the triangulation of methods allow us to create a general procedure for interhospital medical air transport?

In the logistics/transportation process of patient transfer, the following actions are necessary: making a decision about the transfer and communication, stabilizing and preparing the patient for the transfer, choosing the appropriate mode of transfer, involving the staff accompanying the patient, protecting equipment monitoring the patient's condition during the transfer, preparation of documentation, and transfer of the patient to the receiving institution.

The complexity of this process has a significant impact on healthcare supply chain coordination, and it determines patient safety. Maintaining patients' safety and providing them with a highly advanced level of care in the complex air ambulance environment require dealing with serious life threats and rapidly evolving medical issues without the support and facilities available in a hospital environment.

The patient flow between hospitals by means of the air medical transport led to the identification of 13 factors that affect reliability. These factors are environmental, systemic, technical, technological, and organizational concerning the patient's condition. These following factors are relevant:

1. Legal—including regulations standards.
2. Administrative—at the specialist and internal level of hospitals.
3. Geographical and climatic (weather, terrain, elements of the area).
4. Technical—flight range; distance; conditions of airport infrastructure.
5. Infrastructural—dedicated to patients' air transport.

6. Means of transport—quantity, quality, equipment, availability, rate of wear and tear.
7. Staff—the availability and qualifications of staff health and psychophysical conditions of staff to any fear of flight.
8. Patient's condition entitling to and allowing transport—patients who may pose a threat to the mission's safety are not eligible for air transport.
9. Documentation—completeness of patient's medical documents, referral to the hospital, confirmation of procedures followed, technical standard of documentation.
10. Being equipped with medications and medical supplies necessary to ensure patient safety during transport.
11. Communication—hospital and interorganizational communications.
12. Human factors—personal predisposition, psychophysical condition, ability and willingness to make decisions under pressure, reaction to stress, reaction speed, and involvement of staff accompanying the patient at all stages of the process.
13. Time—related to the needs of the patient—time necessary to prepare the patient, time of flight, time related to readiness of service of all groups involved in transport.

Patient air transport is one of the key challenges in providing adequate medical care to patients, maintaining its continuity and the availability of highly specialized medical procedures. Therefore, this process requires proper planning of procedures, standards, and rules of conduct; organizing human resources, equipment, and infrastructure; and coordinating the processes of patient inter-hospital transfer.

Transportation barriers is not the only challenging situation facing the healthcare supply chain.

The availability or lack thereof of health commodities—medicines, vaccines, and other health products—is pivotal to achieving a non-constrained medical resource world. The uninterrupted availability of health commodities depends on well-functioning, robust supply chain systems. We define the healthcare supply chain as the network of systems, components, and processes that collectively work to ensure medicines and other healthcare supplies are manufactured, procured, distributed, and provided to patients at health service delivery points. Effective supply chain performance is, therefore, crucial to the success of a healthcare delivery system.

Chapter 13

Healthcare Supply Chain in a Resource-Constrained World

Gaps in health supply chains in low- and middle-income countries contribute significantly to inefficiencies and underperformance of their health systems. Some important elements hindering the performance of these supply chains include small human resources, vulnerable structures for monitoring supply chain performance, ineffectual in-service and pre-service training programs, chronic underfunding, lack of transparency, and an overdependence on obsolete methods. Although proven health-supply-chain-strengthening techniques exist, the level of adoption of these practices has varied across countries, resulting in multiple capacity gaps and underperforming supply chains. The resulting challenges require complementary practices to address the gaps. While it is recognized that there is no "one-size-fits-all" solution to these issues, we demonstrate that real benefits can be achieved by using "best practices".

Although progress has been made on many fronts, significant gaps remain in the capacity of lower- and middle-income countries to ensure the availability and delivery of health commodities at the right time, place, and cost. Health systems remain weak, depicting them incapable of responding in the best way possible to the healthcare needs of the population. The need for strategies to strengthen the structural weaknesses and stabilize the performances of health supply chains in these economies is urgent. Epidemics like Ebola have exposed the vulnerability and lack of resilience of health supply chains in these countries. Challenges requiring interventions range from low capability in strategic planning and management, lack of clarity of roles and authority, absence of supply chain risk management planning at all levels, all-encompassing human resource capacity challenges, weak in-service and pre-service training programs, unstable currency exchange rates, and frequent diversion of funds from drug funds for unrelated activities like salary supplements, dependence on outdated methods of data collection, and feeble emergency supply chain protocols.

Strategies for countries to address these challenges are varied and complex, and each requires their own and unique specific interventions. An in-depth understanding of a country's SCM needs can be obtained through supply chain process mapping. This exercise provides information on key stakeholders, their roles, and responsibilities in the supply chain. In addition, it provides maturity assessment on functional areas and cross-cutting elements like human resources, forecasting and planning, warehousing, logistic management information systems, and financial implications.

DOI: 10.4324/9781003668732-15

A useful tool for this exercise is the United States Agency for International Development (USAID) National Supply Chain Assessment 2.0.2 toolkit, which enables a holistic approach to analyzing country supply chains as opposed to traditional approaches that tend to focus on isolated processes within the supply chain. Other complementary effective tools for evaluating a country's supply chain information systems include the Interagency Supply Chain Group's key performance indicators (KPIs).

The supply chain is not simply a set of warehouses, trucks, and carton boxes but rather embraces the ecosystem of organizations, people, technology, activities, information, and resources that have to come together to ensure the delivery of the product from the point where it is manufactured to the end user. A highly functional supply chain must have structures at all operational levels to include features that return critical information regarding need, demand, and consumption to health system planners. It is a complex system of operations requiring significant levels of expertise. While there is no "one size fits all" approach, major improvements in SCM can be made by accurately diagnosing challenges and adopting and implementing targeted interventions.

Initiating supply-chain reform is a delicate and complicated endeavor. Solutions are context specific. In the absence of data driven by well-controlled scientific evaluations and analysis, interventions from different contexts should be adopted with caution because external validation of the evidence is weak. To promote efficiency in supply chain functions in resource-constrained environments, the scale-up activities should extend beyond public health institutions to include faith-based and private sector health providers.

I reiterate that SCM is a management science that requires expertise to ensure the availability of vaccines, medicines, and other life-saving health technologies when and where they are needed. Ineffective and poorly designed supply chains for health commodities have negative effects with health workforce shortages, creating barriers to achieving the sustainable development goal of good health and well-being for all.

In a healthcare supply chain world where health institutions of all kinds must learn to deal with this new world, is it likely or imperative that the structure of the healthcare supply chain should alter itself?

Chapter 14

Should Healthcare Supply Chain Be Restructured?

Healthcare supply chains face unique challenges, from sourcing critical medical supplies to managing sensitive data and adhering to regulatory requirements. In a sector where supply chain disruptions can impact patient outcomes, resilience isn't just a competitive advantage—it's often a matter of life and death. In this chapter, we'll examine these challenges and explore best practices for building a new structured healthcare supply chain that can withstand any uncertainty and unexpected situations that do not disrupt patient care.

As with businesses in other industries, healthcare organizations are susceptible to supply chain disruptions from a variety of sources. Some of them are listed below.

Global health crises can lead to heightened demand and shortages of critical medical supplies. This will lead to revealing of vulnerabilities and creating supply chain bottlenecks. Furthermore, labor shortages due to widespread illness or burnout from difficult pandemic working conditions can slow or halt supply chain operations.

Extreme weather events like hurricanes and earthquakes can damage infrastructure, turn shipping routes impassable, and disrupt logistics. Changing climate conditions not only make some natural disasters more common, but they can also affect the long-term availability of resources and impact the viability of living and working in areas that may be essential for certain functions.

Healthcare providers and drug and device manufacturers face strict regulations to ensure patients' safety and privacy, which can complicate the SCM. Regulations can change following shifts in political power, resulting in moving targets for organizations relying on the healthcare supply chain.

Fragmented data systems between manufacturers, distributors, transporters, and customers can lead to communication gaps, hindering decision-making and real-time responses. Even a short communication delay can cause a torrent of slowdowns across a supply chain.

To alter or change the healthcare supply chain, these five steps, while not being the full menu of what needs to be changed, offer a small insight into the restructuring. Supply chain re-structure can help healthcare organizations maintain operational continuity in the face of these challenges and other disruptions. Operational continuity in healthcare supports patient safety and access to

DOI: 10.4324/9781003668732-16

essential treatments and supplies. But it also helps to reduce supply chain costs, minimize waste, and avoid penalties associated with regulatory noncompliance.

Your supply chain is ultimately dependent on the efficiency and reliability of its primary suppliers. By cultivating strong supplier partnerships, you can get more out of these critical relationships.

Work with suppliers to develop flexible, transparent contracts that can meet demand surges and, ideally, provide some forecasting insight into expected disruptions or other complications. A close relationship with your supplier can give you an edge in negotiations and may provide other useful insights.

Relying on a single supplier is a surefire way to disaster and increase your business's weaknesses. You need to diversify your supply chain by partnering with multiple suppliers across different regions. This will reduce the risk of complete supply disruption if a single supplier falls through.

Where possible, source the most critical supplies locally. This will reduce your reliance on long, complex international logistics chains as well as support the local economy and cut the cost impact of shipping.

Shortages and overstocking can have very different patient outcomes effects for a healthcare organization, and both situations should be avoided. These strategies are used to avoid the negative aspects of shortages and overstocking.

Adopt demand forecasting tools that leverage artificial intelligence (AI) and machine learning algorithms to predict future demand based on historical data, demographics, diagnosis, and other factors. These will help you adjust your inventory levels in real time to meet evolving needs.

Determine appropriate safety stock levels for essential supplies using historical demand and keep enough buffer inventory around in case of unexpected demand surges.

Utilize JIT and just-in-case (JIC) models in tandem rather than relying on one or the other. The JIT approach minimizes stock levels and optimizes resources at the cost of higher risk during periods of high demand. Incorporating a JIC approach for essential supplies gives your business the flexibility to adapt.

For patients and/or healthcare organizations, your product is only as useful as long as it's there when it's needed. A relatively minor delay can have huge impacts on your users and thus on your brand reputation. Improving logistics and distribution can be resource-intensive, but it's usually worth it to prevent delays and ensure that your product is in the hands of the people who need it most.

One of the best tactics is to establish warehouse locations near target healthcare facilities or other key client bases to reduce lead times and maximize access during emergencies. Within the warehouses themselves, establish organizational practices that make it easier to move materials in and out. You'll also want to maintain high standards for staff—warehousing work is far from unskilled labor; a fully trained, professional team can have a massive effect on your bottom line.

At the local warehouses and along your logistics chains, should invest in real-time tracking and Internet of Things (IoT) technology, including RFID and GPS. These technologies can provide a window into shipment locations and potential delays, allowing you to respond to problems as they arise. Also keep in mind the maintenance requirements of the warehouses, equipment, and shipping fleet.

As with your suppliers, try to partner with a diverse array of logistics providers to reduce the impact of disruptions. This is especially important when you're moving essential and perishable items like vaccines, biologics, or lab samples.

Healthcare supply chains are held to strict standards to protect the safety and privacy of patients and providers alike. Here are a few ways to ensure your company stays compliant from procurement through distribution:

Maintain comprehensive records and documentation of all supply chain transactions to stay compliant with the FDA's Unique Device Identification System and HIPAA requirements.

Conduct regular audits among suppliers, warehouses, and distributors to uncover their weaknesses to uncover safety concerns and prevent legal issues before they attract the attention of regulators.

Build a risk management framework that routinely assesses risks and provides contingencies for emergencies including cyberattacks, data breaches, or sudden regulatory shifts.

Do your due diligence by researching suppliers and other partners to ensure they meet industry requirements and conduct business in a way that supports human rights and sustainability.

Sustainable supply chain practices reduce waste, cut costs, and support overall re-structure. The long-term effects are beneficial too—a protected environment is a more stable environment.

Where possible, use environmentally friendly suppliers who prioritize sustainability and reduce their carbon footprint. Use energy-efficient transportation options, recyclable packaging, and renewable energy for warehouses. It's also worthwhile to consider opportunities to recycle, repurpose, or reuse materials across your supply chain, reducing costs and reliance on suppliers.

The healthcare supply chain is the backbone of the industry, with impacts on patient safety, operational efficiency, and regulatory compliance. Whether you're in life sciences, selling drugs and devices, or a medical supplier manufacturer, the restructuring of your supply chain should be a top priority.

The restructuring of healthcare supply chain of course includes patient safety, efficiencies, and regulations. However, the same restructuring must include and make way for future developments in the field of healthcare—AI, digitalization, end-to-end relationships, and span of control. These will be discussed in the next chapters.

Chapter 15

How Is Artificial Intelligence Changing the Healthcare Supply Chain?

AI is transforming industries worldwide, and healthcare is no exception. AI is leading a significant revolution in healthcare supply chains, driving efficiency, reducing costs, and ultimately enhancing patient outcomes. By leveraging advanced algorithms, machine learning, and predictive analytics, AI optimizes every aspect of the healthcare supply chain—from inventory management to logistics and distribution. We will now explore the various ways AI is being applied across different areas of the healthcare supply chain.

Inventory management is a critical component of the healthcare supply chain, and AI is making significant strides in this area. AI-driven demand forecasting allows healthcare organizations to analyze historical data, seasonal trends, and external factors to predict future demand for medical supplies and medicine accuracy. This predictive capability optimizes inventory levels, minimizing the risk of stock-outs and overstock situations, which is costly and harmful to patient care.

Moreover, AI enables automated replenishment systems that can reorder supplies when inventory reaches a predetermined threshold. This automation ensures that essential items are always available, reducing the burden on healthcare staff and minimizing the risk of human error. By maintaining optimal inventory levels and streamlining replenishment, AI augments operational efficiency and contributes to cost savings.

AI is also revolutionizing procurement processes within the healthcare supply chain. Supplier selection is a crucial aspect of procurement, and AI tools can evaluate and rank suppliers based on criteria such as price, quality, delivery times, and reliability. This data-driven approach allows healthcare organizations to make informed procurement decisions, leading to better supplier relationships and cost savings.

Contract management is another area where AI is making an impact. AI systems can analyze and manage supplier contracts, ensuring compliance with agreed-upon terms and identifying opportunities for cost reduction. By automating these processes, AI reduces the risk of human error and enhances the efficiency of procurement operations.

DOI: 10.4324/9781003668732-17

In addition, AI-driven analytics enable healthcare organizations to monitor supplier performance over time. This ongoing evaluation helps make data-driven decisions about which suppliers to partner with, further optimizing the procurement process and ensuring the timely delivery of high-quality medical supplies.

Logistics and distribution are critical to ensuring that medical supplies reach their destinations on time and in quality condition. AI is pivotal in optimizing these processes through advanced algorithms that determine the most efficient delivery routes. By reducing transportation costs and ensuring timely deliveries, AI enhances the overall efficiency of the healthcare supply chain.

Transporting temperature-sensitive medical products like vaccines is called cold chain management and is another area where AI makes a difference. AI monitors and controls the temperature of these products throughout the supply chain, ensuring they are stored and transported under optimal conditions. This capability is crucial in maintaining the integrity of vaccines and other sensitive medical supplies.

AI is undeniably transforming the healthcare supply chain, driving efficiency, reducing costs, and enhancing patient outcomes. From inventory management and procurement optimization to logistics and distribution, AI optimizes every supply chain aspect. Through automation of routine tasks, predicting demand and providing timely insights, AI ensures that healthcare providers can deliver better patient care by having the right supplies at the right time. AI's role in the healthcare supply chain will only become more essential.

As AI evolves further into a vital tool in the healthcare supply chain, in order to better understand this, perhaps an actual example of a company adapting to its uses would be a good fit at this time. This is how one company is channeling the power of AI to improve the healthcare supply chain.

The company is a healthcare icon—Johnson & Johnson. The following are a few ways they are utilizing AI to improve the healthcare supply chain.

In the operating rooms, surgical video captures procedures that can provide medical professionals with opportunities for education, research methodologies, and quality-improvement strategies.

Johnson & Johnson is developing digital solutions for the operating room, which use AI algorithms to allow surgeons to re-watch significant moments from their procedures. Without AI, this process could take hours to complete. New and learning surgeons want to see how they performed and learn from their performances and how others performed. But it's a lot of work to sit and watch hours of footage from the full procedure and cut it down to clips.

Once you get enough of these enriched surgical videos, there is potential to explore algorithms on the behaviors, tactics, and movements that could in the future provide further information to care teams.

Cardiac ablation is one example. This minimally invasive procedure delivers energy through a catheter to correct an irregular heartbeat in patients with heart conditions like atrial fibrillation. During cardiac ablation, a small flexible tube is inserted into a vein in the groin and guided through the arteries up into the heart, where the location of the abnormal tissue that is responsible for the condition is identified.

The company's CARTO™ 3 System enables electrophysiologists to create 3D maps and navigate inside the heart during catheter ablation procedures. The system's newest Version 8 is shown in Figure 15.1.

Discovering and developing new drugs to treat diseases are long and complex undertakings, but AI can help to reduce the time of the process.

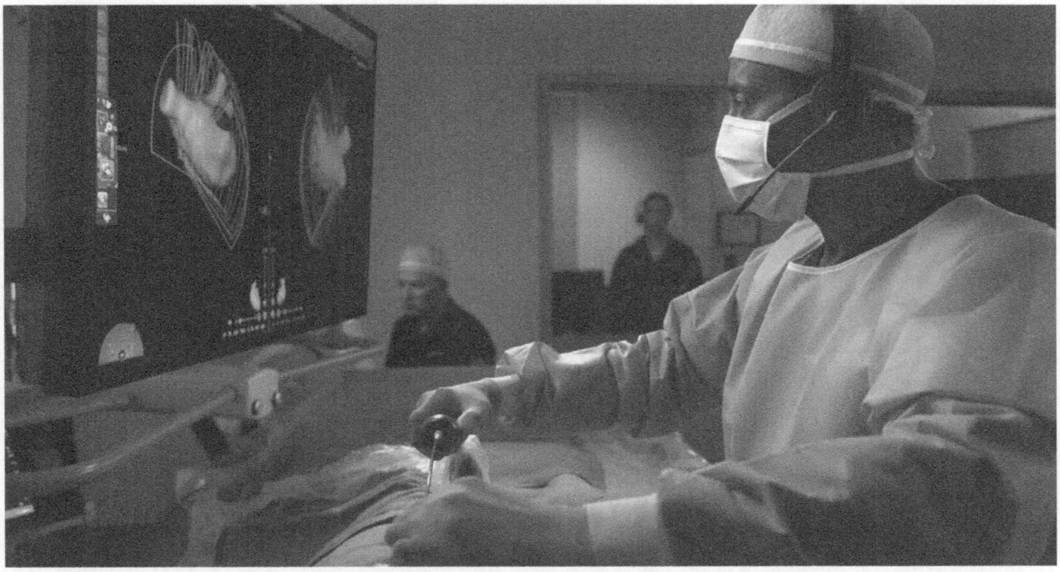

Figure 15.1 An electrophysiologist uses the SOUNDSTAR™ Ultrasound Catheter with CARTO-SOUND FAM™ Module to create a CARTO™ 3 System map of the left atrial geometry.

To develop medicines, researchers need to understand which biological and genetic variations cause diseases. By applying AI to identify medical data, such as EHRs, lab results, or genetic sequencing, scientists can shed light on what drives specific diseases.

Once promising disease targets are identified, Johnson & Johnson is then using AI to help discover molecules that could interact with the disease. AI can also design and optimize those molecules to develop drug candidates that are fit to combat the disease and minimize side effects. The company is doing this through its own state-of-the-art technologies.

Drug discovery is an extremely challenging process with only a small percentage of lead compounds moving into clinical trials and an even smaller percentage becoming approved medicines. By applying AI, we can advance the most promising drug candidates into clinical development, with the goal of improving the probability of successfully bringing a drug to market and rapidly getting new treatments to the patients who need them the most.

Enabling more personalized care by understanding diseases, AI can be a game changer. By applying AI to clinical data derived from or generated by common diagnostic tests such as CT scans, MRIs, electrocardiograms, and echocardiograms, AI can enable more personalized targeted treatment and accelerate clinical trial enrollment.

For example, bladder cancer is the tenth most common cancer worldwide. Treatments exist for patients whose tumors have a specific alteration in the Fibro Blast Growth factor gene. Patients with Fibroblast Growth Factor positive tumors don't always receive the targeted, personalized treatment that could significantly impact their care and outcomes.

To help address this challenge, Johnson & Johnson is developing an AI-powered biomarker test that, when applied to digitized images of biopsies, can detect whether patients' tumors are likely to have Fibroblast Growth Factors or alterations. The company is evaluating the clinical utility of this technology and exploring its potential future use for patients.

First come the discovery and development of therapies, medications, and other healthcare products. Then comes the step making sure that these products reach patients. AI can help with that, too. Stocking products in hospitals, pharmacies, clinics, and other healthcare facilities where they're needed requires an accurate prediction of supply and demand. This can be challenging, as a wide range of factors can affect the supply chain, including market trends, economic disruptions, supplier issues, and more.

AI-powered solutions can help prioritize which locations will be greatly impacted in order to quickly respond to risk factors that may otherwise affect the ability to deliver products to people who count on them. It's the responsibility of the company to make sure patients and customers have reliable access to the transformational therapies it creates. AI is helping them build a stable, efficient, and resilient supply chain so they can deliver on that obligation.

Chapter 16

How Digitalization Has Generated Benefits and Increased Deliverables

Rising healthcare costs force healthcare organizations worldwide to reconsider their business strategies. Hospital managers are tasked with lowering operating costs while upholding the high quality of care, two goals recognized as contradictory by many healthcare professionals.

Attempting to contribute toward reaching these goals, the plan is to study the digitalization of the healthcare supply chain through the adoption of ERP systems and studying its impact on hospital supply chain costs.

Public healthcare spending cuts force healthcare organizations across the globe to reduce their operating costs while being required to ensure the quality of care. One of the focal points is the healthcare supply chain, which can be defined as a complex system managing the flow of products, services, and information to satisfy the needs of patients. Supply chain costs are estimated to account for 40 to 50% of a healthcare provider's total costs, suggesting that supply chain performance improvement could be a major facilitator for increasing the operational efficiency and reducing costs.

While other sectors deploy various SCM practices to lower their supply chain costs, the healthcare sector is clearly lagging behind. Some healthcare practitioners attribute this fact to the complexity of healthcare supply chains—the existence of strong national and international regulatory frameworks, the difficulty of demand forecasting because of patient heterogeneity, and limited knowledge by pharmacists and physicians who are key decision-makers regarding the procurement of drugs. The small adoption rate of ERP systems that support the management of hospital supply chains is an additional reason. The hospital supply chain encompasses the process of procuring, manufacturing, and delivering goods and services from providers to patients, including medical and nonmedical products, such as pharmaceuticals, medical devices, food, and cleaning supplies.

ERP systems are comprehensive software applications designed to integrate the main functional areas of an organization's business processes and are known to impact the adoption of supply chain practices significantly. Despite their importance in making hospitals more efficient and

DOI: 10.4324/9781003668732-18

deliver their services more promptly, research studies involving the digitalization of healthcare supply chains and ERP implementations in healthcare are sparse.

The following framework serves as the foundation that guides the understanding, explanation, and prediction of the extent of ERP systems adoption in hospitals and how they help on hospital supply chain costs. This assistance is captured by the inclusion of the following six elements: technological context, organizational context, environmental context, perceived benefits, extent of ERP systems adoption, and hospital supply chain costs, all of which are discussed below.

The technological context is represented by the hospital's technological readiness, which comprises IT infrastructure and IT expertise. IT infrastructure establishes a platform that provides the foundation for implementing ERP systems, and IT expertise entails the knowledge and skills to implement ERP systems. Research has shown that firms with sophisticated IT infrastructure and skilled IT resources have increased chances of successfully implementing technology innovation.

Various organizational factors have been suggested to impact innovation and technology adoption. One factor in many technology adoption studies is organizational readiness, which reflects an organization's internal capability to accept new technologies. Organizational readiness is impacted by the organization's culture and the availability of skilled, knowledgeable, and well-trained employees regarding new technologies. An additional aspect of organizational readiness considered crucial in many IT adoption studies is top management support and commitment, as they are necessary to ensure adequate resources and to overcome barriers and resistance to change inherent in the organization.

The organization's size constitutes one of the most commonly researched variables in the organization adapting new technology. Some arguments have suggested that smaller organizations are more likely to be innovative as their sizes can translate into a more flexible environment. However, the opposite may be true, as the organization's size can positively lead to innovation as larger organizations are more likely to have the financial resources to invest in new technologies. The extent of new technological systems adoption in hospital supply chains is positively affected by hospital size.

Influential factors from the external environment in which an organization conducts its business will affect the technology. There are two external environmental factors that affect systems within healthcare institutions. They are business partner influence and government influence. Pressure from supply-chain partners and government influence constitute environmental factors that may influence an organization's adoption of technologies. Suppliers may advocate certain technologies and suggest their adoption or even use their power and influence to pressure their business partners to do so. Governments can provide incentives or even mandate technology adoption, especially in highly regulated sectors such as healthcare.

Supply chain costs, encircling all costs related to the purchase, distribution, and management of supplies, are critical to improving the hospital cost performance as they account for about one-third of the operating costs of healthcare facilities. Considering the global trends toward healthcare cost reductions and the fiscal policies aiming at public healthcare spending cuts, the focus is placed on the cost side of hospital performance. Cost performance has to be used in conjunction with quality performance when assessing overall hospital performance.

The insights discussed earlier concerning ERP systems adoption in hospitals and their demonstrated impact on hospital supply chain costs bring attention to this less-explored area of research and reinforce the role of ERP systems as a strategic asset for the digitalization of the healthcare supply chain. There is a growing push for hospitals to urgently digitalize their supply chains by implementing and leveraging Enterprise Resource Process (ERP) systems to deliver quality care at a lower cost. To support the new technology, there is a need for hospital executives to secure adequate financial and organizational resources, provide active support, remove barriers during the implementation process, provide incentives to those involved, and promote the benefits of ERP systems to employees. Encouraging a learning and continuous improvement culture is crucial for increasing technological readiness. The government, as a major public health stakeholder, top management of healthcare institutions, and the research community, should engage in coordinated actions toward increasing the awareness of the role of ERP systems. A greater understanding of their potential benefits and positive impact on hospital cost performance may lead to a faster and more comprehensive adoption.

Chapter 17

It Is Time to Clinically Integrate the Healthcare Supply Chain

Yes, it is time to clinically integrate the healthcare supply chain. But it is not that simple to accomplish. First, there is the basic design to think about and to implement. Part of this layout are four major areas of interest that need attention as well as the relationship between healthcare at large and the frontline clinicians. The four major areas of interest are engagement, knowledge, insights, and change management. To begin, let's consider the design and layout of such an undertaking.

We've learned many lessons based on the experiences of healthcare supply chains in recent years, and one thing has become clear. Hospitals and health systems need to connect the supply chain to the EHR of the patient and other clinical systems in order to homogenize, streamline, and automate business processes. The depth of integration and automation helps to lower costs, track supplies throughout the organization, maintain caregiver and patient safety, and ultimately improve outcomes.

In recent years, health systems have put a large focus on improving their clinical operations, but what quickly emerged during the pandemic is that business engines also play a vital role in keeping systems running smoothly. The ideal model is to combine next-generation clinical and business platforms that integrate and optimize enterprise-wide value creation. Aligning business systems with clinical investments will enhance organizational performance, accountability, and sustainability. Following this alignment, the model becomes the trusted source of cost and support for real-time decision-making.

The clinically linked healthcare supply chain plays a crucial role in lowering costs and improving outcomes. Supply leaders need the flexibility to experiment with new procurement procedures and quickly find new sources of supply to keep up with demands for equipment and supplies needed to treat patients. The bottom line is that they need to have critical supplies on hand.

Clinically integrating the supply chain (see Figure 17.1) will reap many rewards. Here are some ideas on how and where to begin:

DOI: 10.4324/9781003668732-19

- **Establish a data-driven, outcome-focused environment.** A comprehensive data management strategy that relies on delivered system integrations and data standards is key to ensuring data integrity. Not only does information need to be accurate, it also needs to be easy to understand and consume.
- **Reassess your "value-analysis" program.** Today's programs should include thoughts and ideas from physicians, nurses, and other specialists to ensure a comprehensive perspective that goes beyond cost, efficacy, and reimbursement. A more holistic assessment will also consider how supplies affect clinical labor and patient outcomes. It only stands to reason that the more involved clinicians are in the process, the more readily they will adopt their organization's supply chain strategy.
- **Keep communication lines between the supply chain team and clinical team leaders open.** Supply leaders must begin working with the chief of medicine to make sure all members of the team understand policy and changes in that policy. Having open lines of communication not only keeps everyone informed but also can spur innovations.
- **Keep your eye on the recall.** Even before the pandemic, recall management in healthcare faced a variety of challenges that were compounded by the way recalls are handled by manufacturers, distributors, third parties, and the FDA. Reliance on manual processes can lead to financial exposure and, more importantly, carry the potential to put patients and caregivers at risk. Automation is the way to go. When business and clinical systems are connected, identification of where these products are located is efficient. This capability ensures that recalls are dealt with promptly and documented appropriately.

Before implementing such a plan, we need to see how those four areas of interest and the relationship of frontline clinicians relate to this integration.

Over the last decade or so, clinical-supply integration has been created as a process to aid in fulfilling the clinical integration of healthcare supply chain. The shift from volume to value-based care shows that healthcare organizations must dig deeper; think longer term; and form a

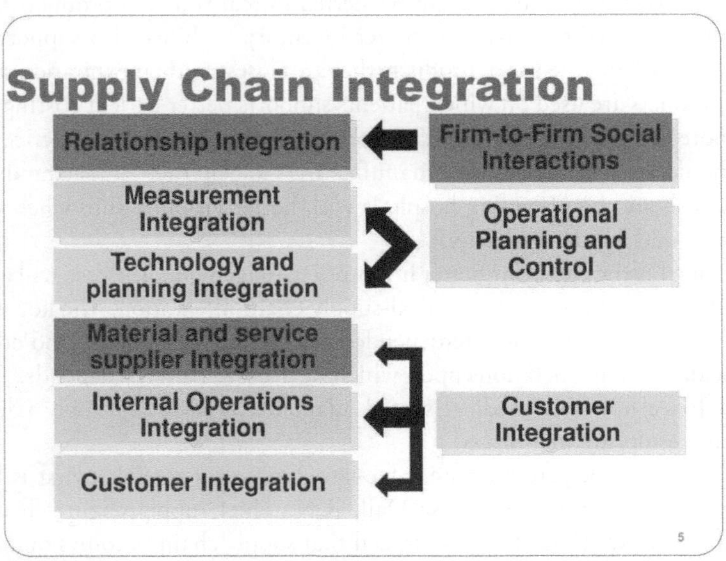

Figure 17.1 Clinically integrated supply chain value.

sustainable, committed partnership between supply chain and clinicians. With many of today's razor-thin operating margins, clinical-supply integration is a necessary financial shift. Leadership, supply chain, and clinicians must work together to make data-driven decisions for the good of the organization if it is to succeed well into the future. Safety is another strong motivator to pursue clinical-supply integration because improved resource utilization and standardized practices decrease the chance for mistakes.

Achieving this clinical-supply integration requires all stakeholders to understand where the organization stands currently and where it still needs to go. The CSI maturity model demonstrates how a healthcare supply chain can evolve over time. It is a guide designed to help the organization through the journey. It also provides the various challenges the organization will encounter. After determining what your organization has accomplished and where the organization stands today, your team can design a line of attack to reach the next phase.

There is no better way to illustrate the importance of clinical integration with the supply chain than to use an actual living and breathing example from the organization that first proposed and implemented their idea—AHRMM: Association for Healthcare Resources and Materials Management—through an assigned task force for the Clinically Integrated Supply Chain. In the following paragraphs, we will review one of the first hospitals and medical schools to implement this process—Vanderbilt University Medical School.

In 2017, the AHRMM launched its Clinically Integrated Supply Chain Task Force, under the direction of Jimmy Chung, MD. This task force was assigned to find an interdisciplinary approach to deliver patient care with the highest value—high quality, best outcomes, and minimal waste at the lowest cost of care. The goal was to achieve this level of care through absorption, coordination of clinical and supply chain knowledge, data, and leadership across the healthcare spectrum.

The use of clinical evidence can help both clinicians and supply chain collaborate to determine the best products that deliver the best care at the best price. Fortified with this information, hospitals and health systems can standardize specific products and suppliers. Standardization and fewer suppliers will also increase clinician familiarity with the product, which will reduce errors in their use.

With tracking inventory, clinicians can be alerted in real time if a product that is expired or recalled is about to be used on a patient. Better inventory visibility also supports practices that reduce waste by prioritizing the use of products that are closest to their expiration dates. Capturing data on which products are used on which patients supports better patient costing, and it can also help generate more evidence on how products perform in routine clinical practice.

Hospitals should be sharing data with manufacturers to help them understand actual demand. In turn, suppliers should be providing hospitals with better visibility into when they can expect product shipments and in what quantity.

There is a strong business case for better inventory management. The case will only get stronger as more hospitals seek and implement clinical-supply chain integration. The key will be broadening their view as they recognize the interdependencies between the quality and cost of healthcare delivery and the day-to-day operations upon which healthcare delivery depends.

Now we shall see how one medical school adapted AHRMM's Supply Chain Integration Program, and the results are manifested.

As health systems participate in more value-based payment models, what is the role of supply chain executives? According to Teresa Dail, R.N., chief supply chain officer at Vanderbilt University Medical Center (VUMC), it is crucial that supply chain becomes more clinically integrated and that decisions about purchasing and deployment are equitable and patient-focused. Dail oversees VUMC's $1 billion supply chain, which includes everything from value analysis, contracting, procurement, and accounts payable to the logistics of receiving and inventory and equipment management.

VUMC, a leader in the healthcare supply chain world, in 2018 established the Vanderbilt Supply Chain Collaborative and Supply Chain Consulting Group. This group offers new service model creation and sharing of ideas with approximately 50 hospitals, a number of non-acute care facilities across the country and medical suppliers. With this collaboration of data and ideas, the 1,000-bed VUMC gets better pricing on everything from spine implants to pharmaceuticals, saving about $4 million to $5 million annually as a result.

The traditional thinking of supply chain being only focused inside the four walls of the hospital needs to change. Care trends are changing—more care is being provided outside of the emergency room and hospital admissions—and supply chain executives need to be involved in these trends. When considering interoperability of medical devices, health systems need to get the right language into the technological systems.

At Vanderbilt, teams of clinicians and supply chain executives come together to study data and look at how closely clinicians are adhering to agreed-upon contracts with vendors about which supplies will be used. Even though Vanderbilt has strong processes in place, it seems to be a struggle to get leaders to take ownership. Supply chain executives can share this data but can't manage changes in process at the physician and clinician level by themselves.

Supply chain executives can remind financial and clinical executives that savings achieved through volume contracting get re-invested into the organization, as well any savings from waste reduction.

But, beyond cost, VUMC now has the capability to pull together quality data and cost drivers to look at the entire patient population. This will allow each hospital which adapts this program to see how they are performing against their peers, not just on cost but also on LOS, complication rates, and readmissions.

In addition, VUMC has created a startup for-profit subsidiary called Carefluent Connect to support home medical equipment needs of patients as they transition from VUMC care into the home. Additional service offerings include patient transportation and nutritional needs. The company will either contract out for those services or provide them itself. With this new subsidiary, VUMC believes they will impact patient outcomes in a positive manner, outside the walls of the hospital and reducing admissions.

Chapter 18

The End-to-End Healthcare Supply Chain

In the healthcare supply chain, span of control and end-to-end relationships are related concepts. Span of control relates to areas influenced by the supply chain. End-to-end relationships refer to the goal of evolving a true end-to-end supply chain and the involvement of all in it. Both remain a challenge in the healthcare industry.

An end-to-end supply chain (Figure 18.1) combines a business's supply chain functions into one continuous workflow, from procurement of raw materials through delivery of finished goods to customers. This is in 180 degree contrast to the series of loosely connected operations in a traditional siloed supply chain. An end-to-end supply chain focuses not only on the operations involved but also on how they interact with one another to create a complete view of a company's supply chain. Each function is optimized in a way that emphasizes collaboration, connectivity, and integration. Visibility across the entire supply chain, of a business, can identify optimizations to create a more streamlined and efficient operation, leading to cost savings, reduced waste, and increased customer satisfaction.

This visibility is a necessity for businesses to effectively communicate, solve problems, and provide service to partners and customers Any change made to one operation should

Figure 18.1 Different perspective of end-to-end supply chain.

DOI: 10.4324/9781003668732-20

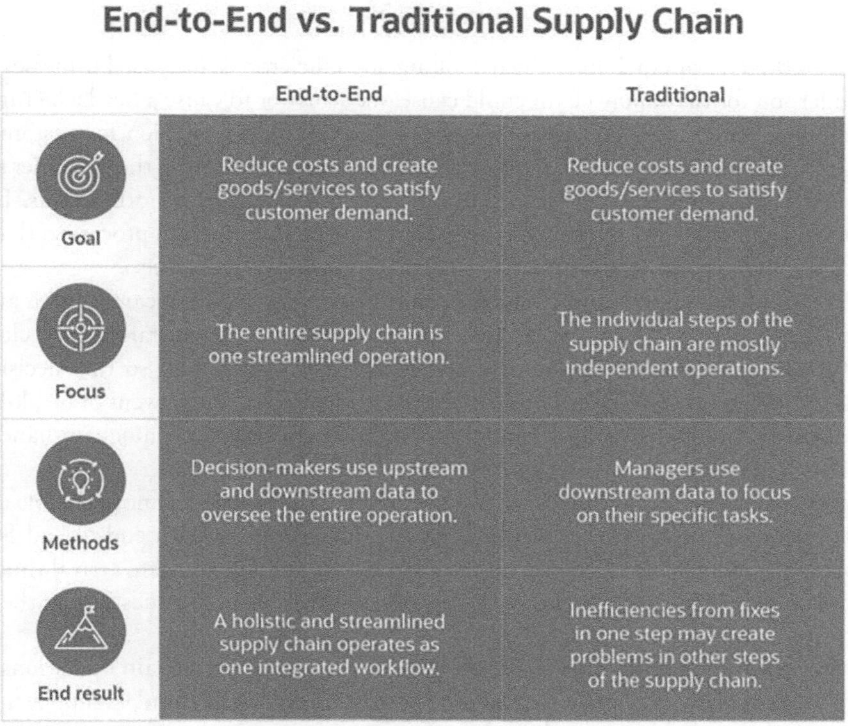

Figure 18.2 Comparison for perspective.

be analyzed from two perspectives: How does this impact the internal operation and other internal departments, and how does it impact any other operations in the supply chain? The objective of end-to-end SCM is to optimize each function without negatively impacting the rest of the workflow.

The best way to show this is with a comparison between the end-to-end supply chain and the traditional supply chain (see Figure 18.2). End-to-end and traditional supply chains have the same overall goal of reducing costs and providing customers with goods or services. Both types of supply chains involve many of the same functions, such as manufacturing, shipping, and customer service. However, a traditional supply chain primarily looks at each function of a business's operation as an individual, stand-alone process with its own needs and goals. Not the case in an end-to-end supply chain, which views each function as a single step in a larger integrated process.

A traditional supply chain typically focuses on downstream information, with managers focusing on data based on the inputs they receive from prior steps in the supply chain. Downstream visibility is focused primarily on how a business's products are traveling to the customer. In an end-to-end supply chain, decision-makers concentrate on upstream information, which provides visibility into how all the raw materials necessary to make those products are moving through the supply chain. Downstream and upstream information together creates the end-to-end supply chain.

End-to-end supply chain can provide a business with the same benefits, challenges, and best practices as other types of SCM. Here is the breakdown of those three.

Benefits

- **More efficient operations:** When looking for efficiency solutions, businesses that have blinders on for the supply chain could cause one's answer to cause a headache further down the chain. For example, a faster sales process could lead to confusion for customers exploring returns, warranties, or service options and end up complicating the customer service and reverse logistics process, tying up staff who could be focusing on other tasks. End-to-end management helps streamline and integrate the entire supply chain process so that improvements aren't negated by unforeseen collateral damage down the line.
- **Less risk of delays and supply chain breakdowns:** A breakdown can occur at any point in the supply chain, from an unexpected supplier shutdown to a natural disaster, closing delivery routes. End-to-end SCM provides visibility across operations so that decision-makers can see where vulnerabilities lie and plan for contingencies in the event of breakdowns such as diversifying suppliers and shipping companies or changing how much on-hand inventory is distributed throughout a region.
- **Increased customer satisfaction:** The goal of SCM is to create a more reliable and affordable operation, both for the business and for the customer. With end-to-end SCM, businesses can establish detailed tracking information and more accurate arrival times. Even in the case of delays, quick customer notification and updated timelines can be the difference for patient satisfaction.
- **Better vendor relationships:** End-to-end visibility into supply chain operations goes both downstream and upstream, benefiting the healthcare institutions and its suppliers. Managers using an end-to-end supply chain have a transparent and organized ordering process for their needed medical supplies and services. Vendors can avoid rush orders or frantic emergency shipments by having a more thorough understanding of what their clients need are.
- **Transparency in operations and inventory:** Businesses with visibility across their supply chain can see a detailed view of every step of production to prevent manufacturing delays. In today's economy, with many companies operating as e-commerce businesses and the amount of data needed for a comprehensive end-to-end supply chain, many businesses use software and a fully integrated business platform to keep the data organized and accessible.
- **Better data for analysis, forecasts, and improvements:** All the data collected during the end-to-end supply chain process can be used to better forecast customer demand and production schedules. Instead of flying by the seat of one's pants and hoping to produce enough for a potentially busy season, accurate demand forecasts can keep shelves stocked just enough and minimize carrying costs and waste.

Challenges

- **Complexity:** The intricacies of the supply chain can make visibility into every function and operation of a healthcare institution difficult to achieve. Measurements, such as inventory levels, available supplies, and shipment tracking, can be delayed, and communication breakdowns can occur. For many smaller hospitals or other healthcare institutions implementing end-to-end SCM for the first time may require an investment in a more sophisticated business platform than they currently use.
- **Delays in cost-cutting improvements:** End-to-end supply chain managers need to focus on the big picture and the interconnected elements of the supply chain. But that can sometimes cause delays in cost-saving measures as decision-makers miss the trees for the forest. For example, if a medical supplier is offering customers a lower price than a business's

current vendor on comparable-quality those supplies, managers may spend too much time weighing the impact on the supply chain and miss out on the opportunity. Quicker thinking can create benefits that analysis can miss. What is the balance in healthcare?

- **Overpromising and underdelivering:** To gain customers' trust, businesses may unintentionally give too much visibility to customers and create unrealistic expectations. For example, if a business is overconfident in its delivery tracking system and processing times, it may promise estimated delivery times or give automatic tracking information to hospitals for "shipped" items that are still being processed. If a shipping label is printed and the information is forwarded to the healthcare institutions days before the goods end up on a transportation mode, it will cause an unforeseen delay and danger in patient care. Over time, familiarity with end-to-end analysis should close the gap between new features and how best to use them.

Best Practices

- **Share information throughout the supply chain.** It's important for every manager or team leader throughout the supply chain to have access to current data and strategies. By creating a well-connected network that includes suppliers, the workforce, and customers, businesses can create stronger relationships than their competition, leading to higher quality and loyalty from every party.
- **Emphasize demand planning to keep inventory just lean enough.** Demand planning is one of the most important ways to control the supply chain and inventory levels. Overstock limits warehouse space and storage facilities. It increases carrying costs, and it slows fulfillment. Understock drives customers to competitors. Companies using demand planning can stock just enough to meet demand and keep customers.
- **Prioritize a reliable workforce.** End-to-end supply chains are only as effective as the staff handling each step. Managers with a knowledgeable staff can implement changes and avoid breakdowns in the supply chain. Companies with high employee retention and effective training programs are better suited to the complexities of the end-to-end supply chain than companies that rely on new hires because of heavy turnover.

The supply chain is the route through which a business's lifeblood must flow, from the first design blueprint to the final sale to the customer. But businesses facing unexpected breakdowns in their supply chains are often left scrambling to find new suppliers, distributors, or delivery services. Thanks to advanced technologies, such as cloud-based software and Blockchain, companies can collect and analyze data to effectively manage end-to-end supply chains, which look at the supply chain as one holistic operation instead of as being separate and independent processes.

By managing the healthcare supply chain as a single streamlined workflow, medical institutions can optimize their complete operations instead of one task at a time. End-to-end SCM can help all medical and healthcare institutions—no matter the size—create highly efficient and reliable operations that have the flexibility to withstand supply chain breakdowns while reducing costs and increasing customer satisfaction.

III

CHANGES IN HEALTHCARE SUPPLY CHAIN OVER THE LAST TEN YEARS

Now that we have explored some of the major challenges facing the healthcare supply chain, we can discuss the changes healthcare institutions have endured while facing these challenges:

- The size and role of government regulations
- Medical packaging and labeling
- Environmental social initiatives
- Solving structural challenges in supply chains
- The circular supply chain in healthcare
- New administrations tariffs and effect on healthcare

Healthcare is a complex and multifaceted industry that requires a series of interconnected systems—the ones listed earlier—to function efficiently. One of these key systems is the healthcare supply chain industry. It comprises a network of resources and processes that coordinate and manage the transportation of goods and services from manufacturers and suppliers to healthcare providers.

The healthcare supply chain industry has come a long way in a relatively short time. Just a few decades ago, hospitals managed supplies manually with pen and paper. Today, technology drives healthcare inventory management, providing real-time visibility into medical resources. However, the supply chain industry still faces roadblocks. Shortages, waste, and inefficiencies persist. Innovative solutions are revolutionizing healthcare supply chain operations and resilience.

DOI: 10.4324/9781003668732-21

Chapter 19

Medical Packaging and Labeling in Healthcare Supply Chain Industry: Or How to Stay Compliant

Understanding regulatory frameworks is a crucial first step in ensuring compliance with medical packaging standards, especially as many medical products are made overseas. Different regions are governed by specific agencies, and familiarity with these entities is essential for adhering to guidelines. In the United States, the Food and Drug Administration oversees medical packaging standards and prioritizing safety. In Europe, the European Medicines Agency plays a key role in regulating packaging standards. Depending on the location of operations, other relevant regulatory bodies may also be involved. These agencies establish and enforce guidelines to safeguard the quality and integrity of medical packaging. Businesses in the production and distribution of medical devices and pharmaceuticals need to stay well informed of all labeling requirements, as shown in Figure 19.1

To ensure compliance with these two regulatory agencies, most manufacturers of medical equipment and supplies have implemented standard certifications from the International Organization for Standardization. This organization has created a number of certifications to ensure that manufacturing standards are met for packaging and labeling. There are three certifications created by this organization to ensure complete compliance throughout the medical supply industry and, thereby, the healthcare supply chains.

The first one is ISO 13485. ISO 13485 serves as the foundation outlining the requirements for a Quality Management System within all medical supply manufacturers. This standard provides a comprehensive framework that organizations can adopt to ensure the consistent production of safe and effective medical devices. A well-structured Quality Management System, together with ISO 13485, covers all facets such as developing quality policies, managing risks, controlling documents, and incorporating continuous improvement processes. Adhering to this international standard enables companies involved in medical packaging to establish and maintain a systematic approach to quality.

DOI: 10.4324/9781003668732-22

Figure 19.1 Proper labeling in healthcare.

Second, there is ISO 11607. This standard scrupulously outlines requirements and test methods essential for materials and overall packaging systems within the medical industry. ISO 11607 provides a framework to guarantee the integrity and safety of medical packaging—critical aspects such as the suitability of materials for maintaining product sterility. With exact observance of ISO 11607, companies involved in medical packaging can establish and maintain a reliable and standardized approach to packaging design, validation, and process control. This commitment to compliance reinforces the assurance that medical products are packaged in a manner that preserves their quality and meets the stringent requirements of the healthcare supply chains and patients.

Lastly, the third certification is ISO 14971. This standard guides organizations in identifying, analyzing, and mitigating risks throughout the product lifecycle. Aligning risk management practices with ISO 14971 enables companies to reinforce their ability to anticipate and address any and all issues that might arise. This ensures that packaging processes have met industry best practices.

Throughout these medical certifications, there are three validation processes that need to be followed to ensure the effectiveness of packaging—labeling, environmental conditions, and traceability.

Compliance with thorough labeling standards is of utmost importance in the field of medical packaging to guarantee the transparency and safety of the enclosed products. It is essential that all labeling on medical packaging adheres to regulatory requirements, providing accurate and clear information. This labeling should include details about the product, exact instructions for use, expiration dates, and warnings. Meeting these requirements not only facilitates regulatory approval but also plays a crucial role in ensuring that patients, healthcare professionals, and regulatory authorities can easily comprehend the information presented on the packaging. With labeling compliance, companies in the medical industry supply chain provide user safety, mitigate risk, and contribute to the overall effectiveness of the healthcare system.

The impact of environmental conditions is central to maintaining the integrity of medical packaging. It is essential to thoroughly consider and test how factors like temperature, humidity, and light may affect the packaging. Rigorous testing ensures that the packaging materials can withstand diverse storage and transportation conditions without compromising the safety or effectiveness of the contents. This conscientiousness is particularly critical for pharmaceuticals and medical devices, where the preservation of product quality is of the utmost importance. Fortifying packaging against environmental challenges contribute to the reliability of their products throughout the supply chain.

Medical supply companies need to establish a strong traceability system to ensure transparency and accountability within the medical packaging supply chain. Traceability functions as a meticulous record-keeping mechanism which will facilitate a comprehensive tracking of materials from initial sourcing through every stage of manufacturing and distribution. It involves tracing raw materials, documenting manufacturing processes intricacies, and monitoring the subsequent journey of products through the distribution network. By adopting a traceability system, companies in the medical packaging industry enhance their ability to tackle quality control concerns, mitigate risks, and comply with industry standards.

Companies who stay up-to-date on regulatory requirements ensure success of their medical packaging operations. Companies should establish a proactive approach by regularly monitoring updates and changes in regulations. This involves active participation in industry conferences, where insights into standards and best practices are shared. Subscribing to relevant publications and maintaining open lines of communication with regulatory agencies further enhance awareness of any modifications that may impact packaging processes.

Chapter 20

The Circular Supply Chain and Its Implications in Healthcare

The circular supply chain or economy (see Figure 20.1) is one that eliminates wastes and prefers the reuse of products as opposed to discarding after only one use. There are a number of moving parts to this circular supply chain, so we will concentrate only on two—surgeries and medical supplies. A circular economy would advocate for reusable products that would be more resistant to supply chain disturbances and minimize environmental impact.

Surgical operating care is one of the most energy-intensive healthcare practices with a high dependency on medical devices. This is an opportune area for the circular economy. Operating rooms are more energy intensive than clinical wards. While the application of a circular economy

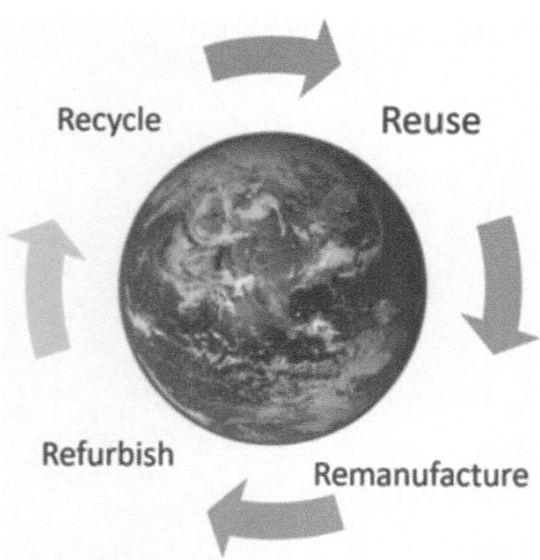

Figure 20.1 Perspective of a circular supply chain.

DOI: 10.4324/9781003668732-23

to healthcare has been discussed more generally, we describe its specific applications to the operating room environment.

A circular economy involves eliminating waste, circulating products and materials, and reinvesting resources into the environment. Within the operating room, it involves the repair, reuse, reprocessing, and recycling of surgical devices and materials. The first step is an assessment of environmental impact across the entire life cycle of products and materials used in surgery. Many life cycle assessments have been conducted in surgery, without standardized protocols and without data available for certain devices and procedures.

One example of a circular economy in surgery is reusable operating room attire—gowns and face masks. Reusable textiles, such as surgical drapes and gowns, have shown multiple environmental benefits over single-use textiles, including reduced natural resource expenditure, solid-waste production, and carbon footprint. Shortages of single-use face masks forced many systems to adopt novel reuse protocols. While healthcare systems should be lauded for their immediate adaptations, a circular economy framework relies on the reuse of materials at the outset. Reusable devices can be both environmentally beneficial and cost-effective. A circular economy could incentivize manufacturers to create surgical products that last longer or reengineer their processes to maximize the recovery of materials used.

There are several barriers to creating a circular economy in operating rooms supply chains. First, data regarding the environmental impact of surgical materials and devices are needed as well as greater transparency of manufacturers' emissions. Hospitals can apply pressure by selectively purchasing from manufacturers who provide rigorous proof of emission control. Policy change at the national level is also needed to enforce emissions reported by manufacturers. With such environmental impact data, hospitals can better assess outcomes in accordance with their financial bottom line and clinical outcomes.

Second, greater alignment is needed between the U.S. Food and Drug Administration, manufacturers, and hospitals. Although the FDA provides guidelines for medical device reprocessing, the approval process can be onerous and does not encourage medical supply manufacturers to engage in reuse. Instead, there is the challenge of planned obsolescence in device design that favors single-use processing in order to drive revenue. Policy changes that either tax environmental impact or incentivize reuse are therefore needed to align economic and environmental demands.

Third, hospitals need to invest in the infrastructure and resources for reuse and reprocessing associated with surgery. Although third-party reprocessing is one alternative, hospitals should be equipped with the staffing and services to cope with on-site reprocessing. However, on-site reprocessing requires upfront financial investment and adherence to regulatory and infection protocols.

Finally, hospitals could increase advocacy, transparency, and communication to promote best practices and motivate cultural shifts in healthcare. Patients may be willing to support sustainable healthcare and be more satisfied with hospitals that engage in sustainable practices, providing a dual benefit of serving patients' interests while conferring a competitive market advantage.

During the past 30 years, the healthcare industry has become increasingly reliant on single-use disposable medical devices, particularly in high-income nations. Medical devices include all equipment used in the provision of medical care. The healthcare supply chain can be grossly dichotomized into medical devices and pharmaceuticals. We will focus exclusively on medical devices. Single-use disposables are emblematic of a make-waste economy in which products are manufactured, used once, and disposed. This unsustainable model of production and consumption contributes to global ecological issues by depleting natural resources and generating excessive solid waste.

A more sustainable framework that has gained traction within the healthcare supply chain industry and policy makers is the circular economy, where products are maintained in use for as long as possible without terminating in disposal.

In contrast to a one-use economy, a circular economy is restorative by design. Manufactured products flow throughout the system—reuse, reprocessing, repair, repurposing, and recycling, maximizing material value and minimizing waste disposal. Some medical devices are best designed as single use. These are typically low-complexity devices that are difficult to clean such as intravenous catheters, tubing, syringes, and needles. For these products, recycling to recover the base materials may be the best option. At the other end of medical supplies are high-complexity devices such as medical imaging equipment, maintained with cycles of maintenance, repair, and refurbishment. In between are devices for which circular design coupled with reprocessing protocols offers the possibility of maintaining product integrity. The more complex the device, the higher the economic and environmental savings of maintaining product integrity. Transition to a circular economy requires the cooperation of diverse stakeholder groups moving toward a shared goal of systemic transformation. This must be built around the respective roles of hospitals and healthcare providers, original equipment manufacturers, regulators, and patients.

Achieving a circular supply chain economy in healthcare will require transformation with buy-in from device consumers, original equipment manufacturers, regulators, creditors, and professional standards organizations, like the ISO. This will require the introduction of a policy based upon solutions driving toward the objectives of eliminating waste and maximizing material value.

Hospitals and healthcare providers can take a number of important steps to create conditions that promote a circular economy—value care, organizing for reuse, updated procurement policies, circular product design, and new emission targets.

High-value care encompasses the mitigation of waste and inefficiency while maximizing patient outcomes. This framework can drive efficiency of facilities operations with respect to energy and waste management and can push clinicians to be mindful of resource consumption and to select environmentally preferable drugs and devices where choices exist. Adoption of such high-value principles in procurement will foster circular and ethical supply chains.

Hospitals should have the infrastructure for collecting recyclable materials for which reuse or reprocessing is not possible, such as packaging. Although recycling is the lowest-yield circular solution to reduce waste and emissions, clinical plastics are typically high grade, with the potential for recovery of embedded material and emissions. The challenges of securing recycling vendors for clinical materials have been successfully overcome in many systems.

When healthcare facilities adopt procurement policies that favor reusable devices over single-use disposables, they send a strong market message that innovation toward reuse will confer a competitive advantage. Procurement policies can stipulate that the disclosure of product environmental emissions through life cycle assessment is a necessary condition for entering into a service contract. Large health systems and group purchasing organizations can leverage their considerable purchasing power for procuring ethically and sustainably sourced products and helping ensure a living wage, safe working conditions, and job security along the global supply chain.

The design of durable products that are easy to disassemble for reprocessing is becoming increasingly important. Modularity, adaptability, and versatility are hallmarks of circular design. Because the original equipment manufacturer is responsible for product performance and safety, it is in its best interest to devise reprocessing protocols that are safe, effective, and easy to perform. When a product is worn out, the original equipment manufacturer is motivated to repurpose materials efficiently for new applications.

Governments shape the regulatory landscape in which private- and public-sector innovations occur. Environmental targets for emissions and waste reduction can influence healthcare facilities' operations and help drive supply-chain reform.

The ongoing manufacturing of single-use disposables in the healthcare supply chain has arisen from a multifactorial tie-in of healthcare stakeholders. A circular healthcare economy, built on principles of resource conservation, efficiency, and cycles of reuse and material recovery, offers an alternative to the unsustainable consequences of current practices. This requires comprehensive industry transformation driven by user demand and new business models, encouraged by a favorable regulatory and professional environment that values public health and sustainability as highly as individual patient safety.

Chapter 21

Solving Structural Challenges in the Healthcare Supply Chains

How could health systems enhance their ability to withstand supply shocks and deliver quality care in ordinary times and when crises strike?

This question will be addressed by discussing these priorities that remain as challenges to improving the healthcare supply chain. These are examining ways to mitigate risks, forming strategic partnerships with suppliers, and streamlining logistics.

The COVID-19 pandemic exposed challenges in U.S. health system supply chains. Persistent and prominent supply shortages, together with economic uncertainty and rising inflation, have exposed that this may well be the most opportune time for health institutions to improve their supply chains.

Health institutions are habitually familiar to dealing with supply shortages. However, many were not prepared to respond to the scale of the supply chain blows when the pandemic struck. For example, overnight, PPE including N95 masks, latex gloves, face shields, eye masks, and gowns were depleted and unable to quickly be restocked. Many health institutions and systems ignored their standard procurement practices. They purchased from suppliers or resellers without their typical level of vetting, guaranteed future purchase volumes, and paid significantly higher prices. These unusual practices brought undesirable results—overstocking, accepting lower quality standards on medical supplies, or not receiving a product at all.

Due to the pandemic and ongoing supply chain disruptions, health systems continue to experience shortages of critical medical supplies. Health systems are now shifting their focus from managing severe pandemic-related shortages to creating more resilient, efficient, and economically viable approaches to procurement for the long term. All health institutions must be prepared for ever-present threats such as another global health crisis, a regional health emergency, or a mass-casualty event of any origin.

Health institutions that fail to adequately plan for future supply chain shocks will severely hinder patient care and incur reputational, financial, and other risks. Caught short of critical

DOI: 10.4324/9781003668732-24

supplies, health system leaders could face difficult challenges, including providing care of lesser quality, canceling certain types of care, or paying substantially more from alternate vendors for the same supplies. Supply chain shortages will place even higher pressures on a workforce still recuperating from the pandemic. Supply chain leaders will need to devote considerable time and effort to find alternatives, and clinicians may lack the supplies they need to properly do their jobs in the meantime.

It isn't possible for health systems to fully mitigate themselves from all future supply shocks, as they are unpredictable and come with their own level of severity. But the supply chain leaders must learn from their experiences during the pandemic and build strategies to minimize risk and augment resistance moving forward.

One of the most important challenges for healthcare supply chain leaders to recognize and learn is the benefits of forming strong strategic partnerships with medical suppliers. The benefits of these partnerships are incremental cost savings or revenue, increased sustainability of long-term savings, access to additional resources, and expanded reach into those communities.

The healthcare industry is rapidly changing on a local level with competing hospitals establishing strategic relationships around the community, which can significantly increase competition for patients. With an ongoing shift toward outpatient care in the market, hospitals continue to evaluate opportunities to increase outpatient offerings. Hospitals are often turning to suppliers for partnership opportunities to increase patient reach.

Ensuring a beneficial outcome for all parties involved in a partnership is not an easy-to-accomplish feat. From the start, the partnership must agree on their mutual purpose to keep everyone committed on a common goal. Many partners will develop a charter and detailed work plans to keep on track. Sharing institutional knowledge and best practices can be invaluable to help each party achieve their mutual and individual goals.

Although collaboration in the healthcare industry is commonplace today, limitations do exist regarding those that can collaborate and the degree to which they do. This is especially true for physician-hospital relationships because of Stark Law, where potential conflicts of interests can carry the threat of litigation and hefty fines. What makes matters more complicated is that Stark Law does lack clarity which is why you should pay careful attention to any relationships that may involve physicians.

The right leadership is a key success factor for strategic alliances. Without this, the best designed and well-intentioned alliance will often fail. Collaborative leadership teams that effectively utilize Steering Committees to manage key decisions should be required to help work out any issues and review progress toward the mutual goals.

Lastly, some supply chain leaders might argue that healthcare institutions' most important challenge is to streamline their logistical operations. To that point, there are four strategies to aid in streamlining healthcare logistics. They are the following:

- Ensure product integrity
- Adapt to fluctuating demand
- Navigating regulations
- Good manufacturing practices or GMP compliance

Maintaining the integrity of medical products and safeguarding sensitive data are critical priorities in the healthcare industry. Temperature-controlled storage and specialized handling procedures and strong cybersecurity protocols are essential to preserving the quality and safety of your products. Logistic partners with advanced technological capabilities—drug packaging and labeling licenses and cold storage—can provide the solutions needed to protect the medical supplies and ensure they are safe to send for patients.

The healthcare supply chain is characterized by unpredictable demand patterns, driven by factors such as seasonal flu outbreaks, natural disasters, and global pandemics. Effectively managing these sudden shifts in demand is crucial to ensuring the timely delivery of critical medical supplies and equipment. Logistic providers with growing operations and flexible logistics solutions can help healthcare organizations adapt to these fluctuations.

The healthcare industry is subject to a maze of regulations and compliance requirements, especially in a global economy, where each country has their own governmental healthcare regulations. GMP compliance refers to the adherence to a set of guidelines and regulations that ensure the quality, safety, and efficacy of pharmaceutical products and healthcare items. These guidelines cover various aspects of manufacturing, storage, handling, and distribution and are designed to maintain the integrity of the products throughout the supply chain. Failure to adhere to these stringent guidelines can result in costly fines, product recalls, and reputational damage. Logistical providers with expertise in this healthcare field can navigate these regulatory complexities with ease, ensuring that your supply chain operations remain secure.

These are some of the reasons why GMP compliance is important in healthcare logistics and supply chain:

- Compliant warehousing ensures that pharmaceutical products and healthcare items are stored and handled in controlled environments that meet specific temperature, humidity, and security requirements. This helps to prevent product degradation and maintain their quality and effectiveness.
- Adhering to GMP guidelines helps companies avoid regulatory penalties, product recalls, and reputational damage. It also demonstrates their commitment to patient safety and product quality.
- GMP compliant warehousing practices help mitigate the risk of product contamination, cross-contamination, and mix-ups during storage and distribution. Proper labeling, lot tracing, segregation, and handling procedures minimize the chances of errors and ensure the integrity of the products.
- Well-organized storage, accurate inventory management, and efficient distribution processes reduce lead times and minimize stock-outs.
- Compliance in healthcare logistics directly benefits patients by ensuring that the products they receive are safe, effective, and of high quality. Proper storage conditions and handling practices prevent the distribution of counterfeit, expired, or contaminated products, protecting patient health and well-being.

In the vigorous and highly regulated healthcare industry, managing the complex maze of logistics and supply chain operations is a constant challenge. Healthcare and wellness product companies often grapple with complexities such as ensuring product integrity, data security, regulatory compliance, and the timely delivery of products. These challenges can divert valuable resources away from a company's core competencies, hindering growth and innovation.

However, the solution to these supply chain puzzles lies in partnering with a trusted logistics provider. By outsourcing logistics and SCM to a specialized logistic company, healthcare organizations can solve benefits that streamline operations, enhance efficiency, and ultimately improve patient care.

Chapter 22

Environmental and Social Initiatives in the Healthcare Supply Chain

If the major industrialized nations' healthcare industry has a tremendous impact on both the environment, generating 8.5% of greenhouse gas emissions, and the socioeconomic health as the largest source of jobs representing 17.7% of world's gross domestic product, *then why have so few health systems and hospitals made progress in addressing environmental, social, and governance issues?*

One primary reason is the lack of accountability. There are several recent initiatives aimed at driving healthcare toward measurable ESG improvements, such as the Joint Commission's Sustainable Healthcare Certification Program, which went into effect on January 1, 2024.

But, it is not merely reputation based upon certifications. Lack of accountability can be seen as part of dollars being spent on these programs. Healthcare organizations that show their commitment to ESG criteria can access lower rates from lenders.

For healthcare organizations faced with unmatched economic and labor challenges, costs and competing priorities are major barriers to ESG improvements. While ESG is something most health leaders would like to embrace, many can't afford to allocate human and financial resources to these initiatives as they struggle to deliver care to their communities.

Another major barrier to ESG improvements is identifying initiatives that will have a measurable impact. It's one thing for a health system or hospital to say that ESG is a priority, but quite another for an organization to back this statement with proof that they are reducing their environmental footprint or improving health equity in their community.

But the pressure to show and or to implement ESG programs is on the rise. The U.S. Securities and Exchange Commission proposed that climate disclosure requirements would require publicly listed companies, including healthcare organizations, to report on their ESG programs. ESG reporting requirements for nonprofit healthcare organizations will be next.

The supply chain presents innumerable opportunities for a health institution or an individual hospital to make appreciable improvements in its social and environmental initiatives

DOI: 10.4324/9781003668732-25

through the purchases it makes—from the selection of diverse suppliers to products with less packaging waste.

But given financial, labor, and accountability barriers, healthcare organizations need to drive procurement departments responsible for purchasing without extra burdens like costs. At the same time, they also need to automatically capture metrics on this purchasing activity for both voluntary and mandatory reporting.

Chapter 23

The Role of Standards in the Post-Pandemic Healthcare Supply Chain

After the crisis created by the COVID-19 pandemic, healthcare organizations throughout the entire supply chain are turning their attention to the future to look for answers to the questions, "What could we have done differently?" and "How should we prepare for future pandemics and other crises?" Federal, state, and local government agencies are reacting similarly with a number of supply-chain-related proposals. Much of this activity could have possibly been avoided if unique identification standards had been adopted across the healthcare supply chain.

Where should the healthcare industry focus its attention to cause the most impact when there are so many other issues that need to be addressed? The exchange and coordination of reliable, trusted quality data seem to be of the utmost importance to all opportunities for improvement. One place to start is with swift and total adoption of standards. Those standards are already in action as a result of specific regulations such as unique device identification and the Drug Supply Chain Security Act. Full adoption of the global standards supporting these regulations could help address two critical themes that have been shown to adversely impact patient care.

- Product transparency
- Data-driven demand planning and forecasting

These themes could have been dramatically mitigated with the adoption and use of global standards for both medical devices and pharmaceutical products. The challenge is in getting universal acceptance of these standards. The following sections provide an overview of how global standards would support improvement in these two areas.

Products used in patient care—prior to the virus of 2020—were well scrutinized by healthcare professionals before they were ever brought in for use in the treatment of patients. This surge of new products and suppliers created a huge backlog of supplies that still were yet to be

DOI: 10.4324/9781003668732-26

inspected before these medical products could be properly added to the healthcare inventory. Supply chain professionals lacked insight into all of the necessary product attributes for these to be efficiently and accurately added to any patient care. Without basic information about these products, healthcare supply chains were not able to categorize "like" products in order to confidently shift from one product to another equivalent. This led to possible poor judgment on the part of clinicians as they were unsure of the new product use and its far-reaching effect on patient care. Without efficient supplier and full product knowledge, a hospital's ability to maintain the flow of inventory for even the most basic types of devices and pharmaceuticals was hindered. This lack of product transparency contributed to slower patient care and created supply chain shortages, thus risking patient care.

Poor medical and product knowledge proved to be a significant issue during the pandemic. This impacted both medical devices and pharmaceuticals and, in some cases, delayed the product from being available or sent where it was most needed. The resulting lack of the existing inventory level accuracy, coupled with limited demand planning and forecasting, contributed to significant product shortages. Furthermore, understanding changes in product use to drive patient care requires quick and accurate identification. This was especially true during the height of the COVID pandemic as unique uses of both devices and drugs depleted the availability of certain products. Tying product usage to patient-driven outcomes allows for an accelerated recognition of what products are in play for the treatment of patient care situations. The use of standards for the globally unique identification of both products and locations would provide consistent identification by all supply chain stakeholders of products used at the point of care. Armed with these product and demand specifics, both manufacturers and providers would be better positioned to forecast demand and position the available products to align with normal and/or immediate needs.

The adoption and use of data standards across the industry and with all the manufacturers of medical equipment and supplies will serve as a foundation for improving supply chain transparency, planning, and resiliency of medical devices and pharmaceuticals.

The use of unique device identifiers to positively identify products improves product transparency by supporting automated systems that can:

1. Confirm the product being used is the correct one
2. Link the unique devise identifier to other product attributes such as latex, expiration date, and other clinical data.
3. Allow for similar products to be classified together to improve flexible usage at the patient care.

Supply chain professionals in healthcare routinely engage in manual efforts to manage and analyze data in order to complete tasks and processes that most consumer goods industries have automated. As a result, reactions to changes in utilization or sourcing and obtaining clinically acceptable substitute products from new sources can take longer and delay critical supplies in reaching the patient care setting. The broader use of identification standards within healthcare would support the automation of these processes streamlining the process and expediting the delivery of these products to front line healthcare workers.

The ability to quickly and confidently identify a product anywhere in the supply chain is a necessary condition to implementing systems that will provide an understanding of what is used and where it is located or consumed.

U.S. regulations exist for both medical devices and pharmaceutical products, which require these products to be uniquely identified and marked in both human and machine-readable formats. These regulations are intended to provide a standardized way to confidently and uniquely identify medical devices and pharmaceuticals across all information sources and systems. Unfortunately, these unique identifiers are not in use by all players in the healthcare supply chain, so many of the benefits to patient care are haphazard.

Chapter 24

Tariffs and the Healthcare Supply Chain

There is much discussion and discernment concerning the possible tariffs that President Trump wishes to impose on a number of foreign nations and products. The tariffs we are most concerned about for this book are the healthcare tariffs on medical equipment, supplies, and medication—most, if not all, are made overseas.

The question to ask is: Will President Trump be able to impose these tariffs on everything he has described? Every politician running for any office often promises more than they can deliver. Perhaps, we need to see what he actually delivers before sounding the alarm bells.

While we are all waiting, we can explore the possible impacts and effects on the healthcare supply chain if any or all of these tariffs do take effect.

The COVID-19 pandemic challenged the U.S. healthcare supply chain in a way in which hospitals purchased and used equipment. Decades of focusing on cost reductions were replaced with considerations about device reuse, PPE, shortages, and securing supply chain reserves. Single-source contracts went away, while supply chain leaders sought new and creative ways of securing the medical supplies they needed through multi-supplier arrangements. Suddenly, price took a backseat to assurances of keeping the supply of material ongoing.

After the pandemic was over, healthcare institutions returned to their normal manner of securing medical supplies—price, price, and price. However, healthcare supply chain leaders took a lesson with them: While cost may be the king, the healthcare system needs to fundamentally update its supply chain system to understand that cost is not the only measure of value—delivery, damages, quality reduce vulnerability and bring hospital procurement up to date with the newest technologies.

In December 2024, healthcare supply leaders again found their roles to be evolving and becoming the most important ones in U.S. healthcare. It's not because the demand for value was causing internal pressure. It's because of the President's position about tariffs. This position is causing great concerns about the availability of the needed products. In reaction, hospital supply chain procurement departments are buying as much as they can within disposable product categories that are either expensive or critical. Whether this reaction is warranted, time can only tell us.

DOI: 10.4324/9781003668732-27

To combat any tariff plan of President Trump, many healthcare institutions have plans in place focusing on group purchasing power, real-time supply analysis, adapting to more ambulatory surgeries, and adopting new technologies throughout their respective institutions.

Healthcare institutions are at a serious disadvantage within the current healthcare supply marketplace. Alone, even the largest hospitals have no negotiation power. Nearly every healthcare supplier is ten times bigger than the biggest hospital buyer, and they usually can operate in a monopolistic manner. These suppliers of medical products are more sophisticated in their sales processes than hospitals are in their buying processes.

To catch up with technology, manage new product adoption, reduce risk, and optimize bargaining power, health systems cannot continue to act alone. They need to come together around the same platforms, and they need a system of mediation, negotiation, and demand to successfully navigate these supplier market.

The way many have found is through group purchasing organizations—the agent for healthcare procurement to address these needs. In the eyes of supply leaders, GPOs today do not perform this role—if they ever did. Healthcare needs a better purchasing structure that transcends the individual health system.

Healthcare supply chain leaders want an actionable, real-time understanding of life cycle of all medical supplies as opposed to historical numbers. Getting to advanced, actionable analytics is key. This can mean the use of AI and other advanced tools.

In terms of technology, healthcare supply chain has a lot of catch-up to do, compared with other industries. There are examples of companies and solutions that enable healthcare systems to benefit from technology and adopt newer technologies to make the supply chains more efficient and effective. Inventory management is the right place to start but the most compelling progress will be made with predictive analytics, demand planning, and better forecasting models.

The ever-growing occurrence of ambulatory surgery centers and other specialized care services like imaging can be seen as a threat to hospitals. Hospital administrators fear that high-margin procedures could disappear, leaving their facilities with only low-margin procedures and a downward spiral to financial issues.

This is happening on some key healthcare service lines, including orthopedics, spine, and cardiology. Most hospitals are still running with a 2% operating margin, and they can't afford this migration. On the other hand, this development also represents an opportunity for healthcare facilities to specialize and get the care closer to the patient.

Fragmentation and decentralization of care represent an opportunity for hospitals, and supply chain leaders know that it should be embraced rather than feared. From a capacity standpoint, specialization helps with throughput. However, hospitals must be deliberate and strategic in this area in order to retain revenue and not break the universe of healthcare. Hospital leaders should start by learning how successful surgery center systems manage centralized purchasing and apply those lesson within their own organizations.

Supply chain leaders in healthcare are still battling the increasing cost of new technology pursued by doctors who are insisting that they and the hospitals be the vanguard of any new technological advances and head of any competition in their fields. The hospitals created the Value Analysis Committees (VACs) to ensure that these new and expensive technologies were not just new shiny toys for physicians. If they are to be adopted, new technologies should make a difference in terms of patient care quality.

The VACs are not scientific tools to evaluate the value of new technology. Supply chain leaders want this to change and looking at the Medical Device Technology Cost Efficiency Index. This is a standardized index that calculates cost-per-procedure improvement to clarify the value of any and all new technology. This index would be extremely useful in the healthcare supply chain as an objective, data-based tool for deciding whether to adopt new technology. This type of index could be used as an industry guide, and at the same time, it could also be tailored to allow the hospital to calculate value based on its own pricing.

In conclusion, we are presently watching how President Trump's tariff plans will affect the delivery of medical supplies to all healthcare providers. At the same time, supply chain leaders will also be absorbed in trying to solve the above structural challenges that have become flawed in recent years. The need for healthcare supply chain leaders and healthcare institutions to come together to strengthen their procurement methods and business models is evident.

IV ETHICS AND SOCIAL RESPONSIBILITY IN HEALTHCARE SUPPLY CHAIN

The thought of social responsibility and ethics has been examined in a range of different industries. There is delicate but implicit relationship between morality and responsibility. Individuals are responsible for their actions and take responsibilities for themselves. Global companies have been involved in a slew of corporate scandals such as product safety, labor exploitation, and data security issues. Stakeholders tend to lose confidence in purchasing their major products, questioning the quality of services and validity of the disclamation of product labeling. Governments and industries—private or public—tend to develop different legislations, standards, and guidelines to enforce compliance. In order to restore public confidence and minimize reputational risk and prevent tighter regulations, companies tend to follow international reporting guidelines, industry standards, and codes of ethics in the particular industry. This section introduces the concept of morality and ethical considerations in the healthcare supply chain, which often encompass patient safety, transparency, equitable access, environmental responsibilities, labor rights, and regulatory compliance. These criteria foster better decisions and guide trust in the healthcare delivery systems.

DOI: 10.4324/9781003668732-28

Chapter 25

Ethical Sourcing

In light of the increased scrutiny of human rights issues in global supply chains, a number of healthcare institutions undertook a comprehensive and months'-long process to review their present sourcing policies and procedures. As part of this review, they earmarked policies versus international best practices to ensure that those new ethical practices are consistent with the latest international guidance.

Approach to human rights of healthcare institutions and their supply chain leaders is guided by the international standards set forth by the United Nations Guiding Principles on Business and Human Rights ("UNGPs"). In this environment, the healthcare supply chain must reinforce UNGP's commitment:

- Promoting human rights throughout our business and supply chains
- Setting expectations and requirements for suppliers
- Assessing and, when necessary, investigating credible allegations of human rights violations in our operations
- Empowering our employees and suppliers with information and training on best practices related to ethical sourcing and human rights

The UNGP's 11 criteria of human rights standards are laid out in detail below for all healthcare institutions to follow:

- Roles and responsibilities—the commitment of senior leadership is essential to advance the key priorities of any ethical sourcing program. Senior leadership must take the healthcare institution's ethical sourcing commitments seriously as well as all employees. Implementing ethics programs across an institution or a diverse and complex medical supplier organization requires cross-functional participation. That's why many partners in the healthcare supply chain have new Ethical Sourcing Committees to take the lead. Such a team needs to be represented by employees from the following internal departments—Legal, Office of Ethics and Compliance, Corporate Social Responsibility, and the Technical Affairs department.

DOI: 10.4324/9781003668732-29

- Ethical Sourcing Standards—healthcare institutions must be committed to ensuring that business activity does not adversely impact internationally recognized human rights. The Ethical Sourcing Committees put forth the core standards under the following categories:
  1. Labor and human rights—all forms of forced and child labor are prohibited. All workers shall be treated with dignity and respect, and they shall have the right to join or form trade unions or other workers' organizations of their own choosing and to bargain collectively. Workers shall be paid at least the legal minimum wage, and working hours must comply with national laws and collective agreements, whichever affords the greater protection for workers.
  2. Health and safety—a safe and hygienic working environment shall be provided, and workplaces shall consist of structurally sound and safe buildings that meet national law and international best practice, including emergency procedures. Production facilities and any worker dormitories shall have access to an adequate number of clean toilet facilities and clean drinking water, and employers must ensure that facilities have the appropriate health, safety, and industrial hygiene certificates in place.
  3. Environment—it is expected from all healthcare systems and suppliers to carry out their activities in a manner that ensures substantial compliance with all applicable environmental laws and regulatory requirements.
  4. Other ethics and governance issues—suppliers and healthcare institutions will not tolerate bribery, corruption, extortion, and embezzlement in the business or supply chain. All must conduct business fairly and transparently in line with applicable laws while ensuring that workers who disclose information or report concerns about noncompliance in good faith are protected from retaliation. We safeguard confidential information received from third parties and protect the personal data of our employees, customers, and other individuals.
- Global risk assessment—with best practices, these institutions should prioritize the risk assessment efforts where the risks are greatest and where healthcare institutions have the ability to assert a positive change.
- Supplier engagement on ethical sourcing—healthcare institutions should be striving to conduct business with suppliers that share their commitment to high ethical standards. When new or existing suppliers accept any purchase order from them, they agree to adhere to the standards in our Supplier Code of Conduct. When evaluating new suppliers, conduct a risk-based approach to due diligence of suppliers. This means that new suppliers must first fill out comprehensive self-assessment forms, and then healthcare teams should conduct a full assessment of the new supplier against the criteria set out by the UNGPs. If a potential supplier is rated as high risk, an in-person audit of that supplier should commence.
- Social compliance audits—social compliance audits are designed to identify deviations from the Ethical Sourcing Standards and Supplier Code of Conduct established by the healthcare and the UNGPs. The healthcare institutions should insist on a risk-based approach to the audit. The audit needs to focus on suppliers with a "High" Risk Rating and high-risk issues in Ethical Sourcing Complaints. Any supplier may be subject to an audit—at any time—as an audit provides a snapshot of working conditions at a certain point in time. In order to ensure that social audits uncover violations, these points must occur, educating, training, and equipping our social auditors to perform at the highest level, conducting unannounced audits and have a holistic approach to audits that includes worker input and an assessment of relevant work and living spaces.

- Grievance mechanisms and incident response—consistent with the effectiveness criteria set out in the UNGPs, healthcare must ensure its grievance procedures are legitimate, accessible, predictable, equitable, transparent, and compatible with internationally recognized human rights standards.
- Remediation—all involved in medical supply and the supply chain must be committed to providing effective remedy where it has caused or contributed to adverse human rights impacts. All stakeholder engagement is a fundamental component to remediation.
- Customer engagement—any retail customer of medical supplies must keep abreast of human rights abuses in the global supply chains. When this has failed, it has resulted in pressure on major retailers to enforce strong and viable ethical sourcing requirements. Increasingly, institutional and public sector customers are advocating for similar requirements.
- Training all stakeholders—a fundamental component of ethical sourcing compliance is training and equipping all employees to identify and respond to risks in the global supply chain. All employees should be familiar with the ethical sourcing program in new hire training and onboarding.
- External reporting and communication—the healthcare institutions are committed to transparency and accountability around their Ethical Sourcing Standards and practices, including to all legal reporting requirements in the countries in which we operate.
- Assessing the effectiveness of ethical sourcing programs—compliance programs must evolve to effectively address risk. Any and all of the ethical sourcing programs must be reviewed on a yearly basis.

In conclusion, ethical sourcing in healthcare and its supply chain must include the following;

1. Setting clear expectations for suppliers
2. Continuous monitoring of supplier relationships
3. Proactive risk mitigation
4. Regular training and engagement on health, safety, labor, and human rights issues
5. Ensuring that suppliers meet ethical standards on sustainability and labor practices
6. Environmental practices in procurement

If ethical sourcing is taken seriously and by all accounts it seems to be—at least by some of the largest healthcare institutions—the outcomes for patient safety and product integrity are boundless.

Chapter 26

Patient Safety and Product Integrity

In the healthcare industry, the supply chain is a critical component that directly impacts patient safety and the quality of care provided. An efficient healthcare supply chain ensures that medical facilities have timely access to necessary supplies, equipment, and medications, which is essential for delivering high-quality patient care. Now we will explore how the healthcare supply chain enhances patient safety and discuss strategies to optimize its effectiveness.

The healthcare supply chain includes all processes involved in the procurement, management, and distribution of medical supplies, devices, and pharmaceuticals within healthcare organizations. This is a multifaceted system that includes manufacturers, distributors, and healthcare providers who work together to ensure that the right products are available at the right time, in the right amounts, and in the right place.

There are six pillars of patient safety that ensure proper care, and, thereby, good patient outcomes can be best assured. They are the following:

1. Timely Access to Critical Supplies—one of the most significant ways the healthcare supply chain enhances patient safety is by ensuring that critical supplies are readily available when needed. In emergencies, every second counts, and having immediate access to medical devices, surgical instruments, and medications can be a matter of life or death. By implementing effective inventory management systems and maintaining the right stock levels, healthcare institutions will reduce the risk of shortages and, thus, delays in treatment.
2. Quality, Control and Compliance—the healthcare supply chain plays an important role in maintaining the quality of medical products. Strict observance to regulations and quality control processes ensures that all supplies meet safety standards. Hospitals and clinics must establish strong relationships with reputable suppliers who prioritize quality and compliance. By following these regulations, healthcare organizations can mitigate risks tied to counterfeit products and substandard medical devices.
3. Data-Driven Decision Making—with the increased availability of data, healthcare organizations can make better and proper decisions about their supply chain operations. By analyzing usage patterns, demand forecasts, and supply chain performance metrics, healthcare providers can identify potential vulnerabilities and take proactive measures to address them.

DOI: 10.4324/9781003668732-30

4. Streamlined Operations—a well-run and organized healthcare supply chain modernizes processes and procedures within medical facilities. This allows the staff to focus more on patient care rather than managing supply issues. By executing advanced procurement systems and automating routine tasks, healthcare providers can improve workflow efficiency. This ensures that healthcare professionals can spend more time with patients leading to better outcomes.
5. Customization of Care—the healthcare supply chain enables providers to customize care for individual patients. With easy access to a diverse range of medical products, healthcare organizations can tailor treatments based on specific patient needs. This personalized approach fosters a positive patient experience.
6. Collaboration Among Stakeholders—collaboration and communications are the keys to improving patient quality care in the healthcare supply chain. By fostering strong communication and partnerships among suppliers, distributors, and healthcare providers, organizations can ensure that everyone is aligned on goals and objectives. Collaborative SCM leads to better forecasting, reduced lead times, and more effective problem-solving.

However, patient safety and the above pillars are only a part of the larger picture. The other part is to ensure and to recognize how the lack of product integrity can lead to poorer patient outcomes.

Medical product shortages represent a significant threat across the entire medical scene of both public and private healthcare delivery by undermining the ability to provide timely and high-quality care to patients. The persistence of shortages in the United States and across the globe caused by a convergence of many factors raises the need to better understand the root causes and effects of shortages.

The manufacturing of medical products is usually performed by multiple companies. What this means is that supply chains are not centrally controlled systems but instead distributed networks with multiple decision-makers that have different goals. This can lead to a window of losing product integrity, as shown by Figure 26.1, and the lack of central control leads to disparities in supply and demand. The challenges presented by decentralization during non-crisis times grow even greater when and if the supply chain is disrupted by a natural disaster, infectious disease

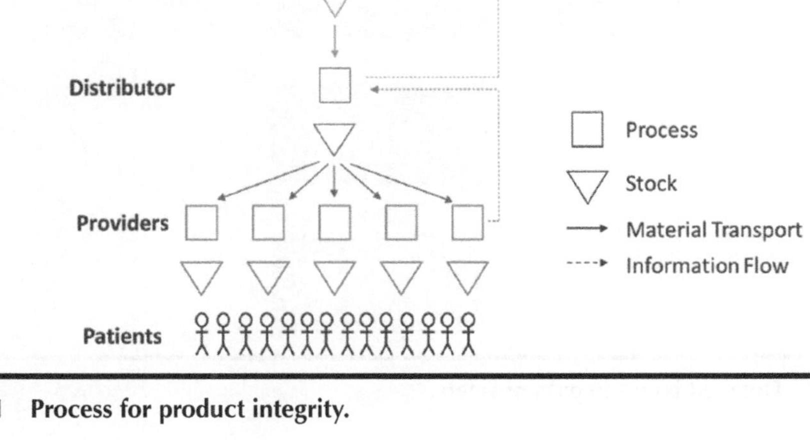

Figure 26.1 Process for product integrity.

outbreak, or a manufacturing process problem. Any disruption in the production of any medical supply can cause a rise in demand, a capacity issue, and coordination issues.

Shortages of medical products have dangerous consequences that extend not just from the individual patient but through healthcare facilities, manufacturers, and suppliers. Shortages can potentially lead to poor clinical outcomes that are caused by substitutions, medical errors, treatment delays, or even lack of treatment if no alternative is available. Healthcare facilities across the entire spectrum of medical care must contend with the effects of increasing product shortages. As well the above issues of patient safety, these shortages come with a variety of other costs—from higher drug budgets to lost revenue to additional labor costs required to mitigate those effects. During periods of shortage, manufacturers and suppliers of critical medical products may face intense pressure to compensate for supply chain disruptions, but they are often unable to ramp up production to meet unpredicted surges in demand.

Figure 26.2 shows the many faceted manners that shortages can occur in the manufacturing of medical supplies and medical equipment—the three causes of medical supply shortages with examples of each.

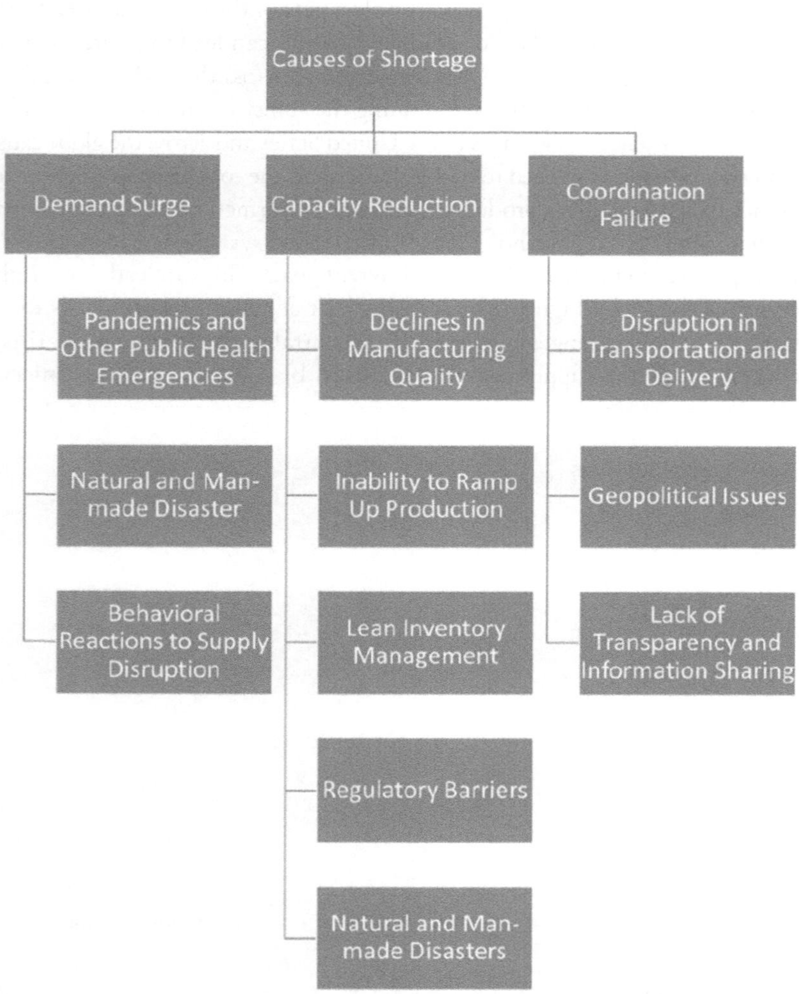

Figure 26.2 Detailed issues in patient safety.

There are approximately 11 examples or possibilities of shortages, and that discussion is meant for another time. However, I will delve into three that I believe outweigh all the others in their effect on patient safety and product integrity—decline in manufacturing quality, disruption in transportation and delivery, and inability to ramp up production.

The single biggest cause of drug product and medical equipment supply chain disruptions under normal operating conditions is the failure of maintaining quality. Declines in quality can often be traced to factors such as the use of older facilities, the lack of modern processes, the lack of proper employee training on the new procedures and processes, companies sharing production facilities, poor third-party contracts and practices that lead to lack of oversight and poor quality, and increased price competition.

Declines in manufacturing quality and subsequent supply disruptions occur frequently among medical manufacturers. Drugs given through injection are the most common products in shortages due to the fact that there are fewer manufacturers of these type of drugs, and these manufacturers operate at full capacity. Full operating capacity makes Production respond to changes in operations and from disruptions.

All manufacturers must adhere to the FDA's current good manufacturing practice regulations, which include minimum requirements for methods, facilities, and controls used in manufacturing, processing, and packing of a drug product. Buyers, therefore, assume that the product is safe for use and contains the ingredients at the strength it claims to have and do not distinguish between the quality of any given generic drug. The market does not reward for production quality. Without a price premium for quality, and with low margins that minimize the value of protecting continuity of supply, drug manufacturers typically do not invest enough in QSs or equipment modernization to prevent quality failures. The words "minimum requirements" need to be revisited by the FDA.

Furthermore, the lack of transparency into the quality of the manufacturing processes used for medical products—thus the quality of the products themselves—prevents the market from rewarding quality manufacturers and causes supply disruptions and shortages. The FDA's examination of quality-related shortages highlights the importance of how to make medical products safer and the supply chains unbroken. Supply chain data analyses have shown that quality problems are largely responsible for drugs that become shortages. There have been repeated calls for more mature quality management systems to ensure consistency and quality drug manufacturing. However, there is still no overriding system in place, thus the quality problems persist.

In emergency situations, supply may be available but cannot reach the people who need it the most. This is due to challenges in transportation and delivery, not of their making. This happens frequently in hurricanes and other natural disasters. This is exactly what happened in 2017 during and after Hurricane Maria hit Puerto Rico. There was extensive damage to the electrical grid, roads, airports, and fuel supplies, disrupting delivery of raw materials and components. Due to this damage on all fronts, Baxter International's drug manufacturing plant which made saline had to halt operations. Backlogs in shipping caused widespread delays—as the existing saline could not get to the port. The cost of shipping containers quadrupled since then and ports in Puerto Rico have been backed up. Many medical products such as saline must be kept in temperature-controlled environments from the time they leave the production facility to the time they are delivered to patients. This posed yet another threat to the quality of drug supplies and challenges in transportation and delivery to rural and remote locations.

Inability of the manufacturers of medical supplies to quickly increase production is a factor that increases volume disruptions. Manufacturers may face multiple barriers to step up production in response to intermittent supply disruptions of raw materials. For most companies, maintaining normal or historical capacity to boost production is not financially feasible. Drug manufacturing is a low-margin business attempt to limit idle production. If a competitor experiences a supply disruption of some sort, there will likely be insufficient capacity available for other manufacturers to increase the production to fill the gap.

There are other situations that limit the ability of manufacturers to boost production such as regulatory risks, packaging and labeling capacity, limits on production, constraints on plant or shipping capacity, and problems with distribution. If the disruption is caused by a disaster or public health emergency, the risks involved included could be employee absenteeism, restrictions to the number of work shift, and limits to certain parts of supply chains, like temperature control storage.

Regulatory risks that manufacturers may face when increasing production are facility inspection delays for new products, revision of old products, and generics, which can lead to longer approval and inspection times. The packaging and labeling needed to contain, transport, distribute, and administer products often rely on foreign sources for components such as resin-based bottles and films, paper cartons and labels, and stainless steel needles. If those raw materials are not readily available, it will delay the supply of the finished product.

Manufacturers may not increase their manufacturing capacity during a shortage. After the 2009 H1N1 influenza pandemic, the mask manufacturers like Prestige Ameritech ramped up production during this emergency. When the emergency waned, they were left with excess inventory and financial problems as the demand disappeared. As a result, the company was very reluctant to increase N95 mask production during the early weeks of the COVID-19 pandemic. The company did eventually install several new mask-making machines and secured investments and multiyear contracts from facilities to make additional masks, which enabled them to ramp up production significantly.

It usually is quite difficult to identify the cause of any particular medical product shortage due to the lack of transparency throughout supply chains, but the root causes can be classified into one of these three categories: demand surges, capacity reductions, and coordination failures. Medical product shortages can have injurious effects on patients by undermining the ability of the healthcare system to provide high-quality care. Some strong supply chain measures, such as stockpiling inventory, provide protection against a broad range of disruptions. Others, such as improving oversight of quality assurance systems, reduce the risk of very specific types of disruptions. To select the appropriate cost-effective strategy for increasing the resiliency of critical medical product supply chains, an agenda is needed for listing and evaluating options.

Chapter 27

Access and Equity

The entities involved in healthcare supply chain—which includes manufacturers, distributors, providers, and patients—all have critical roles in ensuring cost-effective and timely delivery of medical products and services. However, access to these resources is hindered by several significant disparities impacting health outcomes. Some key barriers to equitable healthcare supply chain access include geographical disparities between rural and urban areas, socioeconomic factors such as income inequality, racial and ethnic disparities, technological gaps, and regulatory challenges. This chapter hopes to explore these barriers and offer some strategies for improving access to all. Some of these strategies for improving equity are policy interventions, technological solutions, community-based approaches, supply chain optimization, and workforce development. The goal is to spur future research in healthcare SCM and health equity.

Equity is only one part of the healthcare equation—access is the other part. This equation goes beyond mere equality but must also focus on fairness or equity. Health equity is defined as the absence of unfair and avoidable health disparities, occurring irrespective of people's sociodemographic status and geographical location. This idea is founded on the premise that all people should have the opportunity to achieve the best possible state of health, free from limitations due to social status or any other social factors.

Inequities in the supply chain may lead to severe consequences and widen gaps in healthcare by limiting access to medical supplies and medication in at-risk communities. This connection becomes quite evident when analyzing problems like drug shortages, which have previously been seen to have a direct impact on the susceptible populations including racial and ethnic minorities and people in rural and other underdeveloped regions. These subjects highlight the need to examine and address equity in healthcare supply chain access.

The healthcare supply chain is a complex system that involves several stakeholders. The system faces challenges in the equitable delivery of medical supplies and equipment to all communities. These gaps in the healthcare supply chain have an acute impact on health and have the potential to worsen health disparity across different populations in the United States. Understanding these differences—geographical, socioeconomical, ethnicity, technology, government policy, environment, and workforce—is important in the formulation of strategies to improve equitable access to the healthcare supply chain.

DOI: 10.4324/9781003668732-31

1. Geographical—one of the major issues is geographical disparities, especially between rural and urban areas. Rural healthcare facilities struggle with long supply chains, high costs of transport, and sometimes inadequate storage facilities. These issues lead to an inconsistent supply of vital medical supplies.
2. Socioeconomics—socioeconomic factors play a crucial role in the creation of supply chain inequities. Low-income areas are unable to invest in robust supply chain infrastructure, which will lead to high cost of goods that results from low-volume production and high transportation costs. Included in this factor is the lack of or the inadequate insurance status of healthcare institutions as major barriers to the acquisition of requisite medical equipment and drugs.
3. Ethnicity—this follows the challenge for the unequal distribution of healthcare resources due to race and ethnicity which have historical and systemic racism roots. These inequities are often accompanied by language and cultural factors that impact supply chain interactions and product choices and difficulty with patient well-being.
4. Technology—lack of access to high-speed internet and modern technology in some areas, distinguished as "the digital divide". This "divide" affects the effectiveness of the healthcare supply chain and its management. This divide is evident in the low implementation of EHRs and inventory management in under-resourced areas. The lack of fully integrated data systems in some healthcare organizations and suppliers results in poor tracking of supplies.
5. Government Policy—the regulations governing healthcare are complex and often fragmented in the United States, leading to varying standards in the healthcare facilities across the states. Local and rural health facilities, which mainly operate in minority-populated areas, are most affected by the cost of regulations. Without a coordinated national strategy for healthcare equity, the distribution of supplies will result in failure for any makeshift system.
6. Market dynamics—increased market share consolidation by the larger healthcare institutions reduce competition and lead to higher prices, while small healthcare providers and those serving minority communities often lack bargaining power with large suppliers.
7. Environment—climate change and other natural disasters are other causes of supply chain disruptions, and such disasters affect vulnerable communities the most. In addition, the management of temperature-controlled supply chains in areas with unreliable power infrastructure represents significant challenge for some medical supplies and pharmaceutical products.
8. Workforce—the demand for supply chain professionals in the healthcare industry is high, particularly in rural regions. The lack of training and education opportunities in healthcare SCM in rural areas also contributes to this problem.

Now that we have enumerated the challenges, allow me to offer some strategies that might improve access and equity to the healthcare systems which will automatically default to the healthcare supply chain. The strategies we will look at are policy intervention, technological solutions, community-based approach, supply chain optimization, and upskilling the workforce.

1. Policy Intervention—these are those that argue for government policy interventions for the improvement of equity in healthcare supply chains. In the recent past, there were government plans like the Affordable Care Act. This plan's idea was to expand healthcare coverage and reduce disparities. The overall goal was to influence the healthcare supply chain by increasing demand for medical supplies among a diverse population. The Centers for Medicare & Medicaid Services has added a value-based care program that induces healthcare providers to improve patient healthcare outcomes. As the Affordable Care Act was on the federal level,

some states have enacted the Certificate of Need laws. These laws attempt to regulate the equitable distribution of both health facilities and equipment. Are these policies merely window dressing? Implementation requires continuous evaluation and adaptation to the changing needs of a diverse population.

2. Technological solutions—telemedicine and remote care have emerged as two technological advances for improving access, especially in rural areas that lack physical healthcare infrastructure. Telemedicine may relieve the pressure on supplies as it decreases the number of patients' visits to healthcare facilities during pandemics or other emergencies, and it enables healthcare providers to deal with chronic ailments without frequent hospital visits.
3. Community-based approach—this approach is deemed to be vital in improving equity in the healthcare supply chain in rural areas. One of the strategies that can be used is collaboration between healthcare providers and community organizations. These collaborations can target specific local healthcare demands and try to effectively muster up resources to improve supply chain in disadvantaged regions. The cooperation and collaboration with the local governments, nonprofits, and private sectors can help provide medical supplies and improve the quality of healthcare services to disadvantaged regions. The creation of mobile health clinics is key to tackling healthcare issues in rural areas as they provide preventive, diagnostic, and treatment services directly to patients. These mobile clinics can reduce healthcare differences by ensuring access to care for isolated populations.
4. Supply Chain optimization—optimization means having the right supplies, in the right place, at the right time, and in the right amounts. This tactic will minimize shortages in healthcare facilities. This approach can effectively reduce costs and facilitate accessible healthcare supplies to low-income areas. Collaborative purchasing agreements between healthcare providers can also enhance supply chain efficiency. Through regional purchasing coalitions, it is possible to deliver affordable and accessible healthcare products by negotiating better prices and terms with suppliers.
5. "Upskilling" Workforce—"upskilling" is basically training your employees in new processes and procedures to meet the challenges of today's healthcare environment. It is important to develop and educate the workforce involved in healthcare SCM for improved equity in healthcare supply chain access. This approach acknowledges that the workforce has to be well trained and knowledgeable to support the implementation and sustenance of equitable supply chain practices. These programs aim to equip professionals to operate within healthcare supply chains while keeping equity considerations at the forefront. Such training has been emphasized, in that healthcare SCM is a specialty that requires the combined knowledge of supply chain and healthcare industry knowledge.

This review highlighted a number of complex challenges hindering equitable healthcare supply chain access in the United States, such as geographic disparities, socioeconomic factors, and technological barriers. This chapter also explored some promising strategic solutions like policy inventions, innovation, and community-based approaches to mitigate such disparities. Despite successful implementations and emerging knowledge, a multifaceted approach is necessary to improve healthcare supply chain equity. Addressing them not as silos but as one interrelated discipline is important for the improvement of overall health outcomes.

Chapter 28

Corporate Social Responsibility

The healthcare supply chains support life-saving health institutions. They supply medical institutions with quick turnaround deliveries while prioritizing consumers through each step of each company's operations. Putting consumers first directly connects those supply chains with corporate social responsibility policies.

But first, what is corporate social responsibility?

Corporate social responsibility is a modern business model that bridges the interest of the consumer with that of corporate interests. It includes four factors: The company's environmental, social, philanthropic, and ethical self-regulation standards to consumers. Government regulations and laws are the primary factors setting the groundwork for corporate social responsibility. It all starts with corporate social responsibility policies, pushing corporations to stick with their eco-friendly values.

Companies have a direct influence on their supply-chain partners. The supply chain is the network of businesses making products a corporation needs. When companies with purchasing power enact corporate social responsibilities, they experience new benefits. Corporate leadership teams use sustainability to set goals of higher profits, more market share, and a better environment.

As those benefits become daily advantages, corporations expect their supply-chain partners to follow their set path. Without eco-friendly supply chain support, the corporation's corporate social responsibility policies wouldn't produce the same effective results.

Supply chain companies depend on their corporate partners' purchasing power to keep the lights on. If most of their partners go green, the SCM teams must find ways to provide eco-friendly support. They may change their purchasing methods or business models to continue their economically beneficial partnerships.

SCM plays a direct role in CSR policies. Those policies continue to exist when they receive external support through supply-chain partners—manufacturers, clinicians, medical suppliers. A sustainable healthcare supply chain makes its supplies more readily available to other companies. Supply chain healthcare also has responsibility toward the environment. Producing goods and services requires using electricity and limited resources like water or fossil fuels. Those actions harm the environment, creating direct effects.

 DOI: 10.4324/9781003668732-32

How do healthcare supply chains and their institutions implement corporate social responsibility programs?

Corporate healthcare supply chain leaders can start these programs in SCM by reexamining the existing business practices. They should evaluate current practices for environmental impacts and consider the following strategies.

Well-meaning business practices may create wastefulness that goes unnoticed. Something as routine as laser cutting materials for implants could indicate serious waste.

Corporate social responsibility policies would address this by seeking alternative options. 3D-printing implants would remove the need for lasers, resulting in faster production and less waste. These advancements can also help patients, like how 3D-printed implants improve the restoration of bones and cartilage.

Healthcare supply chain leaders may also upgrade their equipment. Supply chain companies use equipment to provide daily goods or services. The machinery may not have Energy Start approval or modern technology that reduces its electricity consumption. Medical supply shipments pose an industry-wide issue. Twenty to thirty percent of hospital medical supply costs get swallowed up by warehousing expenses, while an additional 10–34% vanish into thin air through multiple "transportation waste" events, with as many as 3 to 5 shipments occurring between importers and end users.

Companies could reflect on current procurement practices and the average number of their monthly deliveries. Making larger, less frequent orders would reduce supply costs and transportation waste events. Products go through a long journey from makers to sellers, and every stop adds cost and takes time. It's time for healthcare providers to team up directly with producers and main sellers.

Corporate social responsibility includes employee well-being as a part of the social and ethical self-regulation pillars. A supply chain manufacturing plant could install windows where employees spend the most time. Letting more natural light into the workplace boosts employee energy11 while creating a better environment. Sunlight decreases stress, which healthcare supply chain employees feel intensely. Employees within healthcare supply chains living with these or other burnout symptoms need more support. CSR standards prioritize this through policies that put employee well-being on equal standing with sustainability goals.

Transparency is another fundamental concept in corporate social responsibility. Companies must explain where they fall short in their sustainable, social, and ethical business models. Consumers and shareholders then get to see exactly how the companies plan to achieve their CSR goals.

Corporate social responsibility policies are increasingly important for healthcare supply chains. CSR standards make companies align with consumer demand, increase profitability, and support the environment more effectively.

V

TECHNOLOGY TRANSFORMING THE HEALTHCARE SUPPLY CHAIN

The healthcare industry is undergoing an insightful transformation driven by technological advancements, particularly within its supply chains. SCM in healthcare is critical to ensuring that the right products reach the right place at the right time, impacting patient care quality. Innovations in technology are not only streamlining supply chain operations but also enhancing overall patient outcomes. This section will examine how several different technologies are revolutionizing healthcare supply chains. The keys driving this change in healthcare technology are telemedicine, AI, machine learning, Blockchain, and robotics. We will show how all of these have affected the healthcare supply chain and, hopefully, how they act in unison to affect change.

DOI: 10.4324/9781003668732-33

Chapter 29

Amazing Things Happen When Care Is Available, Anytime and Any Place

This is what has occurred since hospital institutions and some clinicians brought telehealth into their overall medical and well-being plan. Let's explore in further detail.

The ways that healthcare providers use technology continue to evolve. Connected care solutions such as telehealth and remote patient monitoring tools have become more widely implemented in recent years. This has allowed clinicians to deliver care and connect with some remote patients more effectively. The next step in this evolution requires all health providers to connect these tools throughout their processes.

Healthcare providers need to understand how deploying new tools such as automated solutions powered by AI will affect the experience of patients and clinicians. They must plan to overcome obstacles such as staffing shortages and cultural resistance. Providers also must find ways to optimize the technology tools they use, such as secure and fully integrated software throughout entire medical processes.

The use of these connected care solutions has declined from the pandemic peak, but they are still being used in much larger numbers than before 2020. Many patients—those unable to visit in person or unable to travel long distances—have come to rely on virtual options to conveniently access the care that they need. Providing effective, quality-connected care not only helps healthcare organizations to attract patients and clinicians but can also lower costs and improve outcomes for patients.

Hospitals and other healthcare institutions, like clinics and surgi-centers, competed to start up connected care solutions as quickly as possible, but many of these systems remain disconnected from healthcare organizations' larger IT environments. Connected care solutions that are disconnected from organizations' cybersecurity tools and processes may expose vulnerabilities that hackers can exploit. Healthcare organizations must unify their IT environments and deploy cybersecurity tools and frameworks such as mobile device management.

DOI: 10.4324/9781003668732-34

In addition to telehealth solutions, which facilitate direct patient-to-practitioner interaction, healthcare providers need to make headway in the use of remote patient monitoring, virtual nursing, and digital front-door. With remote patient monitoring, clinicians can extend their reach beyond the traditional bounds of medical facilities. With the help of the aforementioned technologies, they can quickly analyze data to arrive at knowledge about patient outcomes. Together, these technologies form a connected system that can change healthcare making it personal and patient-centered.

Across the country, especially in rural areas, telehealth has significantly expanded options and accessibility for patients and clinicians. Videoconferencing platforms, fully integrated with EHR systems, make it easy for patients to connect with general practitioners and specialists. Clinicians in rural settings can use telehealth to consult with specialists remotely, bringing the expertise of larger health systems to underserved areas.

Remote Patient Monitoring that influences videoconferencing platforms and connected medical devices to manage at-home care is becoming a more important component of the total healthcare system.

Virtual nursing lets clinicians see patients without visiting their rooms in person. It saves clinicians time and effort by enabling them to check in with patients quickly and easily, while also maintaining social distancing practices that help prevent the spread of transmissible diseases.

Financial pressure is one of the top concerns that healthcare organizations face. Connected care can help reduce the cost of care delivery. There is grant funding from programs such as the Healthcare Connect Fund that can provide financial assistance to healthcare organizations to enhance broadband connectivity, improve community outreach, and ultimately provide telehealth to more patients who need it.

Chapter 30

Blockchain Ramifications on Healthcare Supply Chain

Data management in healthcare supply chain is a complex arrangement where multiple organizations provide proper supply chain services in day-to-day life. Incorrect data disrupts the supply chain, which has a long-term impact on the healthcare. Various issues in the present supply chain must be addressed. Blockchains are well known nowadays for their ability to create safe and visible solutions. The growing use of these types of technologies also includes healthcare applications. Blockchain solutions are effective in the health sector for secure data retrieval and storage, resulting in more effectual product creation and tracking. We will try to get a better understanding of Blockchain's significance in the healthcare supply chain.

Healthcare organizations must determine why their supplies are almost always insufficient, as well as the obstacles that made tracking the volume and location of crucial supplies so difficult. It is time to start revising processes and figuring out how to close breaches in supply chains. Blockchain technology is considerably suited to tackle this issue. Blockchain solutions are transparent, traceable, and secure. Currently, most medical and pharmaceutical supply chains are facing significant logistical challenges, including lack of shipment locations, uncertainty, transportation disruptions, product quality tracking, cross-border customs reporting, and complicated invoicing and payments.

Before we go any further, definition and the workings of some types of Blockchain are necessary—please excuse some of the technical verbiage. Blockchain is a collection of records linked with each other and strongly resistant to alteration and protected by cryptography. It is a technology that allows users to store data in a decentralized manner. The advantage is that the information is available multiple times in the network, making it difficult to modify.

Participants join the Blockchain network with transaction in a structure known as a *Block*. Blocks are being used to store groups of transactions. Each block in the network carries a cryptographic hashmark of the preceding block. A chain is formed by the connected blocks. A block is often digitally signed to ensure the integrity of the data stored inside it. If someone seeks to add a transaction to the chain, it will be validated by all the network participants. The transaction must then be approved by a majority of the parties. Afterwards, a group of accepted transactions is bundled into a block and delivered to all nodes in the network. They confirm the new

DOI: 10.4324/9781003668732-35

block in response. Every subsequent block contains a hash, which is the preceding block's unique fingerprint.

When developing and implementing a Blockchain solution for a healthcare supply chain, we must choose the type of Blockchain which would be the most suitable for the project. Figure 30.1 shows the different types. Therefore, it is essential to have a clear understanding of the options available for Blockchain structures.

1. Public Blockchain: A public Blockchain is one that does not need permissions to post transactions. A public Blockchain is a decentralized platform that allows anyone to be a part of the network and verify transactions on the network.
2. Private Blockchain: A private Blockchain is a restrictive Blockchain. It only operates in a closed network. It is usually used within an organization where only selected members are participants of a Blockchain network.
3. Hybrid Blockchain: This is a Blockchain that uses the characteristics of both a private and public Blockchain. Hybrid Blockchain is created on the basis of various business needs and is customized to industry needs.
4. Consortium Blockchain: This executes the transactions using both private and public Blockchains. They are operated by a small number of participants and do not enable outside players to validate transactions.

A healthcare supply chain often begins with a producer or manufacturer who manufactures the medicinal things and transfers them to a company warehouse or to a distributor. The manufacturer's

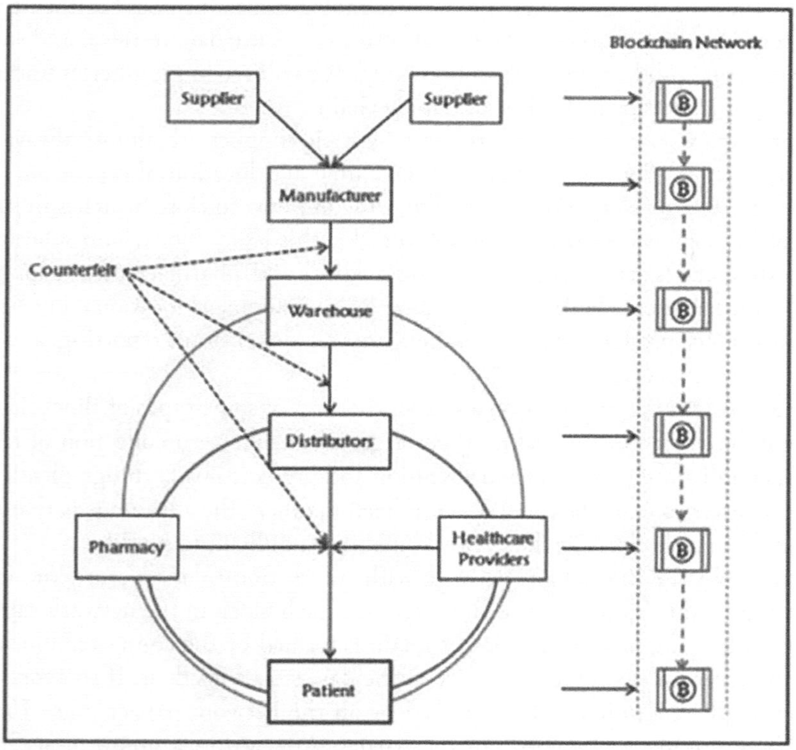

Figure 30.1 This is a Blockchain of healthcare supply chain.

raw materials are supplied by one or more suppliers. Distributors ensure that everything your doctor suggests is safely and securely distributed to your healthcare providers such as hospitals, clinics, pharmacy, or straight to the patient, if needed on an emergency basis.

Healthcare supply networks are complicated, diverse, and constantly evolving. Counterfeiting through intermediaries is possible on multiple fronts—when pharmaceuticals are shipped from the manufacturer to the warehouse; when pharmaceuticals are stocked in the warehouse; when they are shipped from the warehouses to other stakeholders such as the distributor, pharmacy, healthcare professionals, and patients. But identifying and tracking the counterfeit are incredibly tough. We require a powerful technology, such as Blockchain technology, for flawless monitoring and tracking. Blockchain is a transparent and traceable technology that has the potential to solve many of the challenges of traditional supply chains, where all transactions are data secure.

In a traditional supply chain, the interaction between all the stakeholders—manufacturer, distributor, pharmacy, healthcare practitioners, and patients—takes two forms. The product is usually stored in the manufacturer's warehouse once it has been manufactured. A distributor as a middleman picks up pharmaceuticals and any other medical products from warehouse and delivers them to other parties. In another scenario, stakeholders can buy medical supplies directly from the manufacturer, circumventing intermediaries like distributors. The patient is at the heart of the system, and we must serve him or her.

Due to Blockchain network's unassailable feature, every single transaction from supplier to end user will be recorded, and no one can modify the same. Blockchain-based healthcare supply chain is a developed, completely decentralized concept where clients, pharmaceutical, doctors, and others connect with each block of the work.

Even though Blockchain has helped alleviate some of the issues with a healthcare supply chain, there are still a number of impediments preventing the optimization of the healthcare supply chain—traceability, transparency, counterfeits, reverse supply chain and product perishability.

In healthcare, traceability helps to monitor the movement of drugs or medical devices throughout the supply chain. Many existing supply chains are incapable of tracing products. In order to locate something in the supply chain, one must look either upstream or downstream.

A business must know what is happening at every level of its supply chain, and to provide accurate information about its operations is referred to as supply chain transparency. Transparent supply chains may provide the perception that an organization is honest and transparent about its operations and, therefore, trustworthy.

Counterfeit medications are a big concern in the healthcare supply chain. The Health Research Funding Organization revealed that about 10–30% of pharmaceuticals in underdeveloped nations are counterfeit. Additionally, as per the World Health Organization (WHO), around 30% of all medications marketed in Africa, Asia, and Latin America are counterfeit.

When a product is placed on the shelf and not sold, it might be because it has expired or is going to expire, or it has a quality concern. The supply chain has a significant challenge in collecting all of these products from a complicated system that includes thousands of stores, distributors, and wholesalers; bringing them back; and disposing of them properly.

Another major issue in healthcare/pharmaceutical/medical supply networks is product fragility. Medical items have a limited life span and are especially sensitive to temperature variations and light exposure. For example, insulin injections must be stored at room temperature for one month. It is essential to ensure that these items or pharmaceuticals are kept in the proper state until they are consumed.

The goal was to better understand the potential of Blockchain technology in the healthcare supply chain. As we have seen, the healthcare supply chain is vast, multidimensional, and ever-changing. Traceability, counterfeit drugs, reverse supply chain, and product perishability are some of the challenges raised that need further exploration from supply chain leaders. Perhaps, Blockchain technology has the potential to overcome all of these obstacles.

Chapter 31

Does Artificial Intelligence Improve Patient Care in the Healthcare Supply Chain?

The fallout from the pandemic was that the entire healthcare and medical supply chain experienced major disruptions. Those disruptions emphasized the need for organizations to improve their supply chains. Thanks to its ability to understand data and automate tasks, AI has played a key role in those efforts. Supply chain leaders are wondering what kind of assistance they can get from AI as it rises up to C-level agendas.

Traditional automation requires well-defined processes and stagnant procedures and/or decision points. When augmented with traditional AI, those efforts gain added insights thanks to cognitive capabilities. AI pushes insights and processes into action, enabling health systems to vigorously adapt to their environments.

Achieving a favorable balance between patient outcomes, supplies, and equipment costs, quality is the ultimate goal of a healthcare system. Perhaps, one item costs more than another, but it accelerates patient recovery—that's good for the people we serve and good for our hospitals as well. It may reduce overall costs at a system level, accounting for less inpatient care. But such insights are buried within layers and layers of data. This research and documentation challenge become much simpler using AI.

AI becomes an aid with easy-to-read responses, and it can be used in different languages. It can offer data about procedures, cost, and outcomes in general. An example can be the difference between different brands and types of sutures. Are there sutures that have antibiotic properties, but cost significantly more? Are there any sutures which are better for reducing infections, or only in specific clinical uses? AI can help define the best appropriate suture based on data across a single large health system, a group of health systems, or some sort of other collaborative of providers.

Besides using AI to aid healthcare providers alleviate cost and enhance patient care, there are other important areas of the healthcare supply chain for which AI is being put to use and is showing improvement and efficiencies in those areas—risk management, sourcing, inventory management, and logistics/distribution.

DOI: 10.4324/9781003668732-36

AI can help healthcare supply chain leaders and medical providers effectively manage risk and build flexibility for demographics or groups of providers and alert supply chain leaders for course corrections based upon the information of disruptions. The technology can analyze current and historical data involving inventory levels, patient case levels, geopolitical events, and weather. Some organizations rely on control panels fed by this data and alerts and course corrections for disruptions. AI can be questioned to produce risk assessments, scenario simulations, and mitigation strategies. These are in response to shortages or widespread crisis to help supply chain planners manage and proactively mitigate the risks.

Today, the healthcare supply chain industry employs more sophisticated IT systems with vast amounts of data. Being able to accurately analyze data around cost, quality, and patient outcomes can help physicians determine the best supplies or drugs to use, depending on patient needs.

By using these factors as well as supplier performance and risk profiles, AI has algorithms that are able to provide recommendations for making informed decisions for a healthcare system's sourcing strategy. At the same time, supply chain leaders can use this information to facilitate product standardization and the ranking of best suppliers.

Healthcare supply chain leaders and healthcare providers struggle to effectively optimize their medical equipment inventory—such as MRIs, CTs, PET scans—within health systems. Providers can take a page from the playbook of manufacturers to leverage AI to get the most out of their equipment. AI could more effectively match supply with demand and schedule patients to optimize the uses of these limited resources. This applies to the operating room as well. AI can help revolutionize how surgical supplies are used by physicians and which supplies and instruments are needed for re-supply. Imagine a system in which AI can make recommendations for surgical supplies updates based on historic usage patterns, the patient profile/demographic, case types, physician, and forecast. With this data, the surgical inventory can be automatically updated.

AI has the ability to update and optimize delivery and delivery routes based upon factors like traffic conditions, weather, and the priority of deliveries. This could be a boon for the U.S. healthcare supply chain which is responsible for about 5% of national greenhouse emissions, partly because of its transportation footprint within the supply chain. AI can also play a role in more effectively routing patients to the most appropriate and closest care setting, which would be a win-win for the patients and the providers.

However, many providers lack the proper infrastructure. They are still struggling to determine how to get the right supplies and caregivers to the patient, as well as fulfill the logistics and distribution for lab samples and equipment.

Data is at the core of a successful AI platform, but many healthcare organizations are at the beginnings of understanding AI and its capabilities. At the same time, they are facing greater regulation than many other sectors of the economy. This increased and tougher regulations make strong governance a high priority.

The healthcare supply chain, its leaders, and healthcare providers have been challenged like never before. AI offers the much-needed productivity enhancements for the entire industry. The possibilities are endless for the entire industry with strong data integrity and a proactive mindset.

Chapter 32

Robotics Impact on Healthcare Supply Chain and Industry

Robots in the healthcare supply chain and the medical field are transforming how surgeries are performed, streamlining supply delivery and preventing infections, thus enabling providers to focus on engaging with and caring for patients. Robots first started to appear in the 1980s. The first robots in the healthcare industry only provided surgical assistance with the use of a robotic arm. That is as far as the technology was capable of at the time. Over the decades, AI, as discussed in a prior chapter, enabled data analytics, transforming the role of medical robots to be used in many other areas of healthcare supply chain.

Robots are used not only in operating room procedures but also in doctor-patient settings to support healthcare workers and enhance patient care—hospitals and clinics are increasingly using robots to help reduce exposure to pathogens.

The use of robotics even extends to research and development laboratories where they are used to automate manual, repetitive, and high-volume tasks so that technicians and scientists can focus their attention on more strategic tasks that make discoveries happen faster.

Health risk reduction is one of the primary benefits provided by medical robotics. Robots can be programmed to clean and prepare patient rooms, thereby limiting the person-to-person contact in certain wards of a hospital or clinic that are infectious disease wards. Robots with installed AI medicine identifier software will reduce the time it takes to identify, match, and distribute medicine to patients in hospitals.

As technologies evolve, robots will eventually perform these tasks on a routine basis. The result being, doctors, nurses, and other healthcare workers will be able to spend more time providing direct patient care.

Risk prevention is only one of a number of benefits of the use of robotics in the healthcare supply chain. There are others such as high-quality patient care, streamlined workflow for clinicians, and safe work environments.

DOI: 10.4324/9781003668732-37

1. High-quality patient care—robots support minimally invasive procedures, customized and frequent monitoring for patients with chronic diseases, and restorative healing. As robots lighten workloads, nurses and other caregivers can offer patients more empathy and human interaction, which can promote long-term well-being.
2. Streamlined clinician workflow—to simplify the clinician everyday tasks in a medical setting, the healthcare industry and robotics industry created the Autonomous Mobile Robots (AMRs). These robots can assist in staffing issues by keeping track of inventory and placing timely orders to help make sure that supplies, equipment, and medication are in stock where they are needed. These AMRs, as they have become, enable hospital rooms to be sanitized and ready for incoming patients quickly.
3. Safe work environment—to ensure the healthcare workers' safety, these robots are used to move supplies and linens internally where exposure is at its greatest. These robotics movements help reduce employee exposure to any hospital-acquired infections. In addition, there are "social robots", a type of AMR, which helps with heavy lifting, such as moving beds or patients, so that the physical strain on healthcare workers is lessened.

As there are a number of robots employed to perform every day or routine tasks at a hospital or other healthcare institutions, there are now robots that can perform some surgical procedures. These robots help surgeons achieve new levels of speed and accuracy, while performing complex operations with computer vision-capable technologies. Some surgical robots may even be able to complete tasks by themselves, freeing surgeons to oversee procedures.

Surgeries performed with robotics assistance fall into two main categories:

1. Minimally invasive for the torso—these include hysterectomy, prostatectomy, bariatric surgery, and other procedures primarily focused on soft tissues. After insertion through a small incision, these robots lock themselves into place, creating a stable platform from which to perform surgeries via remote control. Open surgery using large incisions was once the norm for most internal procedures. Recovery times were much longer, and the potential for infection and other complications was greater. Working manually through a button-sized incision is extremely difficult, even for an experienced surgeon. Surgical robots make these procedures easy and accurate, with a goal to reduce infections and other complications.
2. Orthopedic surgeries—robots can be preprogrammed to perform routine orthopedic surgeries such as knee and hip replacements. Robots are enabled and trained in specific orthopedic surgeries, with precise directions for where to go and how to perform the procedures.

In addition to the aforementioned robots and their use in the healthcare industry and supply chain, there are several others worth mentioning, showing their use and capabilities within the healthcare supply chain industry—therapeutic robots, service robots, and social robots.

Therapeutic robots can help with rehabilitation after strokes, paralysis, or traumatic brain injuries or with diseases like multiple sclerosis. Outfitting these robots with AI and cameras that have depth perception can monitor a patient's form as they go through exercises—measuring degrees of motion in different positions and tracking progress more precisely than the human eye.

Service robots were created and programmed to perform the routine tasks the clinical employees are burdened with on a daily basis. Some of these routine tasks are issuing reports, setting up patient rooms, tracking supplies, filing purchase orders, restocking medical supplies, and moving bed linens to and from the laundry facilities. Having some routine tasks performed by service robots gives healthcare workers more time to focus on immediate patient needs. Service robots can also help with cleaning and disinfection. These service robots are equipped with ultraviolet light, hydrogen peroxide vapors, and air filtration to help reduce infection and to sanitize reachable places in a uniform way.

Social or so-called "friendly" robots are meant to deal directly with humans. They are used in long-term care environments, like nursing homes or assisted living institutions, to provide social interaction and medical observation. They encourage patients to comply with treatment schedules and provide personal engagement, helping to keep patients alert and positive. Social robots help reduce caregiver workloads, but the verdict is still out on the patient well-being.

Medical and health robotics will continue to evolve alongside advancements in machine learning, data analytics, computer vision, and other technologies to enhance the healthcare supply chain. Robots of all types will continue to evolve to complete tasks autonomously, efficiently, and accurately.

Chapter 33

Big Data Transforming the Healthcare Supply Chain

Increasing costs and operational inefficiency in healthcare supply chain have drawn the attention of all professionals within the supply chain. A capable supply chain can provide tighter control and visibility for greater focus on quality patient care. Big Data Analytics (BDA) is increasingly being adopted for the building of an information depository. This analytic process with the use of Big Data tools improves operational efficiency and reduces human errors that can often be deadly. Better healthcare planning can be done by the usage of Big Data. Suitable methods and practices can be used for healthcare data analytics which can help in better decision-making for an increase in the business value and customer interest. However, the usage and applicability of BDA tools in the healthcare supply chain sector are relatively new phenomena as compared to other service sectors like e-commerce and finance.

This chapter is an exploration of the implementation of BDA tools in the healthcare supply chain settings of hospitals for quality improvements and better patient care. Then I will summarize a number of challenges and opportunities connected with the employment of Big Data in the environment of healthcare supply chain.

Big Data in healthcare refers to the vast volume, variety, and quickness of healthcare-related data that is generated, collected, and analyzed within the healthcare industry. This data encompasses a wide range of information, including patient records, medical images, clinical notes, billing information, and generated health data. The application of advanced analytics and technology to this wealth of data has the potential to revolutionize healthcare supply chain—patient care, disease prevention, and treatment best practices.

While Big Data in the healthcare supply chain offers great potential, it no doubt presents challenges related to data security, privacy, and data quality. Safeguarding patient information and ensuring regulatory compliance are critical considerations in the healthcare data sector of the supply chain. The benefits, challenges, and steps to implementing Big Data for the healthcare supply chain are enumerated and discussed below.

The incorporation of analytics into healthcare supply chains has proven transformative, by dealing with critical challenges and enhancing efficiencies. By using real-time data, healthcare organizations can streamline their operations and ensure patient needs are met promptly. Below

DOI: 10.4324/9781003668732-38

are some of the key benefits and challenges for incorporating Big Data into healthcare supply chain.

Benefits

1. Demand forecasting—unpredictable demand for medical supplies is a constant challenge in healthcare supply chain, which is driven by issues such as seasonal outbreaks, emergency procedures, and sudden patient influxes. Analytics emboldens organizations to create accurate demand prototypes by analyzing historical trends, current consumption rates, and external factors such as health emergencies.
2. Optimized inventory—effective inventory management is the backbone of a resilient supply chain. Analytics enables healthcare organizations to track the flow of supplies, ensure the proper stock levels for all types of healthcare supplies, and mitigate excess inventory.
3. Reduce supply chain risks—supply chain disruptions, whether due to supplier delays, geopolitical issues, or natural disasters, can jeopardize patient care. Analytics provides early warnings by identifying the defenseless areas, determining where disruptions might happen and implementing proactive measures.
4. Improved supplier relations—supplier relationships are vital to healthcare supply chains, and Big Data provides insights to optimize them. By analyzing data on supplier performance, pricing trends, and delivery reliability, healthcare organizations can determine reliable suppliers, receive better contracts, and benefit from reliable deliveries.

Challenges

1. Data quality—healthcare institutions produce huge amounts of data. But the accuracy and consistency of this data are often brought into question. Incomplete or inaccurate data can lead to inaccurate forecasts and poor decision-making. Inaccurate numbers leading to poor decisions undermine the reliability of analytics.
2. Expensive initial investment—the adoption of advanced data requires sizeable financial resources—from investing in sophisticated tools and infrastructure to hiring skilled personnel—the costs can be excessive for smaller healthcare institutions and organizations. Added expenses, such as system maintenance, software updates, and staff training, add to the financial burden. Organizations must carefully weigh these costs against the long-term value analytics can deliver.
3. Resistance to change—the introduction of technology such as BDA into habitually manual processes often encounters resistance from healthcare professionals. Stakeholders accustomed to the existing workflows may be hesitant to adopt new technologies or trust data-driven solutions. Overcoming this resistance requires clear communication about the benefits of analytics, tied to training and stakeholder involvement to foster acceptance.
4. Data privacy—due to the inherent nature of healthcare, data being private and sensitive makes security and privacy paramount. Analytics systems must comply with stringent regulations such as HIPAA in the United States. Organizations must prioritize tough cybersecurity measures such as encryption and secure access protocols.

Now that we have covered a number of benefits and challenges, we will see the best practices to implement and maintain the Big Data information portal. It requires a structured and systematic approach. These are the steps to be taken to have any chance of success.

1. Data collection—the initial step to implement analytics is to gather and combine data from all sources within the healthcare supply chain and organization. This includes data from inventory systems, procurement platforms, EHRs, and patient usage of medical supplies. By combining and collating data from different departments, healthcare providers can obtain a holistic view of their supply chain.
2. Data standardization—data quality is crucial to the success of any analytics implementation. Organizations need to ensure that their data is accurate and consistent. After this data is corrected and accuracy is ensured, then they can build an efficient Big Data information platform.
3. Continuous monitoring—any information platform is a continuous process rather than a one-time solution. To ensure sustained improvement, healthcare organizations must frequently monitor the performance of their supply chain and its use of real-time data. This constant maintenance allows timely adjustments as needed, ensuring that supply chain operations remain efficient and responsive to changing needs.

The healthcare supply chain is the backbone of patient care, and advanced analytics is the key to its continued adoption of best practices. With the influence of Big Data insights, flawless integration, and real-time monitoring, healthcare organizations can mitigate risks, enhance efficiency, and ensure that critical resources are always available in their supply chains. As the healthcare industry and its supply chain continue to embrace digital transformation, real-time data platforms are no longer optional.

VI

BEST PRACTICES AND STRATEGIES IN HEALTHCARE SUPPLY CHAIN

With the growth in recognition of the impact SCM in healthcare has on operational, clinical, and financial outcomes, many healthcare executive leaders are making greater investments in their supply chain operations.

The healthcare supply chain is the lifeblood that sustains the health and well-being of individuals. A healthcare supply chain organization needs to navigate this scene with a deep understanding of the complexities at play—technology, strategy, and best practices. These complexities revolve around the health and well-being of patients.

Figure 0.3 The four best strategies and best practices—Lean Management, Agile Management, Hybrid Models, and Cold Chain Logistics.

DOI: 10.4324/9781003668732-39

Chapter 34

Lean Management and the Healthcare Supply Chain

Healthcare systems are always looking for ways to improve patient care quality, save money, and streamline how they work. Lean Management has materialized as the chief weapon to achieve this objective. Lean Management started with Toyota to after the destruction of World War II as the method to rebuild all their industries. The idea behind this methodology was to mitigate waste and bring more value to car buyers. The healthcare industry began to adapt this methodology to their industry. This helped to produce the same results as Toyota saw—mitigate wastes, improve processes, and improve patient care.

At its heart, Lean healthcare management is about finding and removing non-helpful parts of how care is provided. This waste shows up in different ways like long wait times, unnecessary transport, making more than needed, or errors hurting patients. By dealing with these waste sources, Lean methodology principles allow providers to simplify how they operate and shift resources toward activities that directly improve care for patients.

A short definition and history of Lean will give us a better understanding of the methodology and what it can accomplish when implemented correctly.

Lean healthcare management is a patient-centered philosophy that revolves around identifying and eliminating wastes in the processes. By minimizing these wasteful processes, healthcare organizations can repurpose their resources for activities that directly contribute to improved patient outcomes. Lean principles encourage a pursuit of perfection, but we must remember that perfection is a myth. The Lean healthcare principles allow healthcare organization and providers the great chance to mitigate wastes thereby reducing cost and thus provide higher-quality services to patients.

The origins of Lean principles can be traced back to the Toyota Production System, which created to rebuild the Japanese economy after World War II. It was considered a revolutionary approach and developed by the Japanese automaker to minimize waste and maximize value for customers. Originally adopted by all other manufacturers, the Lean philosophy has since went well beyond manufacturing industries and found its way into the healthcare industry.

In an industry where the margin for error is razor thin and can be life-altering, the importance of Lean principles in healthcare cannot be overstated. Lean fosters a culture of continuous

DOI: 10.4324/9781003668732-40

improvement. Healthcare supply chain leaders as well as healthcare professionals, through this methodology, should be hastened to identify medical and administrative practices which need to be streamlined.

This proactive approach not only enhances patient safety and quality of care but also improves sourcing for resources, leading to major cost savings and improved financial performance for healthcare organizations.

The Lean methodology in healthcare encompasses a diverse array of tools and techniques, each designed to address specific challenges and optimize processes. Some of these tools are Value Stream Mapping, 5S, and Kanban. All are designed to demonstrate how to reduce wastes and improve healthcare medical and healthcare supply-chain processes.

Value Stream Mapping is a basic and sound Lean tool that enables healthcare organizations to visualize and examine the flow of materials, information, and processes involved in delivering patient care. By mapping or showcasing the entire value stream, healthcare professionals can identify holdups and repeat processes and activities that do not add value to any healthcare process, and it shows the way for targeted process improvements.

This is an example of value stream—first mapping the process and then adding information or data. Then it can add time lines to the map.

The timeline for total process times and lead times required in the healthcare supply chain for medical supplies will vary by the type of supply and equipment.

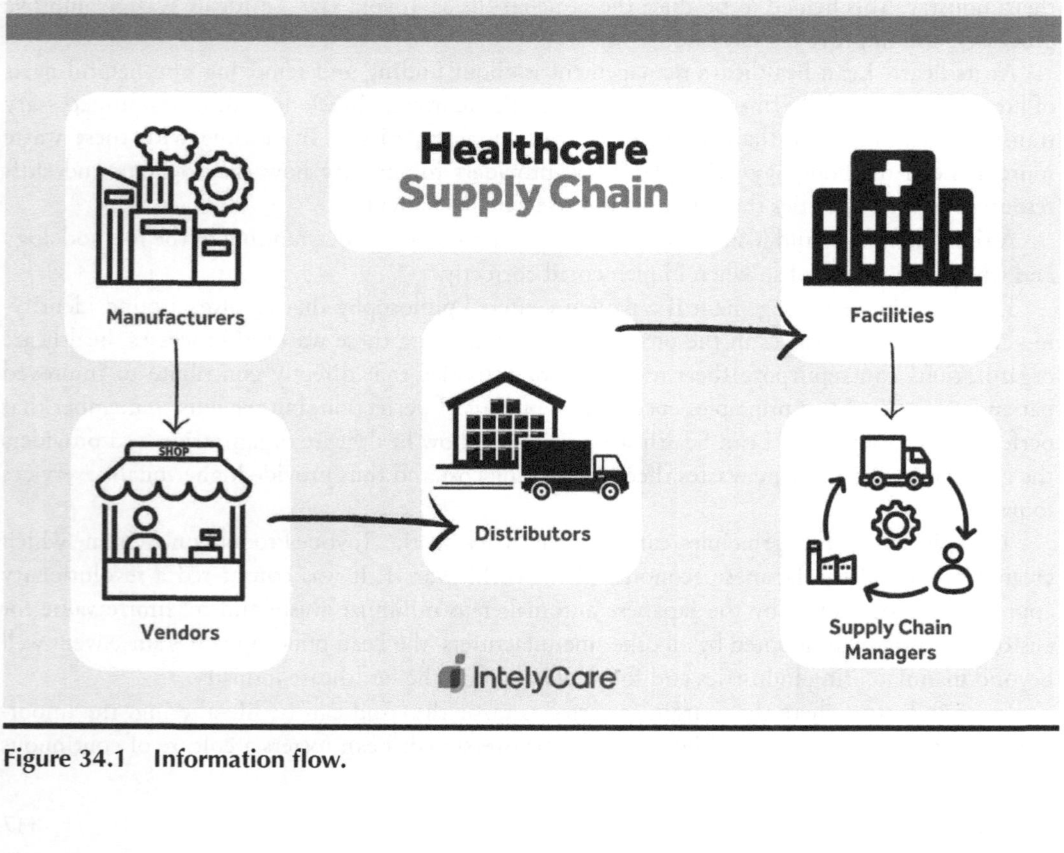

Figure 34.1 Information flow.

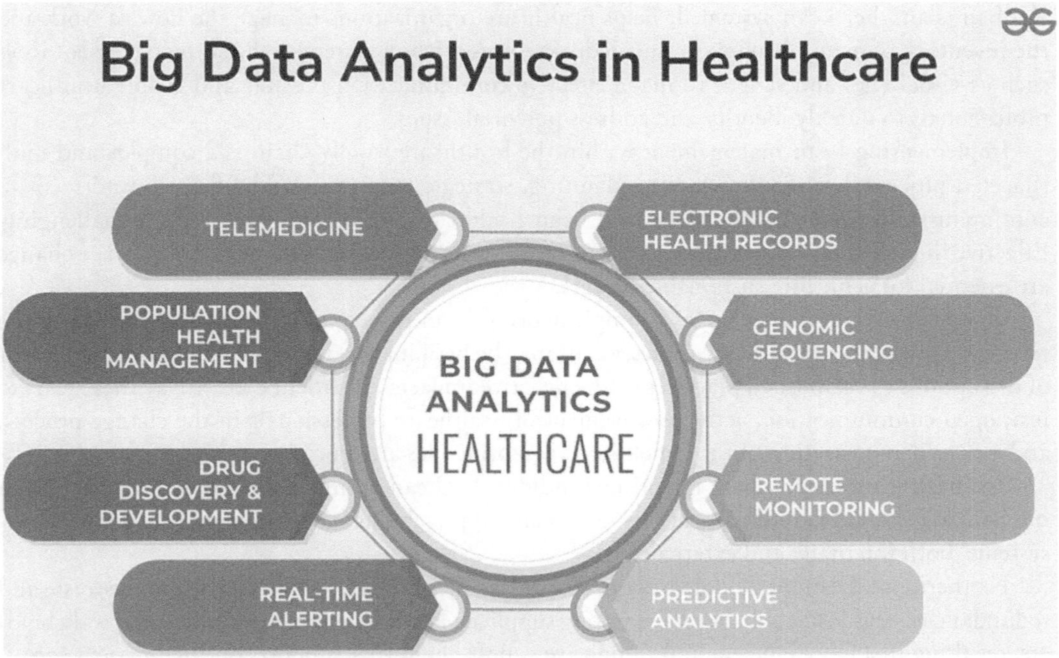

Figure 34.2 Analyze data in healthcare.

The 5S methodology, which consists of Sort, Set in Order, Shine, Standardize, and Sustain, promotes a well-organized and efficient workplace, ensuring that necessary resources are readily available and properly maintained. Below, please see an explanation for each one.

1. **Sort:** You sort through the workplace and keep only what you need. Evaluate what you need and remove parts or tools you do not use. Unused material is something you segregated to another part of the facility. These unused materials are designated as obsolete, hazmat, or other and labeled as such for purposes of proper disposal. This part of 5S requires discipline and supervision. One must check these types of materials on a regular basis so that work place only has the materials needed.
2. **Set Up an Order:** In this part of 5S you set up tools and equipment so that you can readily select and use them. There is no wasted time, and it prevents wasted time for setting up of production. The primary concept here is "First In First Out" or better known as FIFO. FIFO means a company should use the inventory that came in first, as it will prevent newer material or supplies from becoming obsolete—as obsolescence in healthcare must be avoided.
3. **Shine:** With this component of 5S we mean cleaning the workplace at a set interval of time. Cleaning and inspection are tied together. With cleaning, you help to keep equipment and machinery in good working order. This cleaning includes employees workstations.
4. **Standardize:** Standardization means you pick the best practices for a work station and the whole facility and stick to those practices. The standards are always kept high, and every process has a standard.
5. **Sustain:** The sustain part of 5S refers to training, discipline, and the upskilling of employees. Feedback from employees and management is valuable at this point to see the consequences of this implementation.

Kanban is another Lean system. It helps healthcare organizations manage the flow of work and the inventory of medical supplies, thus reducing waste. It is a system of visual management tools such as visual cues and signals to make effective communication possible and enable healthcare professionals to quickly identify and address potential issues.

Implementing Lean management within the healthcare supply chain is a complex and multifaceted process that requires careful planning, strategic execution, and a firm commitment to continuous improvement. The steps to a Lean healthcare organization are indeed challenging. Effective implementation strategies, comprehensive training, and a willingness to embrace change are essential for achieving sustainable success.

One of the primary challenges in implementing Lean principles in healthcare is overcoming resistance to change. Healthcare professionals may be hesitant to adopt Lean methodology for fear of disruptions to established practices or the negative impacts on patient care. To lay these fears to rest, open communication, active involvement of healthcare professionals in the change process, and a clear demonstration of the benefits of Lean principles are crucial.

The healthcare supply chain is a prime candidate for Lean optimization. By adopting the Lean methodology, healthcare organizations and their supply chains have implemented new delivery systems, both internally and externally.

Furthermore, Lean methodologies can streamline procurement processes; minimize waste and redundancies; and foster collaboration among suppliers, healthcare providers, and other stakeholders, resulting in a more efficient and responsive supply chain that supports optimal patient care.

Healthcare organizations must develop an all-inclusive Lean healthcare methodology that aligns with their overall mission and goals. Plans should also include continuous improvement, staff development, and adopting emerging tech over time. By embracing the Lean culture and all it has to offer, healthcare supply chains can endeavor to enlist constant improvement, empower teams, and drive lasting positive change for patient care and operations.

The next chapter will explore the agile methodology. We must remember that they are related but not the same methodology.

Chapter 35

Reasons to Prioritize Agility in the Healthcare Supply Chain

To expand on their definitions, Lean is the methodology that focuses on the mitigation of wastes, while agile perceives that software development and adoption by healthcare will enhance the industry. We will delve into agile more deeply.

Agility is important to the healthcare supply chain as it allows healthcare institutions to adapt quickly to changing patient needs, competition and regulatory guidelines imposed by the government, and/or the FDA. An agile supply chain responds faster to change and new opportunities.

Disruption and massive, rapid change are now the norm. However, the response from supply chain leaders has been largely defensive. Managers endorse measures to guard against supply shortages. Agility, which most supply chain officers would say yes to as a nice-to-have attribute, is harder to measure and is seen as less urgent in a crisis. The outcome most supply chain leaders have focused on is to improve the more substantial elements of the supply chain, such as cost, service, quality, inventory, and asset performance.

Yes, agility is less tangible than Lean, but that does not make it less important. The ability to save money or weather a crisis is insufficient in the long run. Agility can make the difference between operations that thrive and those that just survive. When disruption hits, it upsets and flips over established practices, but at the same time, it can uncover new opportunities. Three of the most important benefits of agility—more timely data and improved visibility, the ability to execute faster than the competition, and collaborative relationships with key supply-chain partners—will enable healthcare supply chains to give better responses to new opportunities.

What makes a supply chain agile? The key performance metrics related to agility are not as well defined as they are for a Lean supply chain. The focus on agility will vary depending on a company's overall strategy and the design of the supply chain. However, there are areas that can be used to build agility into the supply chain. They are the following:

1. Demand sensing—ability to discern and respond to changes in demand. However, the agile supply chain goes a step further and anticipates changes. The agility enables the supply chain to reconfigure production and distribution network and to build robust sources of supply. In an agile supply chain, managers track metrics that include the average number of days between anticipation of demand for a new product and getting it to the market.

DOI: 10.4324/9781003668732-41

2. Collaborative relationships—supply chain managers who excel in this area become centers of information. They take in data and observations from multiple sources to understand opportunities and risks. They excel in collaborating with their key supply-chain partners to respond in a coordinated manner to these opportunities. They collaborate with key customers, exchanging marketplace information and aligning demand forecasts and product flows. They also share information with each other, such as inventory, production schedule, and capacity information to better optimize the entire end-to-end supply chain.
3. Process integration—agile supply chain organizations break down functional barriers and focus on optimizing end-to-end processes. This fundamentally changes the speed at which an organization can respond to change. Process cycle times that were traditionally measured in months will be executed in weeks. The ability to respond quickly will lead to a greater degree of control over the end-to-end supply chain, including manufacturing plants, supply locations, and customer access points.
4. Information integration—advancing technologies such as cloud computing, 5G, the industrial IoT, and AI are driving the digitization of supply chains and increasing information about assets. Organizations often run into trouble because of the inability to easily and quickly share information. This same constraint is even more challenging when sharing information globally across the extended supply chain. The focus is on the depth and the integrity of this information as agile supply chain excellence is driven by accurate data.

Supply chain leaders need to find a new balance that properly weighs the importance of these four building blocks. If that is not intimidating on its own, then supply chains must also reach new levels of customer service and meet ever-more stringent regulatory and governance goals.

The right balance will depend upon one's position and role within an industry supply chain, each company's specific strategy, and how the supply chain contributes to your competitive advantage. Furthermore, this will be influenced by internal priorities and the external environment changes. Investments in building smarter and more digital factories and distribution centers can have a positive impact on all dimensions of the supply chain.

The opportunity is worth the effort. Agile and Lean supply chains that can execute against these imperatives—demand sensing, collaborative relationships, process and information integration—can go to a source of competitive advantage and a driver of profitable growth.

Chapter 36

Is a Hybrid Model Best for Healthcare Supply Chain?

A hybrid model that combines centralized and decentralized supply chains for medical supplies and equipment is promising for the procurement aspect of the supply chain. The hybrid model can minimize costs involving factors such as fleet, location, demand, and delivery time. As with anything else, the advantages and disadvantages need to be discussed and weighed before any decision is made.

The *hybrid strategy* is poised to define the future of the healthcare supply chain. It will merge the Lean methodology with the agility required for less stable markets. The goal is to create an adaptable manufacturing system that can respond quickly to any challenge.

As shown in Figure 36.1, the concept of a hybrid supply chain have emerged as the light at the end of the tunnel in the business world. Implementing this combined strategy allows businesses to meet demand with flexible production capacity.

The supply chain is the lifeline of any business, ensuring the seamless flow of products from creation to consumption.

Throughout the changes in the supply chain over the decades, the drive for efficiency has evolved from the traditional models to the adaptability of agile and Lean methodologies.

Now, it is time for a hybrid strategy and to define the future of healthcare SCM.

The hybrid supply chain represents an important evolution in operations management. It has grown out of necessity in industries where neither a Lean strategy nor an agile strategy could meet the demands of the modern marketplace. This combined strategy demonstrates a shift toward more resilience.

It is particularly effective for companies with separate physical locations for different manufacturing partners, allowing for a more customized response to key customers and final customer orders.

Hybrid supply chains adopt centralization to cut operating expenses by reducing duplicated efforts across various departments. This approach can lead to significant savings in logistics, as seen with global retailers who centralize their distribution model, resulting in less waste and lower costs throughout the supply chain.

DOI: 10.4324/9781003668732-42

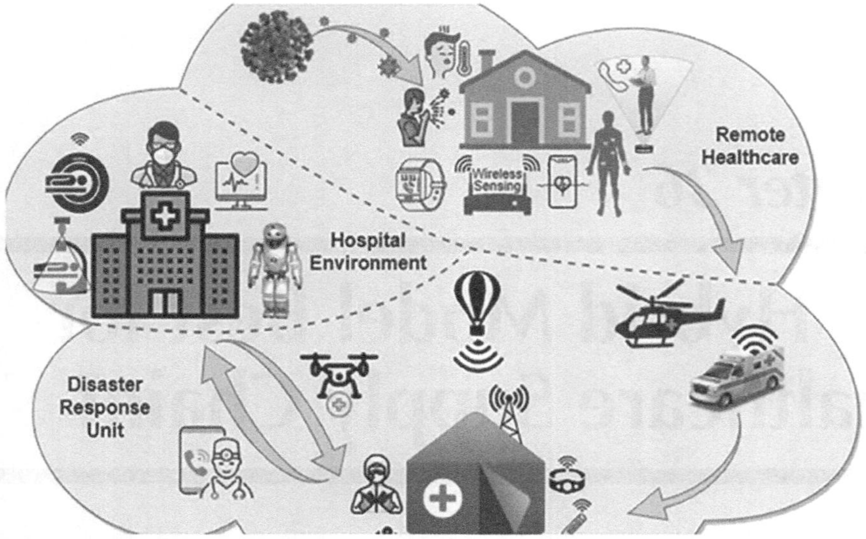

Figure 36.1 Delivery of hybrid healthcare.

However, centralizing a hybrid supply chain can also have its disadvantages. One such disadvantage is increased vulnerability to local disruptions impacting the entire supply chain. It may lead to longer lead times for supply-chain partners located further from the central facility or market. Other important disadvantages of consolidation are higher transportation costs and a potential cut-off from local markets.

In a hybrid supply chain strategy, businesses can exploit the advantages of both Lean and agile methodologies to create a robust supply network. This strategic union allows for a multipurpose agenda, supporting a broad gamut of supply chain activities—from the manufacturing process to final product delivery.

A hybrid supply chain strategy offers the flexibility of an agile supply chain with the effectiveness of the Lean methodology. It supports companies in steering through the complex waters of the modern marketplace. This combined approach can mitigate risks by adapting to customer needs and leading to improved customer satisfaction and service levels.

Chapter 37

Cold Chain Logistics and Healthcare Supply Chain

Cold chain logistics is the movement of temperature-controlled medical supplies along the supply chain (see Figure 37.1). These goods often include pharmaceuticals, equipment, and temperature-sensitive foods. Cold chain logistics doesn't only commence when the product is loaded onto the vehicle; it involves every step of the transportation journey, from initial handling to last-step delivery.

The healthcare industry relies heavily on cold chain logistics for the distribution of biopharmaceutical goods across all borders. These goods can be life saving. Without effective cold storage transportation—controlled room temperature, refrigeration, and freezing—the goods can become unusable. This has serious financial and healthcare consequences for healthcare companies.

Ensuring product integrity and security throughout the supply chain has always been a high priority for the healthcare supply chain and the entire healthcare industry—manufacturers, pharmaceuticals,

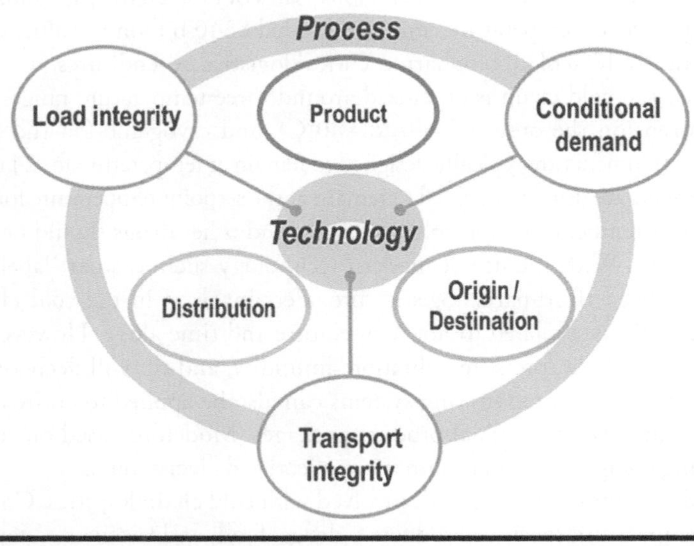

Figure 37.1 Process of cold chain integrity.

DOI: 10.4324/9781003668732-43

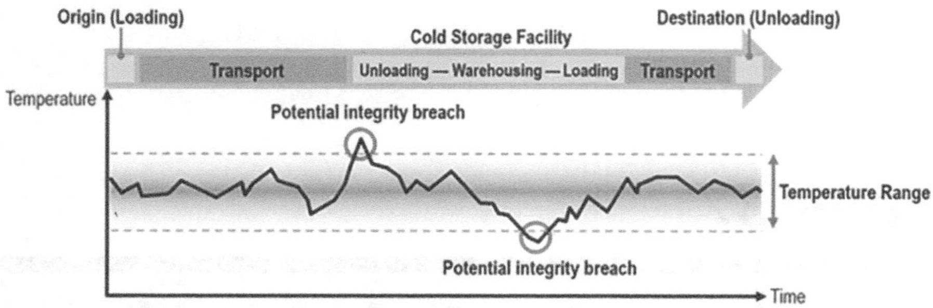

Figure 37.2 Cold chain branches.

medical devices and medical supplies, and laboratories. All of these parts of the healthcare supply chain are duly concerned with ensuring the delivery of viable medical supplies. However, with the changing product portfolio, stricter regulations, extended geographic coverage areas, and increasing risk and cost pressure, the level of concern is greatly increasing. Each facet of the healthcare supply chain just mentioned has their own cold chain criteria for every product they provide.

It would be best to delve into each sector separately as to understanding of cold chain logistics as it pertains to each one. Cold chain logistics has become extremely important in the medical device industry due to the advent of personalized medicine, vaccines, and biopharmaceuticals. It ensures the viability of temperature sensitive medical products with meticulous temperature control.

Figure 37.2 depicts the road ahead for the pharmaceutical cold chain filled with obstacles. Every healthcare company that takes temporary ownership of these high-value medical supplies and equipment must safeguard the capability of these fragile, high-value products. Failure to ensure strict temperature requirements can create enormous financial and clinical impact, as many shipments are often valued at hundreds of thousands and even millions of dollars.

The logistics required to ensure a reliable distribution of temperature-sensitive healthcare products is complex and leaves very little margin for error. Worldwide spending on biopharma cold chain logistics has been rising steadily since 2018, and it is projected to grow by another 25% over the next three years. As of early 2020, annual global sales of biotech drugs, biologic products, and vaccines that require strict temperature control exceeded $340 billion in value. Cold chain logistics accounts for nearly 18% of all biopharmaceutical logistics expenditures.

The pharmaceutical cold chain is organized around three temperature ranges—refrigerated (2 to 8°C), deep frozen (on the order of −40 to −80°C), and cryogenic (on the order of −160 to −180°C). Domestic shipments are typically designed to remain at temperature for 24 to 72 hours, while international shipments are usually designed to remain at the setpoint temperature for up to 120 hours.

The sensitivity of temperature-controlled vaccines and other drugs should be treated with the white-glove treatment. With the use of modern technology such as smart-label technology and RFID, many specialized third-party logistics providers involved in the cold chain distribution can track and transmit data related to not temperature and time alone. However, any continued or multiple exposure to light, pressure, vibration, humidity, and tilt will decrease the integrity of medical supplies. Today, such monitoring systems can also be applied to entire cargo containers, individual pallets, and even individual product packages. Modeling based on real-time and historic data is helping companies to entertain more effective delivery routes.

The medical device industry is, indeed, involved with cold chain logistics. Cold chain logistics ensures that all temperature-sensitive products—drugs, food, and vaccines—stay in their specific temperature range throughout distribution and final delivery.

The global climate change has contributed to cold chain shipping challenges. There is no spot on earth that is immune to this unprecedented levels. Who could have predicted that temperature degrees would reach 30+ degrees Celsius in cities like Brussels and Hamburg? Europe is the main supplier of medical devices and is the fastest warming continent in the world, according to the World Meteorological Organization. In addition to the climate issue, monitoring technologies are increasing regulatory authorities' inclination for more controls on the shippers and importers of medical devices. There are significant challenges the medical devices industry faces that might hinder the implementation of cold chain shipping.

1. Lack of cooperation from suppliers—Complying with cold chain regulations in the buyers' country may contradict the shippers' or suppliers' internal processes for packing and shipping of the goods. Automation or the lack thereof may also be a reason for suppliers' reluctance to cooperate. Adding temperature-controlled devices to the packaging requires human intervention, but automation by suppliers removes human interaction. As well, applying changes to comply with a specific single customer will be costly.
2. Packing and repacking—air freight is done based on passive cooling for cost reduction considerations. Passive shipping may require repacking of goods to include temperature-controlling materials. This will make the buyer request repacking services. This will increase shipping costs that may merely be equal to cost of goods, thus reducing profits.
3. Absence of stability studies—what happens if the temperature of a specific medical product goes outside of the acceptable range during shipping? Do we automatically dispose of the goods? Not necessarily. The buyer of these medical supplies—healthcare institutions—should request a Stability Declaration from the manufacturer. Stability Declaration is a quality document issued by the supplier which includes research proof about the highest and lowest temperature that products can undergo and remain viable.
4. Insurance—insurance policies cover cold chain shipping for medical devices through Food Clause, which stipulates 12 hours of continual damage for the refrigerating compressor, an incident that can happen only for active cooling, which keeps your passive cooling shipments outside any coverage. Despite the fact that both food and medical devices are perishable, the difference in stability and mode of shipping between both types creates a gray area which is for the interest of insurance companies.
5. Temperature-controlled facilities at airports—not all airports have facilities required for temperature control products like chillers, cool storage area, or a refrigerated dollies for the load and offload of goods. Challenges increase in the case of non-direct shipments, where parcel stops at different airports. Think of your refrigerated shipment that includes dry ice that will deplete in 72 hours. It stops at Minneapolis airport for 48 hours as a stopover. Who will be replenishing the dry ice for the products?
6. Regulatory employees—the main responsibility of these employees is to enforce laws. They are book-reliant. This book reliance and lack of product training and knowledge will prevent regulatory employees at customs crossing to fully evaluate the stability and usability of products. This lack of training may lead to unnecessary decisions like destruction or import refusal and inordinate time delays for product clearance.

In this era of Big Data, the more visible data there is, the faster and more accurate your decision and proactive actions will be. Why should a healthcare institution wait till you receive a shipment with temperature issues to request stability data from supplier? Make sure that every Stock Keeping Unit on your system has this data of shipping temperature and storage temperature.

The operation of cold chains is dependent on the required refrigeration and specialized temperature control of healthcare medical products where each cargo unit to be shipped has different requirements in terms of location, medical viability, and transport integrity. Because of the additional tasks involved, as well as the energy required for the refrigeration unit, transportation costs for cold chain products are much higher than for regular goods. The ongoing rise in living standards, life longevity, and economic specialization will remain important drivers for years in the growing demand for perishable goods and the cold chain logistics supporting their transport.

Once all these strategies and methodologies are implemented and maintained, naturally there is a need to measure them to see how successful they have been. That is where Performance Measurement and Improvements come into play.

Chapter 38

Metrics for Performance and Improvement in the Healthcare Supply Chain

Employing the power of real-time data, healthcare SCM has been able to prioritize automation and fully integrated systems. With a multitude of available metrics, healthcare providers can drive decision-making to new heights of accuracy.

This chapter will discuss some of top supply chain metrics for healthcare providers to implement and monitor—how well they can be used to measure and enhance the success of supply chain initiatives within the healthcare industry.

The areas to be discussed include measuring healthcare supply chain success, the top healthcare supply chain metrics, how to use these metrics, and how to track and improve these metrics.

The shift from rambling out-of-date systems and manual processes to cloud-based integration, process automation, and digital data capture in the healthcare supply chain has ushered in a new era of advanced analytics. Health system and hospital supply chain leaders have real-time access to up-to-date insights to guide their decisions. The scope of healthcare SCM metrics at their fingertips can make it challenging to determine which metrics are most critical to measure.

While each individual health organization and hospital has its own distinct challenges and opportunities, the following six are the most critical financial metrics to evaluate the success of healthcare SCM. Figure 38.1 expands on these metrics.

1. **Supply Accounts Payable Days:** Measures how effectively the healthcare organization is managing its payables.
2. **Supply Expense Per Case Mix Index**: Enables the organization to measure and trend supply expense that is adjusted for volume and patient acuity.
3. **Supply Expense as Percent of Net Patient Revenue**: A high-level metric that monitors the relationship between supply expense and net patient revenue.
4. **Spend Under Management**: Provides leadership with a measure of the amount of total expenditures, which is being effectively managed by the organization's supply chain team.

DOI: 10.4324/9781003668732-44

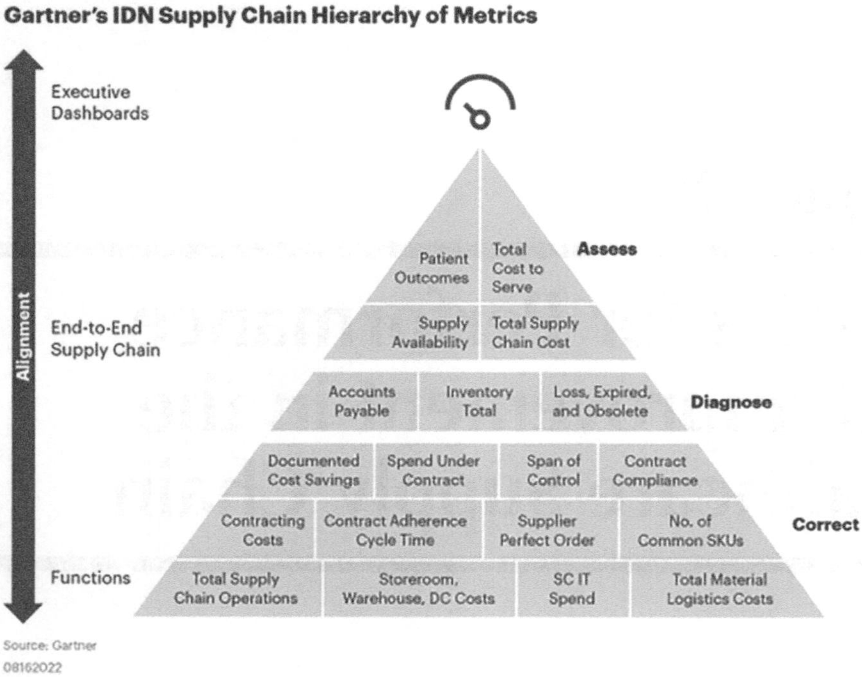

Figure 38.1 Gartner's IDN Supply Chain Hierarchy of Metrics.

5. **Inventory Turns or Movement**: Measures the hospital or health organization's ability to manage its inventory of products in support of delivery of care to patients.
6. **Supply Chain Labor Expense Per Case**: Tells the hospital the labor cost used for in-house supply chain functions. This metric tells the quality of supply chain's cost structure within an organization.

Above are the six best metrics a healthcare organization should implement on a monthly basis to measure financial and supply chain performance. What areas within the healthcare supply chain would have the best use for these metrics?

Benchmarking: A healthcare supply chain team can use metrics to benchmark their performance against similar healthcare organizations. Some of these metrics are similar size, similar product mix, similar volumes, and similar leading practices. An accurate and comprehensive analysis will likely yield some unexpected findings.

Finding Opportunities: The insights found by KPI tracking in healthcare can enable supply chain teams to identify opportunities for savings or improved process efficiency.

Goals: After establishing targets of opportunities for improved performance, a supply chain team can leverage metrics to set achievable goals. If a supply chain team discovered that their supply expense as a % of Net Patient Review was higher than those of a colleague organization, a goal can be set to implement changes.

Measure Looking Forward to Goals: One of the most important aspects of healthcare SCM metrics use is measuring progress toward established goals. As the saying goes, if you can't measure it, you can't manage it. For example, supply chain team sets a goal to reduce its Supply Chain Labor Expense Per Case Mix Index by 10% by the end of the current fiscal year. They implement a technology solution that automates inventory management for process efficiency and productivity. Measuring this KPI, before and after implementation, can help them evaluate the impact of their supply chain inventory investment.

KPIs or metrics, as commonly called, are vital yardsticks in healthcare systems. These yardsticks quantify the effectiveness of supply-chain processes.

They serve as signals for healthcare providers, guiding strategic decision-making and operational improvements. By the use of KPIs, healthcare organizations can enhance their collaboration with supply-chain partners and drive improvements in patient care through continued improvement of resources.

Here are some best practices for tracking and improving these critical metrics, each one of importance on its own merits. However, used as a whole, it can only improve upon the present state of the healthcare supply chain.

Set realistic goals—healthcare supply chain leaders are increasingly pressured—by hospital and medical suppliers—to reduce expenses, operate more efficiently, and contribute to improved care quality. A more strategic approach to measuring supply chain success in healthcare is for supply chain leaders to concentrate on fewer KPIs that are more realistic and achievable. These will yield greater value. It is better to focus on fewer metrics, ensuring that the data driving them is accurate, complete, and up to date, as opposed to moving forward with unreliable data. Take the time to set up your systems, data, and teams for success so that when you leverage healthcare supply chain metrics to quantify the value of the supply chain, there is no doubt that the performance results are real.

Leverage technology—healthcare supply chain leaders rely on modern technological solutions—such as predictive analytic tools—to recognize the growing importance of healthcare supply chain metrics and insights for supply chain leaders.

Healthcare supply chain teams have now started to track Supply Chain Expense Per Case Mix Index and are measuring supply expense adjusted for volume and patient insight over time. Predictive analytics tools using AI can identify trends in the data, which indicate expense increases.

Implement continuous improvement—the healthcare supply chain is famous for continuous change—changes in suppliers, products, contracts, costs, usage. Therefore, measuring supply chain success in healthcare requires a strategy that accounts for impactful changes to the chosen KPI. If the chosen metric is Expenditure Under Management then the expense numbers on which the analysis is performed must be accurate and up to date. The information comes from various sources within a health system and must be shown to be accurate from within the organizations ERP system. Using data that is thrown together from different systems, which is months old, does not provide the supply chain team with an accurate picture of any part of the supply chain. Inaccurate, incomplete, or outdated data that is fed into the computer system renders the end result data useless. The growing adoption of cloud-based ERP systems that are fully integrated with pay applications, EHRs, and SCM solutions bridges the gaps between data sources and faster access.

The healthcare supply chain stands at a critical juncture. As the industry continues to adapt to an era defined by uncertainty, the lessons of recent years have shed light on the persistent vulnerabilities and extraordinary opportunities for change. From technological advancements like AI and predictive analytics to the expansion of care beyond hospital walls, the forces shaping 2025 demand a proactive, innovative approach and drive progress toward a more agile, equitable, and efficient future.

VII THE IMPORTANCE OF MEDICAL AFFAIRS IN THE GLOBAL HEALTHCARE SUPPLY CHAIN

Now, we turn our attention to an extremely rare topic that is indeed part of healthcare, its global aspects, and the supply chain. It has become an integral part of the healthcare supply chain. For some reason, it is either given short shrift or completely overlooked. Here, we shall do neither. The subject I am referring to is: Medical Affairs (MA) Departments.

MA Departments can be found in pharmaceutical companies, medical device companies, and life science companies. This department focuses on the clear communication of data and information between all parties in the supply chain—medical professionals, all types of healthcare providers, patients, and regulatory agencies. With this communication, this department is charged with bridging any informational gaps between all these parties.

MA play a crucial role in the healthcare industry, supporting the delivery of high-quality patient care. Healthcare is a complex field that requires interdisciplinary collaboration, effective communication, adherence to regulations, and a strong focus on research and development. In this section, we will explore the diverse roles and responsibilities of MA professionals and their impact on patient care, healthcare policy, research, and development. We will also discuss the future of MA and the emerging trends and challenges that lie ahead.

DOI: 10.4324/9781003668732-45

Chapter 39

Understanding the Scope of Medical Affairs

Medical Affairs (MA) encompass a vast array of responsibilities within pharmaceutical, biotechnology, life sciences, and medical device companies. Its core is to focus on scientific communication to exchange information about products with healthcare professionals, academics, and regulatory bodies. This exchange is crucial to ensure that healthcare providers have accurate and up-to-date information to make informed decisions about patient care.

The scope of MA is broad and encompasses various functions, among which are the following:

1. Medical Science Liaison Activities: Serve as the primary point of contact between the company and healthcare professionals. They engage in scientific discussions, provide medical education, and gather field information to inform internal stakeholders.
2. Medical Information and Communication: Responsible for providing accurate and timely information about products to healthcare professionals, patients, and internal stakeholders. This includes responding to medical inquiries, developing educational materials, and organizing scientific events.
3. Research and Clinical Development: Critical role in designing and conducting clinical trials to generate data, supporting the safety and efficacy of products. Research and Clinical Departments collaborate closely with clinical development teams and regulatory agencies to ensure that studies meet ethical and regulatory standards.
4. Support for Regulatory Affairs: These professionals work closely with regulatory affairs teams to navigate the complex regulatory landscape. They provide scientific expertise and data to support regulatory submissions and interactions with health authorities.
5. Health Economics and Outcomes Research: Conduct studies to assess the economic and clinical value of products. This includes health economic modeling, real-world evidence generation, and outcomes research to demonstrate the impact of interventions on patient outcomes and healthcare costs.
6. Medical Strategy and Planning: Develop and execute strategic plans to support product launch, lifecycle management, and market access. They collaborate with cross-functional teams to align medical activities with business objectives and patient needs.

DOI: 10.4324/9781003668732-46

The Medical Affairs Departments within the global healthcare supply chain have evolved into that of great importance. Here are several key reasons why this is so:

1. Patient Safety and Care: Patient safety is ensured by providing accurate and comprehensive information about products. By facilitating scientific exchange and education, the department helps healthcare professionals make informed treatment decisions that optimize patient outcomes.
2. Regulatory Compliance: In an increasingly complex regulatory environment, MA ensure compliance with regulatory requirements and guidelines. By providing scientific expertise and supporting regulatory submissions, they help companies navigate the regulatory landscape and obtain approvals for new products.
3. Building Trust and Credibility: They are a reliable source of medical information for healthcare professionals, patients, and other stakeholders. By fostering transparency and communication, MA builds trust and credibility.
4. Driving Innovation and Evidence Generation: Plays a critical role in driving innovation by generating scientific evidence to support the development and marketing of new products. Through clinical research, outcomes studies, and real-world evidence, the department aids the advancement of medical knowledge and the improvement of patient care.
5. Optimizing Market Access and Reimbursement: Collaborates closely with market access and reimbursement teams to demonstrate the value of products and secure favorable reimbursement decisions. By generating health economic data and outcomes research, MA help companies overcome access barriers and ensure patient access to innovative therapies.

As shown in Figure 39.1, the Medical Affairs Department performs an essential function within the global healthcare supply chain industry. It covers a wide range of activities directed at advancing medical science, ensuring patient safety, and optimizing healthcare outcomes. By smoothing the progress of scientific exchange, providing medical education, and generating evidence to support product value, MA has a vital role in innovation and improving patient care.

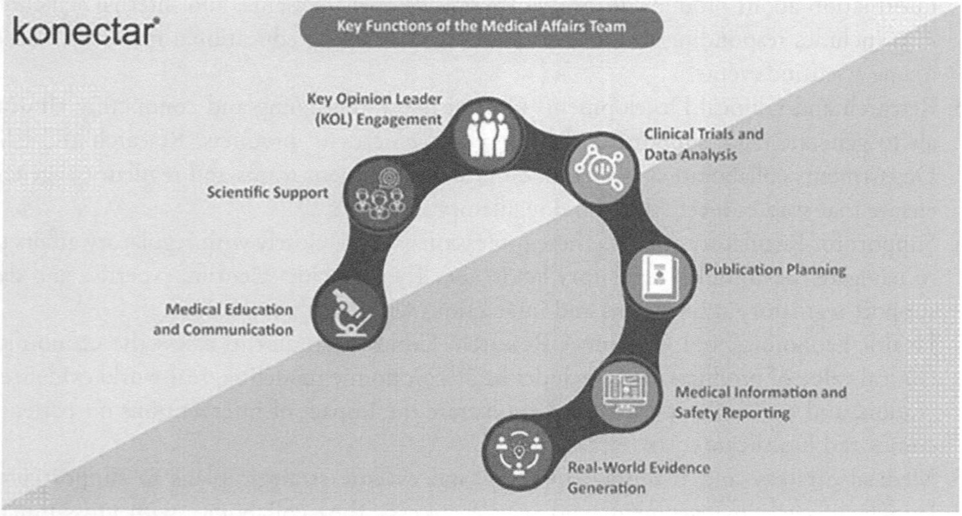

Figure 39.1 Functions of a Medical Affiars Team.

Collaboration and communication between Medical Affairs professionals and clinicians are particularly important in the development and implementation of clinical guidelines. These guidelines serve as a diagram for healthcare providers, outlining the best practices for diagnosing and treating various medical conditions. By working together, MA professionals and clinicians can ensure that these guidelines are based on the most up-to-date evidence and reflect the needs of patients.

The success of MA relies on effective collaboration and communication across different departments within both healthcare institutions and pharmaceutical companies. MA professionals work closely with clinicians, researchers, regulatory affairs personnel, and marketing teams to ensure that patient care is safe, effective, and evidence-based.

Chapter 40

The Key Responsibilities of Medical Affairs within the Supply Chain

Medical Affairs (MA) plays vital strategic function within the life sciences industry, the pharmaceutical industry, the medical supply industry, and all healthcare providers. It operates alongside other key functions such as Research & Development (R&D), forming one of the strategic pillars of the industry. The primary role of MA is to generate and communicate data that assist healthcare professionals, payers, policymakers, and others in making informed decisions that ensure the best use of treatments to benefit patients.

Medical Affairs Department is responsible for the following:

1. Communicating unbiased, evidence-based scientific and medical information to healthcare providers, scientific leaders, patient advocacy groups, payors, policymakers, and others within the healthcare ecosystem.
2. Bringing insights from external sources back to the organization to inform decision-making in areas such as education, research, development, compassionate use, publications, and strategy.
3. Generating new data about marketed and emerging treatments, often through real-world evidence, health economics and outcomes research, investigator-sponsored studies, or pre- and post-approval studies.
4. Collaborating with industry leaders from other functions to drive the strategic direction for the organization to benefit patients.

MA professionals are typically composed of medical and scientific experts, many with advanced, doctoral-level degrees, supported by roles such as data analysts, communications specialists, and business leaders. This department has evolved to become autonomous to ensure that interactions remain uninfluenced by company sales or marketing.

During the last 10 to 15 years, it became apparent that the unbiased, scientific expertise of MA held value beyond direct interactions with healthcare providers. MA teams began to expand

DOI: 10.4324/9781003668732-47

their role as the external voice for the organization's scientific communication. When healthcare providers are seeking information about the actual use and implications of drugs, medical devices, and clinical research, the Medical Information teams within MA provided the answers. Teams dedicated to Scientific Communications, Publications, and External Education developed greater capabilities to serve a wider array of audiences.

With the increasing multifaceted treatments, targeted therapies, and individualized care, MA has adapted to provide comprehensive support. The data from trials are often derived from narrow patient demographics. As a result, the role of MA has expanded to include communicating with patients, advocacy groups, and other stakeholders who expect accurate, timely information across multiple channels.

Alongside the Medical Affairs Information team, there are also the Medical Affairs Strategic, Field Medical teams, Clinical Trial teams, and Regulatory teams. We shall touch upon these in more detail in other chapters. The Medical Strategy team integrates medical expertise with organizational goals, guiding product development, launch, and management throughout their lifecycle. This strategic role ensures effective healthcare outcomes and upholds the integrity and reputation of medical products.

The Medical Affairs Information teams consist of drug, device, and diagnostic experts who develop responses to anticipated or actual questions from healthcare professionals ensuring that concise, accurate, and non-promotional information is provided promptly. Their role is largely responsive, acting as expert resources to answer medical and scientific inquiries. When gaps in knowledge are identified, these teams may employ further studies and educational programs. Medical Information teams utilize digital tools like webinars, interactive platforms, and video summaries to meet the demand for virtual interactions and real-time responses.

In order for all medical information to be disseminated in a clear and concise manner, all employees working within all Medical Affairs Department must be trained in several skills and competencies and show they have mastered them. There are a number of them, and they are as follows:

- MA roles require diverse skills, including advanced scientific training, business, legal acumen, and leadership, with professionals continuously developing these competencies for various roles and careers.
- As MA becomes more strategic, professionals need skills to collaborate with organizational leaders, demonstrating the value of MA in alignment with the company's direction.
- Basic business acumen is crucial for MA to collaborate with other functions, Marketing/Sales, R&D, and the wider healthcare network, to recognize opportunities and deliver value.
- All MA professionals need basic knowledge of properly run clinical trials and evidence gathering to understand all implications of the product.
- Entry into MA requires therapeutic, scientific, and clinical expertise, with proficiency in new technologies for communicating complex ideas to stakeholders with varying levels of scientific competency.
- Understanding global, regional, and local regulations is essential for MA professionals to ensure that activities comply with the legal, professional ethics and standards.
- Effective scientific communication is critical for MA, requiring transparency to engage with external stakeholders in order to create a complete understanding of benefits to the patient.
- Beyond technical skills, MA professionals need personal and emotional intelligence skills, such as listening and learning agility.

MA plays a critical role in the global healthcare supply chain by bridging the gap between clinical research and medical practice. Professionals in this field, including Medical Science Liaisons (MSL) and Medical Information Specialists, ensure that scientific and clinical knowledge is effectively communicated to healthcare providers, medical supply companies, regulators, and patients. This function is essential for maintaining the integrity and usefulness of medical treatments.

As the global healthcare supply chain and industry change and grow to meet the growing and changing needs of the population, MA has adapted by integrating advanced technologies and actual evidence to improve the patient well-being. The continuous development within MA, driven by innovation and collaboration, underscores its indispensable role in advancing public health, nurturing the safe and effective use of medications and the compliance to regulatory standards.

Chapter 41

The Impact of Medical Affairs on Patient Well-Being

Medical Affairs Department plays a vital role in delivering patient well-being. The department has a large scope across the entire global healthcare supply chain. Advanced patient-centered metrics are increasingly more important to medical teams.

In today's rapidly evolving healthcare supply chain surroundings, the MA teams have taken on a pivotal role. They are no longer seen as merely support teams, but are now essential in improving patient care, expanding access to treatments, and shaping the future of medicine.

As healthcare becomes more complex, MA is increasingly focusing on putting patients' needs at the heart of every decision. By concentrating on five key areas, MA can improve patient outcomes and strengthen the reputation of the entire global healthcare supply chain.

Following are the five major areas MA should concentrate on to enhance patient outcomes:

1. **Evidence Gathering:** MA plays a crucial role in generating reliable, patient-centered evidence. With an abundance of data at their disposal, these teams are responsible for relevant and actual patient experiences. They collect real data to show how treatments perform in day-to-day medical practice. This helps healthcare professionals make well-informed decisions, fosters trust in new therapies, and encourages their adoption. By integrating data from clinical trials and actual evidence from these trials and cost-effectiveness studies, MA can accelerate treatment approvals, enhance reimbursement processes, and make essential treatments more accessible to patients.
2. **Adopt Data-Driven Decision-Making:** With access to vast amounts of healthcare data, MA teams are in a unique position to drive accurate decisions. By analyzing actual outcomes and the effectiveness of treatments in real time, MA teams can focus on patient outcomes.
3. **Fashioning Targeted Medical Strategies:** MA is key to creating distinctive strategies that go beyond supporting therapies. By working closely with research and development teams, commercial departments, and external groups like patient advocacy organizations, MA ensures treatments are innovative and aligned with present day and actual patient needs. Collaborations like this make it easier for healthcare professionals to adopt new treatments swiftly and improve patient access.

DOI: 10.4324/9781003668732-48

4. **Medical Engagement:** As global healthcare shifts toward more patient-centered care, personalized engagement has become the forte of healthcare. The Medical Affairs Department has risen to forefront of this engagement. It uses digital tools to provide information to healthcare providers and patients alike. This customized approach helps to increase access to treatments and builds trust. When global healthcare professionals and medical suppliers receive relevant insights, they are more likely to adopt new treatments. In turn, this leads to improved patient health outcomes.
5. **Strategic Medical Leadership:** MA is stepping into a leadership role, changing and re-shaping the strategic direction of global healthcare companies and the supply chain. By supporting resources, talent, and priorities, MA teams ensure that the organization remains committed to improving patient outcomes. Leadership, such as this, promotes collaboration within the company and with external stakeholders stays focused on delivering better health outcomes for patients.

Achieving each of the five priorities as stated earlier will have a considerable impact on patients and on the MA team. As these drivers of patient care are interdependent, the full potential of transformative patient benefits will come from the successful implementation of all five at the same time. However, not all organizations will be or are prepared to invest now in the MA transformation, but this vision of improved patient well-being should be a cross-industry objective for the future.

Chapter 42

Ensuring Quality, Safety through Communications

As Medical Affairs (MA) teams transform in the era of modern technologies and personalized medicines, the discipline of Medical Communications has expanded from only focusing on leading publication-planning activities to driving the development of strategic scientific communications across all global healthcare supply chain platforms. Medical Communications teams have in the past been limited to an execution-focused role, rather than a strategic role when it came to communicating scientific evidence. However, given the new focus on speeding up data communication, with the emphasis on customizing information to various audiences, there has been a clear need for the function to evolve into a more strategic discipline of MA in order to drive a cohesive and consistent scientific communications strategy across multiple channels.

An integrated Medical Communications Strategy, which should include a compelling scientific narrative, is critical in educating both internal and external audiences about the progression and differentiation of assets. The Medical Communications discipline is particularly well placed to drive this process and is increasingly being called upon to be strategic thought partners within and beyond the broader Medical Affairs Department. MA teams create forward-looking strategies by interpreting and framing the data, generating real-world evidence, engaging in peer-to-peer scientific dialogue, and identifying clinical practice insights. Implementing a fully integrated Medical Communications Strategy provides value to these overall strategic approach.

An integrated medical communications plan is the approach to ally Medical Communications with the entire medical strategy for the product. Its main purpose is to articulate a consistent and cohesive scientific narrative across multiple dissemination channels and formats. In order to accomplish this, it must involve insights from cross-functional teams, translating these into impactful communications.

This is a fully integrated medical communications plan for all parts of the Medical Affairs Department to disseminate the accurate information to all other parties in the global healthcare supply chain. As such, these are the benefits of a plan of this magnitude:

1. The plan focuses on consistent scientific narrative while tailoring how data are presented across various audiences and channels across global and regional teams and across all deliverables

DOI: 10.4324/9781003668732-49

created by MA. This helps establish trust in the science and build deeper engagement with the external medical communities.

2. The plan details which stakeholders should receive which communication, why these data are relevant to them, and how to customize to various audiences—healthcare providers, patients, payors, and other key audiences. It also ensures that actionable insights are appropriately captured and incorporated into the communication strategy, which allows MA teams to ensure that all their activities address relevant stakeholder needs in a timely and agile manner.
3. The integrated plan permits the Medical Communications teams to identify areas of overlap and duplication of efforts in their content creation. This helps with streamlining processes to allow for efficiencies, encourages content reuse and repurposing, and ensures a higher return on investment in content creation.

For those of us who do not work in MA or have not heard of such a supply chain department, I think it would be valuable to write down the basic steps to build an integrated medical communications plan. There are five steps to building such a plan. They will be discussed below.

As with any other plan or strategy, one needs to define and lay out the overall objectives that they want to accomplish. They would identify the key scientific communication objectives and priorities for the product. These should be aligned with the overall product vision, the strategic plan for the product, and the Medical Strategy. The plan must include a brief overview of the product, competitor updates, and analysis with any new updates that could affect your communications strategy for the year. It should include insights from the field-based teams or those in customer-facing roles regarding what information the target group of stakeholders is seeking.

Fully understanding your audiences and how they consume content is important. Medical engagement now includes a broader community of stakeholders beyond healthcare providers. which consume information. It now includes clinicians, payees, payors, and medical supply manufacturers across the entire global healthcare supply chain. While traditional plans focus on product data and how to disseminate them to the community, integrated plans are now centered around not only the data but also how the community wants to receive the data. To fully understand your audience, one should be asking of themselves several questions. Who are the target audiences? How do they seek information? What sources do they trust and use? How can we optimize MSL content and field insights?

The medical communications group needs to identify the channels and formats of communication to best engage stakeholders. Given time limitations they have, stakeholders want scientifically accurate and appropriately referenced content. In addition, Field MA teams prefer easy-to-access resources to use with all types of healthcare providers in an era where virtual engagement is increasingly the norm. The amount of medical content and number of peer-reviewed publications are growing at an enormous rate. Stakeholders have limited time to stay updated and thereby use traditional and nontraditional tools to search for and consume information. Stakeholders are also increasingly expecting a Netflix or Amazon-like experience where they can consume medical content when they want it and how they want it.

Medical Communications teams should consider the following digital formats and channels to enhance the reach and impact of the integrated medical communications plan—digital enhancements for publications; plain language summaries for patients, caregivers, and non-specialist healthcare providers; interactive formats for proactive and reactive slide decks; self-service medical information or MA portals; and social media physician networks.

Upon finding and using all digital formats to formulate the message, now it's time to identify the focus areas and detail the tactics to be used in the implementation plan. This step is focused on developing a detailed plan for communication of the scientific narrative that includes input from the cross-functional teams—allows the other functions to have visibility of and plan availability of materials. These could vary depending on the stage in the lifecycle of the product and the target audience. It is best practice to indicate which of the scientific and medical objectives and/or imperatives the tactics are related to. This detail will benefit the cross-functional stakeholders to have a visual representation and knowledge of the various communication tactics that will be available for engagement with stakeholders.

The last step in building this integrated plan is like any other "end of implementation". Measure success, review, reevaluate, and adjust as needed.

MA teams are expected to demonstrate the value of all their activities. The identification and use of appropriate metrics to demonstrate the effectiveness of Medical Communications plans are a hot topic of debate and discussion. There is an increasing need to go beyond reach and readership/usage to engagement and impact metrics. Metrics, when used appropriately, also function as feedback mechanisms for whether a communication strategy has been effective. The following are examples of metrics that are used by Medical Communications teams: Altmetrics, Plum Metrics, Social Media Analytics, Usage of specific content by MSLs, and Google Analytics. Metrics that help capture and demonstrate ROI is still an unmet need in the industry, and we hope that ongoing discussions on the topic will result in innovative approaches for appropriately measuring impact of communication and dissemination activities. In addition to measuring the effectiveness and impact of an iMC S/P, it is important to ensure that the iMC S/P is reviewed at regular intervals (at least quarterly as a best practice) and for cross-functional stakeholders to be part of the review process. This allows for new input to be incorporated in real time and for changes to the overall strategy and plan to be made in an agile manner for the plan to always be current and relevant.

Finally, as with any other program after implementation and metrics, there are the best practices to consider for maintaining fostering cross-functional teams. Some of these practices are listed and discussed below:

1. While Medical Communications teams may not have originally been part of cross-functional team discussions during the development of the Medical Strategy for the product, it is important to include them so that the insights gathered from these discussions can bring to light the creation of the Integrated Medical Communications Plan.
2. Medical Communications teams should plan for cross-functional representation needed for the creation and review of plans. This means that a meeting schedule should be put in place in advance, along with a clear agenda and expected contribution from each stakeholder.
3. Shorter content formats for seeking input on plans to be used: When plans are sent via email for comments from cross-functional stakeholders, getting quality responses can be a challenge. Nontraditional approaches can be used to include summarizing key content relevant to each stakeholder.
4. To ensure alignment between global and regional plans, it is recommended that global teams create a standard template for regional plans. Regional teams can use elements of the global plan and customize relevant sections based on their specific regional needs.

Medical Communications teams, with their expertise in developing a riveting Medical Communications Strategy, have become a major driving force in the dissemination of scientific communication across an organization. The Integrated Communications Plan is an important strategic document that plays a significant role in ensuring that a consistent and cohesive scientific narrative is communicated to the right stakeholder/target audience at the right time and across the right channels.

Chapter 43

Medical Affairs' Influence on Regulations and Health Standards

Medical Affairs Departments collaborate with regulatory bodies or agencies, such as the Food and Drug Agency (FDA), to ensure that healthcare regulations are in place to safeguard patient's rights. Within a global healthcare supply chain, each country has regulatory agencies, with their own compliance rules and laws. Thus, for many healthcare companies, the global supply chain is getting more and more intricate every day.

In MA, building and managing relationships with key opinion leaders—physicians, hospital executives, health system directors, medical researchers, and patient advocacy groups—are a critical component of successful product launches and long-term growth. In today's highly regulated environment, it is more important than ever to make sure that healthcare providers are compliant with all legal aspects of the foreign governments they operate within. Engaging with the right key opinion leaders is a key strategy for all organizations involved in the global supply chain.

First and most importantly, compliance is not simply a box to tick off on a list of tasks. It is a vital component in building trust and maintaining ethical standards in the healthcare industry.

Compliance ensures that interactions between all supply chain parties and key opinion leaders are fair and free from any undue influence. This compliance also protects patients from being exploited or misled by physicians who may be influenced by financial incentives.

Those who work in MA need to understand the regulatory restraints in order to manage their activities in a legal, compliant, and ethical manner. MA personnel need guidelines on the key components of the legal, regulatory, and industry codes of practice in all the countries the organization does business in and how to mitigate the risks.

International government regulations and industry codes of practice provide the requirements and compliance functions needed to advise staff in key areas such as:

- Transparency and Disclosure
- Independence and Objectivity
- Independent Medical Education and Sponsorship

 DOI: 10.4324/9781003668732-50

- Research Collaborations
- Promotion and Marketing
- Conflict of Interest Management

Being aware of areas that can carry potential conflicts of interest, healthcare providers are thereby encouraged to be transparent and to disclose any of these conflicts to maintain the integrity of their products.

Regulations are established by national and local regulatory bodies such as the Food and Drug Administration and Federal Trade Commission (FTC) in the United States. In Europe, there is the European Medicines Agency which covers the European Union, Iceland, Norway, and Liechtenstein and finally the Medicines and Healthcare Products Regulatory Agency in the United Kingdom. These regulatory bodies enforce rules that all global healthcare companies must adhere to. Noncompliance results in penalties such as fines, regulatory audits, reputation damage, or business interruptions.

MA is bound by legal and regulatory frameworks that relate to the promotion of all medical supplies as well as data privacy and anti-bribery and anti-corruption measures, with some leeway for intent, conflicts of interest, and transparency. By adhering to these principles and regulations, the industry can maintain legal compliance and public trust while advancing medical knowledge and patient care.

Medical Governance, though technically part of MA, can operate as a separate function but in conjunction with Compliance or Risk Management. When established as a separate entity within the MA function, Medical Governance usually collaborates closely with Compliance teams to interpret policies and provide strategic guidance, especially in "gray" areas that lack clear industry standards. This partnership is crucial in navigating vague situations to ensure that the company adheres to ethical and legal standards while continuing to innovate and deliver value to its stakeholders.

Medical Governance can play an integral role in shaping how a company conducts itself both internally and externally. It establishes a comprehensive governance framework that guides Medical teams. This ensures that teams make ethical, informed decisions that align with external requirements of the regulatory agencies. Medical Governance helps to safeguard the integrity of business operations while meeting the needs of key external stakeholders, including healthcare providers, decision-makers, patients, and the broader public—the global healthcare supply chain.

To ensure that all types of compliance are met by the entire global healthcare supply chain, codes of practice have been established for each type of healthcare industry and for the countries they have operations. The codes play a crucial role in guiding the behaviors as well as the ethical and compliant conduct of pharmaceutical companies. The scope of these codes is for prescription-only medicines and vaccines but does not include nonprescription medicinal products.

MA personnel have a vital role to play in ensuring that medical activities adhere to regulatory codes of practice. This role is responsible for maintaining the integrity and trustworthiness of interactions between the medical industry, healthcare providers, and the public. These regulations are designed to prevent promotional activities disguised as medical or scientific misinformation. To ensure robust ethical decision-making in the execution of MA activities, Medical Governance applies various strategies and guidelines to distinguish nonpromotional from promotional activities. The Compliance employees safeguard the standards, the laws, and regulations through the monitoring of nonpromotional activities. While promotion and marketing are the roles of Commercial staff as opposed to MA, the latter does have a role in the review and approval of promotional materials.

Maintaining a robust compliance culture within Medical Affairs Departments in the global healthcare supply chain endeavors is sensible and a strategic imperative. This organizational culture must be nurtured from the top to the bottom—from the C-level offices to the lowest line managers and employees. This is the culture that emphasizes governance and compliance standards and where employees feel safe to voice their concerns about a product or service. To navigate all the details of regulations, companies develop comprehensive policy and procedural documents, such as Standard Operating Procedures. Clear demarcation of roles, accountabilities, and responsibilities, especially between Sales and Marketing and MA functions, is crucial to managing ethical application of knowledge and compliant implementation in promotional and scientific activities. The effective management of these operating procedures is a springboard to monitoring, auditing, and, if necessary, disciplinary actions to safeguard the organization, healthcare providers, global healthcare manufacturers, and the patients who depend on the healthcare supply chain.

Understanding and managing regulatory and legal risks are building blocks of an effective compliance program. Companies must conduct risk assessments or audits to identify and gauge inherent risks. This involves documentation of potential risks, interviewing key business stakeholders to grasp the organization's priorities, and ranking these risks using a scoring system. Once identified, risk mitigation plans are developed to outline specific controls and actions needed to mitigate these risks and assign employees responsible for their management.

Policies, like the Standard Operating Procedures, are vital tools for communicating the principles, standards, and requirements for identifying risks. Policies provide the principles that outline the organization's stance on compliance issues, while procedures offer detailed instructions on how these policies should be implemented. These documents ensure that all staff members are well informed about what is expected of them and how to apply their knowledge to empower them to execute their daily activities.

Supporting systems play a crucial role in reinforcing compliant and practical processes. These systems can range from simple databases to sophisticated software platforms that manage and document compliance of activities. For instance, an approval process for promotional or sample materials might use a system that can track submissions, reviews, and approvals. Such systems not only enhance the compliance of processes but also provide an audit trail that can be invaluable during regulatory inspections.

Of course, the implementation of Standard Operating Procedures for regulatory, legal compliance should always go hand in hand with the training of all employees and frequent internal audits to ensure that the procedures are being used and followed properly by all staff.

Training methods come in all different shapes and sizes—from traditional classroom sessions to online courses and interactive workshops. It's important to tailor training programs to the audience's needs, making sure that the content is relevant and engaging. Regular training updates are also necessary to keep up with changes in regulations and company policies and procedures. By investing in comprehensive training, companies will reduce the risk of noncompliance, prevent outside regulatory audits, and promote an internal culture of continuous improvement.

Acknowledging all of the interrelated components, beginning the journey from recognizing the need for a compliance framework within MA to the successful implementation of such a program can seem daunting. The following is meant to give the reader a perspective guide for implementing such a program into Medical Affairs Departments.

1. Strategy: Compliance activities are driven by the company's strategic goals. Integrating a compliance strategy into MA should include benchmarking against industry standards. Starting with these standards, the strategy development continues with risk assessments across

product lines and geographies. Identifying these risks helps the Compliance department anticipate and prepare for challenges that the MA organization will most probably globally encounter.

2. Governance: Creating internal governance groups, especially in MA, will support decision-making and ensure that standards are met for implementation of MA activities. It ensures that MA activities are in internal compliance with other departments and practices—interactions between Medical and Sales/Marketing/Advertising and Research/Development teams.
3. Communication of Operational Procedures: Comprehensive Standard Operating Procedures for the activities identified in the risk assessment should be created. The communication and information sharing will lead to the mitigation of confusion and any dissension between MA and internal and external partners.
4. Monitor and Review Procedures: The practices of MA and the global healthcare supply chain are inextricably intertwined. Initial strategies and SOPs should be reviewed after 12 to 24 months to monitor whether earlier decisions and objectives are delivering the expected outcomes.

Policies and procedures of practice in MA are essential for ensuring legal and ethical conduct, transparency, and protection for all stakeholders involved in the global healthcare supply chain. While these policies add value and reduce risks, MA employees must scrutinize and apply them to ensure that all activities adhere to these regulatory and legal standards.

Chapter 44

How Medical Affairs Is Reshaping the Global Healthcare Supply Chain: Bridging Science and Marketing

Medical Affairs (MA) plays a crucial role in the healthcare industry due to its responsibility in bridging the gap between research and development and marketing operations. By providing scientific expertise, MA ensures that healthcare professionals receive accurate, balanced, and up-to-date information about all areas of the global healthcare supply chain—therapeutic, medical products, and devices. This contributes to better patient outcomes, enhances the credibility of healthcare companies, and supports regulatory compliance. Furthermore, MA teams engage in valuable evidence gathering and engage in survey trials.

In order for MA to excel in the attempt to bridge this gap, these professionals should master five key competency areas. ACMA formulated five areas through a demanding advisory board process involving experts in MA. The five pillars that encompass the necessary competencies for medical affair professionals are life sciences understanding, regulatory compliance, technical competencies, soft skills and business acumen, and processes.

We will discuss in a more detail below:

1. Life science understanding: This area of competency covers medical devices, diagnostics, and drugs. These areas are constantly evolving forcing the MA professionals to stay knowledgeable on current issues. The knowledge and issues are vital as all of these areas fall under their own regulatory compliance. Having a broad understanding of the sectors shapes their ability to express scientific information accurately, efficiently, and in layman's terms to various stakeholders. With this knowledge, MA professionals can stay ahead of others in the industry and anticipate the ever-changing needs of all stakeholders.

DOI: 10.4324/9781003668732-51

2. Regulatory and compliance: Regulatory compliance is a critical pillar that ensures MA professionals operate within the appropriate, ethical, and compliance guidelines. This competency emphasizes understanding the relevant regional regulatory bodies, submission and review of applications, and engaging with external stakeholders. This includes complying with regulations and guidelines established by health authorities, such as those enforced by the U.S. Food and Drug Administration or the European Medicines Agency. Being aware of the regulatory rules can lead to trust, and proper conduct will lead to ongoing collaboration between MA professionals and all global healthcare providers. It is crucial for every individual to possess knowledge of compliance. Regulations can and will differ by region/country, so it is critical that MA professionals have a deep understanding of this competency. There are different regulatory and compliance regulations in each region.
3. Technical competencies: Basic technical competencies such as evidence-based medicine, clinical trial analysis, and health economics and outcomes research are crucial for MA professionals. Clinical trials are the cornerstone of evidence-based trials, and the data they generate forms the backbone of a MA toolkit. Having a strong technical foundation in every role is crucial for successful product development and launches. MA professionals equipped with expertise in evidence-based medicine possess the critical ability to interpret and apply scientific data accurately. Accuracy is imperative to ensure that healthcare providers receive reliable information on the efficacy and safety of medical products.
4. Business acumen: Effective communication and presentation skills are crucial for MA professionals to clearly and concisely explain complex scientific data to diverse audiences—from healthcare providers, patients, to industry colleagues. These professionals must be adept at tailoring their messages to suit different audiences, ensuring that the information is accessible and relevant to each group. MA professionals are not only responsible for presenting data, but they are also responsible for discussing the data. Ultimately, it comes down to the ability for companies to adapt—able to tailor communications based on the needs and personality of the people needed to be dealt with. Whether communicating with a highly technical audience or with patients who may have limited medical knowledge, the ability to adjust the level of detail and complexity is vital. By mastering these communication and presentation skills, MA professionals can ensure that scientific data is accurately interpreted and applied in various contexts.
5. Processes: This focuses on key functional areas within MA that proficient experts should excel in. This includes publication practices, advisory boards, continuing medical education, investigator-sponsored research, and post-marketing studies. Each of these activities plays a pivotal role in advancing medical knowledge, ensuring product efficacy and safety, and maintaining regulatory compliance. Having a comprehensive understanding of processes is essential for MA professionals to succeed and be more efficient in their work. MA professionals are required to work with multiple teams throughout the clinical trial process, and having a solid understanding of each role's responsibility leads to a smoother workflow, ultimately better serving patients.

The department of Medical Affairs in any and all medical organizations plays a vital role between clinical development and marketing operations. With dedication to scientific expertise, regulatory compliance, and effective communication, MA ensures the dissemination of accurate information to all global healthcare professionals and thereby the supply chain.

Chapter 45

Emerging Trends and Challenges for Medical Affairs

The future of Medical Affairs (MA) within the context of the global healthcare supply chain is in the process of being remodeled by innovations in digital technologies, AI, and data. The future leaders of MA must be able to anticipate, shape, and inform the entire global healthcare supply chain on these developments.

MA is no longer merely a supporting function within the global healthcare industry. As we see in Figure 45.1, it is one of the key pillars of the global healthcare supply chain, right alongside the R&D and Sales/Marketing functions. This shift in importance comes with the increased understanding of the role it plays in advancing patient-centered therapies, providing data-driven information, and influencing global healthcare solutions. As its importance grows, so does its impact

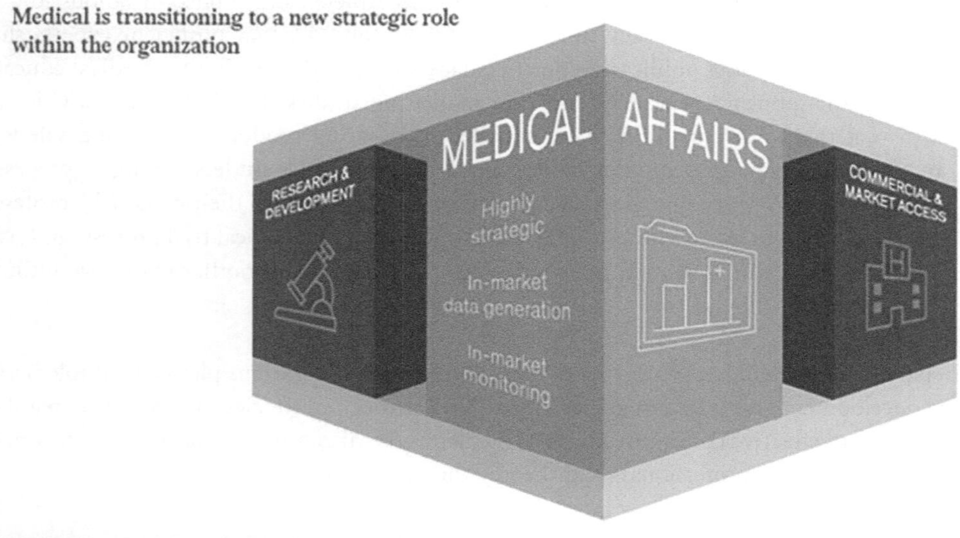

Figure 45.1 Medical Affairs strategic roles.

DOI: 10.4324/9781003668732-52

on the requirements—regulatory and legal. The future is clear; the success of the global healthcare supply chain will turn on how effectively the Medical Affairs Departments use data analytics, generate real-world evidence, and engage stakeholders through both traditional and digital channels.

For MA teams, the challenge lies in transforming data—10 zettabytes and telemedicine platforms—into actionable insights that benefit patients and healthcare providers. Adding to this complexity is the accelerating pace of therapeutic innovation. With global biotech funding reaching nearly $47 billion in 2021, the development of novel treatments has surged, resulting in a 75% increase in available scientific data as per indication over the last decade. MA professionals must navigate this complexity while aligning strategies with patient needs and regulatory requirements. Telemedicine and virtual care became essential, reshaping how patients and providers interact.

For MA, these technological developments demand a digital revolution approach to communication, education, and evidence dissemination. This dynamic landscape requires new capabilities for MA, including leadership development, data integration, and digital education.

To meet these challenges and to "conquer" them in the future, MA must focus on a number of interconnected supports that will change its role to be of healthcare innovation. They are the following:

1. Leadership Change: MA is increasingly recognized as a key strategic voice within the global healthcare supply chain and industry. The increasing complexity of healthcare demands leaders who can campaign for patient-centric innovation. This transition in leadership requires a combination of technical expertise, strategic thinking, and cross-functional leadership.
2. Data Analytics: We know the rise of Big Data actually took place over a decade ago, but MA was not included in that new technology. As stated previously, MA was an afterthought in prior decades. Has Big Data transformed the MA functions or the other way around or have they complemented each other's needs? Real-time analytics, powered by AI, allows Medical Affiars professionals to uncover actionable insights from large data ranging from clinical trial outcomes to patient-reported experiences. However, turning this data into meaningful strategies requires robust tools and a culture of data-driven decision-making. Digital solutions such as *MedAffairsAI* are enabling MA teams to process and interpret complex data with speed and meticulousness. These tools facilitate real-time analysis, automate routine reporting tasks, and provide interactive dashboards that highlight key trends to improve patient outcomes and inform clinical decisions.
3. Evidence Generation or Gathering: Generating strong evidence is essential to MA's role. Traditional siloed approaches fail in today's integrated global healthcare supply chain. By employing AI-driven tools, MA teams can align evidence-generation efforts with stakeholder needs to create real-time data that informs clinical practice. Interactive platforms are becoming essential—dashboards that visualize evidence in real time. Such tools not only enhance the accessibility of evidence but also reinforce MA as a trusted source of actionable insights.
4. Engaging in Digital Technologies: The ways in which MA engages with stakeholders are changing rapidly. With healthcare providers increasingly seeking digital interactions, MA teams adopted a hybrid approach that combines traditional methods with digital platforms. They have offered omnichannel communication, e-learning platforms, and scientifically rigorous content that meets the needs of diverse audiences. Conversion to new content formats to capture physician attention, convey messages, and create scientific narratives reinforces new concepts.

This re-creation or evolution of MA is redefining its role in the global healthcare supply chain. By prioritizing leadership, data analytics, evidence generation, and digital engagement, MA teams can position themselves as vehicles for innovation and organizational success. Tools like telemedicine and AI platforms such as MedAffairsAI empower MA professionals to rise to the challenges of a rapidly evolving industry. As we rapidly draw closer to the future, the opportunities for MA to impact patient care, influence strategy, and drive global healthcare supply chain innovation—supply chain without borders being of utmost importance—we shall see in the next part of this work.

VIII GLOBAL HEALTHCARE SUPPLY CHAIN WITHOUT BORDERS; PARTNERSHIPS AND INTERNATIONAL LOGISTICS

Without doubt, the central phenomenon of our times, globalization is anything but recent. The first explorers took to the seas for new worlds—and new markets—as early as 1500 BC, when Phoenicians living in what would one day be Lebanon established trade routes throughout the Mediterranean and Asia Minor. Consider this: Thirty-five centuries later, in the same place, the Lebanon Ministry of Public Health is providing its citizens with a Pfizer-BioNTech vaccine manufactured in 86 sites across 19 countries.

In the following decades, entrepreneurs around the world were thinking beyond borders. The medical device market expanded dramatically. There has been a growing number of small- and medium-sized enterprises that have started up in Asia, the Middle East, and Europe. Before trade was temporarily halted by the COVID-19 pandemic, the medical device market was growing by 4% annually. By 2019, sales worldwide had reached almost $500 billion.

Today, the medical device market is increasingly shaped by the companies that are most effectively reaching into global markets. By going beyond natural borders, companies are dramatically increasing the access to new expertise, funding sources, suppliers, factories, clinical trials, and distribution channels. With access to countless options in the development and production process, new devices can often be more innovative and faster and cheaper to produce.

Many find the globalization of healthcare to be an exciting trend. Sometimes, people in the healthcare profession will say that they miss the days when American healthcare was mostly a

DOI: 10.4324/9781003668732-53

domestic enterprise that was less exposed to the vulnerabilities in international trade. But the future is already here. Medical centers and research institutions across the United States are becoming more and more reliant on international supply chains.

The future belongs to those who embrace collaboration. As the world leader in biomedical research and development, the United States has a major stake in continuing to champion international networks in the medical device market.

Chapter 46

Models of Collaboration between Government and Private Sector

A public-private partnership (PPP) in healthcare is fundamentally a shared duty between public institutions and private entities, ranging from healthcare providers to technology businesses. This collaborative framework aims to use the capabilities of both sectors to optimize resource allocation, improve service delivery, and provide innovative solutions to the healthcare industry's changing demands.

PPPs, as they are usually called, in healthcare are extremely important as they provide a means of addressing the multiple difficulties that healthcare systems confront across the world. From rising prices and limited resources to the need for technology breakthroughs and better patient outcomes, PPPs provide a strategic and long-term strategy to navigate the complicated landscape of modern global healthcare.

The overview of public-commercial partnerships in healthcare emphasizes the collaborative nature of government and commercial enterprises. The idea has grown as a reaction to the changing healthcare landscape, with both sectors working together to address difficulties and accomplish common goals. This partnership can take different forms—cooperative service delivery, infrastructure development, and technology innovation. The background of this cooperation stresses the transition away from primarily government-provided healthcare and toward acknowledging the potential contributions of the private sector. PPPs have a wide range of aims, including improving access to excellent healthcare, optimizing resource usage, introducing innovation, and achieving cost-effectiveness throughout the global healthcare supply chain.

There are several models in this partnership. They will be discussed below:

1. Service delivery: Private entities manage public hospitals or healthcare institutions. This might include activities like administration, staffing, and day-to-day operations. The private sector's knowledge of effective management techniques, technological integration, and innovation can result in higher service quality and operational efficiency. In contrast, governments may choose to outsource particular healthcare services to private firms. This might involve

DOI: 10.4324/9781003668732-54

diagnostic testing, imaging services, or specialized therapies. Outsourcing certain services allows governments to use the private sector's specialized capabilities, resulting in improved service quality and shorter wait times.
2. Infrastructure development: The infrastructure development starts with "build-operate-transfer" model. This is where private firms invest in healthcare infrastructure development. They run the facility for a set length of time, recouping their investment through service fees or other revenue sources. Eventually, ownership and management of the administration are returned to the government. This concept enables governments to obtain funds and expertise without the requirement for major capital expenditures.
3. Concession arrangements: These arrangements allow private partners to deliver specialized healthcare services or operate facilities. These agreements frequently include a time range within which the private party runs and maintains the infrastructure. The concession agreement may include performance-based incentives to ensure a commitment to providing high-quality service.

These partnerships come with mutual benefits, including improved efficiency, access to capital and technology, risk sharing, and innovations. While public-private partnerships in healthcare have many advantages, as stated earlier, they are not without drawbacks. Navigating these challenges necessitates careful planning and proactive methods. These drawbacks or negatives to forming public-private partnerships are the following:

1. **Ensuring equitable access:** Equitable distribution of gains from PPPs is a key concern for varied socioeconomic groups. Certain communities may be excluded or suffer difficulties in accessing, aggravating preexisting health inequities. To solve this issue, public-private partnerships must include procedures that ensure that healthcare services are affordable, accessible, and inclusive.
2. **Quality assurance**: High-quality healthcare services are vital for the success of public-private partnerships. Maintaining uniform care across public and private hospitals may prove difficult, resulting in uneven care. Implementing defined quality assurance standards, monitoring methods, and regular evaluations are critical for ensuring that patients receive consistent and outstanding treatment.
3. **Balancing both interests**: Gaining the correct balance between public health goals and private sector profit is a challenge. Conflicting interests will happen if prioritizing financial gains above public health goals. Solving these potential issues requires strong contractual structures, open communication, and a common commitment to the overall purpose of healthcare.
4. **Regulatory challenges**: These partnerships face regulatory and legal challenges. Partnership implementation and administration might be complicated by varying regulatory frameworks, licensing requirements, and legal structures. Governments must provide clear, consistent, and regulatory frameworks to promote successful collaboration while protecting public interests.

Public-private partnerships in healthcare provide a flexible and new strategy for solving difficult healthcare delivery. They provide efficiency, creativity, and resource optimization, but they are not without obstacles. Equitable access, quality assurance, and regulatory complications emphasize the importance of cautious planning. Despite their problems, PPPs serve as drivers for positive change, necessitating continual collaboration, openness, and a dedication to the public good.

Chapter 47

Challenges in Cross-Border Healthcare Supply Chain

There are numerous challenges in cross-border healthcare supply chain. To name a few, these include regulatory compliance, inventory management, disruptions of different types and severity, IV fluid shortages, critical product shortages, inflation, and labor issues.

The global healthcare supply chain business faces a complex set of logistical complications in today's linked globe. As healthcare supply chains transcend borders, effective management becomes more important to ensure timely and smooth delivery of medical supplies, drugs, and equipment. This chapter will look at the subtleties of global SCM and the logistics complexities that come with it.

Healthcare supply chains involve the detailed coordination of various entities, including manufacturers, distributors, healthcare providers, and regulatory bodies, across multiple countries and regions. Included in this global scope is logistics—the challenges associated with managing and ensuring the flow of goods and information across the world. For global healthcare supply chain, it encompasses the transportation, storage, and distribution of pharmaceuticals, medical devices, and other critical supplies.

As the global population continues to increase, healthcare needs are rising proportionally, making the demand for a well-functioning supply chain more vital than ever. The healthcare supply chain market is expanding rapidly, driven by factors such as technological advancements, regulatory changes, and the globalization of pharmaceutical manufacturing.

The healthcare supply chain is like no other. It involves the movement of highly regulated and extremely perishable goods. The transportation and storage of pharmaceuticals and medical devices demand adherence to stringent regulations and compliance standards. The need for temperature-controlled transportation and storage further adds to the logistics complexity, requiring specialized infrastructure and expertise. Due to the complexity of global healthcare supply chains, unforeseen events such as natural disasters, geopolitical tensions, and public health emergencies can disrupt the normal flow of operations. Effective risk management strategies are essential to identify potential threats and implement contingency plans.

DOI: 10.4324/9781003668732-55

The main challenges to a global healthcare supply chain come in many shapes and sizes, but we will concentrate on a few of the major factors:

1. Regulatory compliance: Due to globalization and medical facilities all over the world, this looms as a major challenge. Each nation and or region has a myriad of international regulations governing the production, transportation, and distribution of pharmaceuticals and medical devices. From GMP to labeling requirements, each step in the supply chain must adhere to a complex web of standards.
2. Data security: We live in an age where data is "king". Securing sensitive information related to healthcare products and patients is of paramount importance. Healthcare supply chains involve the exchange of critical data, including patient records, product specifications, and manufacturing details.
3. Inventory management: There is a constant need to balance sufficient stock levels without succumbing to the pitfalls of overstocking or understocking. This is a delicate dance in most companies, but especially so in healthcare supply chains. Overstocking can lead to increased carrying costs, the risk of product expiration, and wastage. On the other hand, understocking can result in delays, stock-outs, and compromised patient care.
4. Transportation/Logistical challenges: The world wide nature of healthcare supply chains introduces unique transportation challenges, particularly in regions with inadequate infrastructure. Ensuring the timely and secure movement of temperature-sensitive pharmaceuticals and medical equipment across borders demands a strategic and adaptable approach.

The interaction of all of these factors—logistical complexity, market dynamics, and regulatory compliance—necessitates a deliberate and proactive strategy in the evolving environment of global healthcare supply chains.

Chapter 48

Strategies to Improve Global Healthcare Supply Chain Access

In today's interconnected world, global health and wellness have become increasingly important. As populations grow and migrate, and as diseases cross borders more easily, the need for a relevant global healthcare supply chain to reach everyone is more vital than ever. Despite significant advancements in medical technology and healthcare delivery, disparities in healthcare access remain a critical issue. These disparities, at times, result in unequal health outcomes, where some communities enjoy excellent healthcare while others struggle with limited access to even the most basic services. Finding solutions requires a coordinated global effort. The goal is to provide every individual, regardless of their geographic location or socioeconomic status, with access to quality healthcare.

Global healthcare systems are increasingly adopting a vision that will enable efforts to reduce health disparities. This approach involves recognizing that health challenges in one part of the world can have far-reaching impacts elsewhere. There is a growing emphasis on preparing and training healthcare workers to address a wide range of health issues that transcend national borders. These systems focus on building a workforce that is not only skilled in traditional healthcare practices but also equipped to handle the complexities of global health challenges.

Training and skill development are the core of this global approach. Healthcare workers, especially nurses, are essential to delivering care across diverse settings, from urban hospitals to remote rural clinics. To meet the growing demands of global healthcare, there's a strong emphasis on expanding the skills and knowledge of nurses. This includes training in areas such as infectious disease management, cultural competence, and disaster response.

Disparities in healthcare access are a significant barrier to achieving global health equity. These disparities can stem from various factors, including socioeconomic status, geographic location, and the availability of healthcare resources. In many parts of the world, people living in low-income communities or rural areas have limited access to essential healthcare services. This lack of access often leads to poorer health outcomes, with higher rates of preventable diseases, maternal and infant mortality, and other health issues that could be managed with proper care.

DOI: 10.4324/9781003668732-56

Global healthcare systems are implementing various strategies aimed at improving access to healthcare for underserved populations. One approach is expanding healthcare infrastructure in remote and underserved areas so that more people have access to clinics, hospitals, and other healthcare facilities. In addition, improving the availability of essential medicines and medical supplies is crucial for providing effective care in these regions—improving and maintaining an unbroken healthcare supply chain.

The one major area that has assisted in improving healthcare access has been technology. Physical distance and a lack of infrastructure have long been barriers to quality healthcare in many regions. However, advancements such as telehealth are now bridging these gaps, enabling patients in remote areas to consult with healthcare providers without needing to travel. Telehealth services, along with mobile health apps and remote monitoring tools, allow for timely medical advice and treatment, regardless of a patient's location.

Furthermore, mobile health apps empower individuals to take charge of their health by offering features like medication reminders, chronic disease management tools, and access to educational content. Through these innovations, technology is making healthcare more accessible and efficient, with the potential to improve health outcomes globally.

Tackling healthcare disparities on a global scale requires a coordinated and collaborative approach. No single entity can tackle these complex issues alone. Governments, nongovernmental organizations, healthcare providers, and the private sector must work together to create comprehensive strategies that address the root causes of health inequities.

Aligning global health policies with the principles of equity and justice is equally important. Policymakers must prioritize the health needs of vulnerable populations and design interventions that are inclusive and culturally appropriate. Consideration of social determinants of health—such as education, income, and living conditions—is crucial when developing strategies to promote health equity. Continuous research and data collection are also vital for monitoring progress and adapting strategies as needed.

Dealing with global health disparities and promoting equitable access to healthcare are vital components of improving overall health and wellness worldwide. With continued innovation and a united approach, the global community can work toward a future where everyone has the opportunity to achieve optimal health.

Strategic waste management is interconnected with the global healthcare supply chains' access to healthcare, medicine, and treatment. This involves the safe use of all medical supplies.

Chapter 49

Medical Waste Management in a Global Healthcare Supply Chain

Innovations in medical waste management in a global healthcare supply chain include automation and robotics. These systems can transport, sterilize, and sort with great operational effectiveness. Achieving environmental sustainability in healthcare requires improvements in waste management and reduction, material segregation and transportation, and reduced consumption. Current methods of healthcare waste disposal, such as incineration, land-filling, and chemical treatments, negatively impact both the environment and public health.

Hospitals, clinics, and pharmaceutical companies generate tons of regulated medical waste every day. While strict regulations exist to ensure proper disposal, there have been cases of illegal dumping. In the past, some investigations revealed that some hospitals were improperly discarding biohazardous waste, including infectious waste and used syringes.

Such violations highlight the urgent need for compliant medical waste disposal services and increased regulatory oversight. Improper disposal of sharps waste, pharmaceutical waste, and pathological waste can lead to serious consequences, including:

1. Spread of infectious diseases due to exposure to contaminated materials.
2. Environmental contamination when hazardous substances seep into soil and water sources.
3. Legal and financial penalties for healthcare providers failing to comply with OSHA medical waste regulations.

One of the most alarming incidents in 2024 involved medical waste washing up on beaches, raising concerns about improper medical waste disposal methods. Syringes, medication vials, and hazardous healthcare waste were found scattered along coastal areas, sparking environmental concerns. These wastes could spread dangerous pathogens, harm marine life, and cause ecological damage.

Another factor, previously not seen, are the self-administered medical supplies that the public has access to. The rise in popularity of injectable medications for diabetes, weight loss, and other

DOI: 10.4324/9781003668732-57

conditions has led to a surge in home-generated medical waste. Unlike hospitals, which follow strict red bag waste disposal protocols, individuals often lack clear guidance on how to properly dispose of sharps containers, expired medications, and contaminated medical supplies. To reduce this issue, more cities are implementing medical waste disposal drop-off locations and requiring pharmacies to provide medical waste disposal services. Raising awareness about how to properly dispose of medical waste at home is crucial to keeping communities safe.

With the rising concerns around healthcare waste disposal—whether the public consumer or hospitals—the industry is turning to medical waste treatment innovations to improve efficiency and sustainability. Some of the latest advancements include:

1. Autoclaving: The use of high-pressure steam to sterilize medical waste before disposal.
2. Chemical disinfection: Treatment of infectious medical waste with powerful disinfectants to neutralize pathogens.
3. Microwave technology: Heat and radiation to break down hazardous waste safely.

To address the growing concerns surrounding regulated medical waste disposal, governments worldwide are tightening regulations. New policies focus on increasing fines, mandating more stringent training programs for all healthcare employees, and fostering the use of other medical waste disposal methods.

The healthcare industry is at a critical junction when it comes to medical waste disposal. As more waste is produced, the risks of improper disposal grow—but so do the opportunities for sustainable medical waste solutions. By investing in medical waste recycling programs, safer waste treatment technologies, and more effective regulatory enforcement, we can ensure that hazardous waste doesn't end up in our oceans, landfills, or public spaces.

Medical waste disposal may not be the most glamorous topic, but it's a critical issue in the global healthcare supply chain—impacting public health, environmental safety, and legal compliance.

Chapter 50

One Global Health Approach: Integrating Humans, Animals, and the Environment to Prevent Global Disease

In today's interrelated world, the health of humans, animals, and the environment are without question linked together. The concept of "One Health" recognizes this interdependence and advocates a holistic approach for addressing global health issues. One Health encompasses the understanding that the well-being of humans, animals, and ecosystems is interconnected and that interventions must be collaborative in order to effectively tackle complex health challenges. In recent decades, the increasing occurrence of emerging infectious diseases and environmental ruin has highlighted the limitations of traditional isolated health approaches. These challenges transcend national boundaries and disciplines, demanding innovative strategies that can tackle their complex root causes.

One Health provides innovation by fostering collaboration and cross-disciplinary interaction between medical professionals, veterinarians, ecologists, policymakers, and other stakeholders. By acknowledging the holistic nature of health, One Health paves the way for a more resilient, sustainable, and healthier future for both human populations and the planet.

This chapter will explore the principles and significance of One Health and highlight its potential in addressing some of the most pressing global healthcare supply chain issues.

The concept of One Health is not new. It has existed for at least 200 years under different names such as One Medicine, One World, and now One Health. One Health is an approach that recognizes the unquestionable link between human health, animal health, and the environment. It acknowledges that diseases can pass between humans and animals and that environmental factors play a significant role in disease emergence and transmission. The concept emphasizes the need for collaboration and communication across all branches of learning such as medicine, veterinary science, ecology, and environmental sciences to promote a comprehensive understanding of health issues and develop effective solutions.

DOI: 10.4324/9781003668732-58

The CDC image below tells it all:

> One Health is gaining recognition in the United States and globally as an effective way to fight health issues at the human-animal-environment interface, including zoonotic diseases. CDC uses the One Health approach by involving experts in human, animal, environmental health, and other relevant disciplines and sectors in monitoring and controlling public health threats and to learn about how diseases spread among people, animals, plants, and the environment.

Successful public health interventions require the cooperation of human, animal, and environmental health partners. Professionals in *human health* (doctors, nurses, public health practitioners, epidemiologists), *animal health* (veterinarians, paraprofessionals, agricultural workers), and *environment* (ecologists, wildlife experts) need to communicate, collaborate on, and coordinate activities.

As with Figure 50.1 and the Health and the Three C's, global healthcare issues surrounding the concept of One Health include emerging, re-emerging, and endemic zoonotic diseases; neglected tropical diseases; vector-borne diseases; antimicrobial resistance; food safety and food security; environmental contamination; climate change; and other health threats shared by people, animals, and the environment. Some of these are the following:

- Antimicrobial-resistant germs can quickly spread through communities, the food supply, healthcare facilities, and the environment (soil, water), making it harder to treat certain infections in animals and people.
- Vector-borne diseases are on the rise with warmer temperatures and expanded mosquito and tick habitats.
- Diseases in food animals can threaten supplies, livelihoods, and economies.
- The human-animal bond can help improve mental well-being.
- Contamination of water used for drinking, recreation, and more can make people and animals sick.

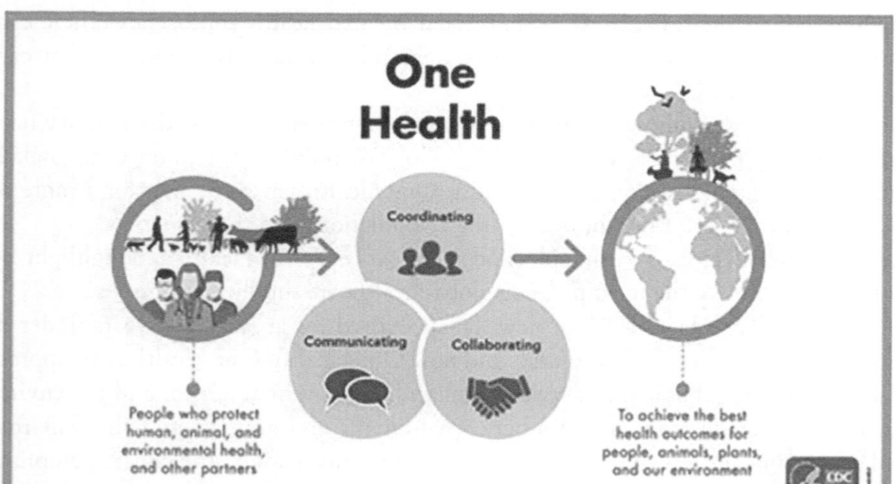

Figure 50.1 Health and the Three C's.

To implement "One Health" into the entire global healthcare supply chain system, major organizational changes will be necessary to integrate the human, animal, and environmental health fields and support the communication, collaboration, and coordination. There are eight critical gaps in the healthcare supply chain that must be addressed to make this implementation a success. They are the following:

- databases and resources to support information sharing
- identification and showcasing of best practice examples for One Health implementation
- mapping of the existing initiatives and capacities for One Health research and building the next generation One Health work force
- a model for an integrated One Health surveillance system
- mechanisms for routine and emergency coordination with relevant stakeholders
- a more complete understanding of the drivers of spillover of zoonotic diseases (transmitted between animals and humans). This includes animal trade, agriculture, livestock farming, urbanization, and habitat fragmentation
- a standardized approach for assessing risks of spillover of pathogens between different animal populations and humans, and emergence of zoonotic diseases, including those arising in food systems
- methods for identifying and reducing spillover risks and spread of zoonotic diseases in ways that minimize trade-offs and maximize co-benefits with other health and sustainable development objectives

Recognizing the importance of a coordinated global effort, the World Health Organization, the Food and Agriculture Organization, the United Nations Environment Program, and the World Organization for Animal Health which constitutes the Quadripartite launched the One Health Joint Plan of Action 2022–2026. This comprehensive five-year initiative aims to foster collaboration and coordination across sectors to address health threats impacting humans, animals, plants, and the environment.

As the importance of the One Health approach becomes increasingly evident, so too does the need for holistic understanding of the intricate relationships among human, animal, and environmental health. After understanding must come collective action, and quickly, if we are to meet successfully the next set of global challenges on a planet that is home to over eight billion people.

Chapter 51

Why Global Health Security in Global Healthcare Supply Chain

The global supply of essential medicines and vaccines is currently highly vulnerable to disruption. To address this urgent problem, we must bring together the leading experts from industry, global health, and governments to identify solutions and induce changes in thought patterns in SCM and procurement.

When the COVID-19 pandemic came along, it allowed us to see the many vulnerabilities within the supply chains of essential health products. These vulnerabilities had been a concern even before the virus. However, this crisis has brought a renewed attention to the importance of the issue.

By bringing together experts from industry, global health, government, and procurement, we can pinpoint strategies to prevent shortages and stock-outs of essential medicines and vaccines.

Challenges highlighted by these experts included shortages, stock-outs, spikes in pricing, sudden peaks in demand, and disruptions to international shipping. The realities of the last two years have prompted many within the industry to adjust their mindsets and to address the risk of future disruptions whether that be another pandemic, a geopolitical crisis, a natural disaster, or climate change. Moreover, there is increasing recognition among both companies and procurers that an overreliance on a small number of suppliers, or suppliers concentrated in one region or country, is a significant liability.

There are various strategies to consider in the security of the global healthcare supply chain. Some of these solutions include switching to a "just in case" model as opposed to a "just in time", smart forecasting and demand planning, dual supply chains for key products and components, measures to ensure better local availability, a shift in criteria for supplier selection, greater communication between suppliers and procurers, and diversifying the supplier base. Furthermore, there are three key criteria we must consider before we implement any of the above solution.

First, global health security must be a top priority. The challenges to global health security can be both the overconcentration of suppliers and/or a sudden crisis which poses serious threats to global access to medicine and essential healthcare.

DOI: 10.4324/9781003668732-59

It is vital that global health security is front-of-mind in decision-making. All stakeholders in the global medical supply chain will benefit from working closely together to prepare for future shocks and then collaborating and cooperating when crises do occur.

Second, the healthcare supply chain should endeavor to strengthen and widen the supplier base. It does not matter the industry one is operating in, all should move away from single source or limited supply chains of both raw materials and finished products.

For companies, this may involve expanding the raw material supplier network and looking carefully at which suppliers to use. For procurers, this may involve awarding tenders to a more diverse range of suppliers. Technology transfers, capacity building, and collaborations between multinational corporations and local manufacturers can boost local availability of essential medicines and vaccines.

Last but not least, identify and strengthen weakest links in access to medicine. The last few years have highlighted the many of the interconnections between different parts of the pharmaceutical and healthcare industries, as well as specific challenges in the global supply chains. In order to make sure that everyone has access to the medicines, vaccines, and healthcare products they need, we must bolster global health security by making sure there are no weak links across the entire gamut of care.

This involves identifying the biggest vulnerabilities in access, in specific healthcare aspects and specific regions of the world, and taking the appropriate action. More parties need to get involved, including those who produce the essential products such as diagnostics, vaccines, and medical gases.

Chapter 52

Why Should Clinicians Care about Global Medical Security?

This chapter one might call Chapter 6; Part II, but it is important to understand the clinicians' changing roles in the global healthcare supply chain. Their role is no longer just one of distributing medicine to the ill, now it includes ethics and morals as well.

A common way to describe the global medical supply chain is complicated due to its length and the interdependent supply chain segments, but along with the varied regulations and laws of other nations. A myriad of international experts exchange ideas about vulnerabilities of medical supply chains and how to make them more resilient. But why should clinicians think and care about a topic outwardly far removed from patient care? Why is this an ethical issue?

One reason is that all clinicians should be aware of weaknesses in medical product supply chains because breaks in those chains generate drug shortages, increase prevalence of counterfeit medicines, and threaten the availability of medical devices or equipment. When medical supply chains break, clinicians' ethical decisions are made more burdened by threats to their abilities to meet care standards as they manage patients' care and try to respond to patients' needs.

Understanding the risks to and the durability of drug supply chains involves the collaboration and diverse perspectives, multiple stakeholders' contributions, and global coordination. A fully integrated approach to medical supply chains' management requires understanding how those chains are enmeshed in a global context.

The interconnectedness of global medical supply chains became remarkably apparent during the pandemic when many frontline healthcare professionals did not have PPE, such as surgical masks and gowns, because of shortages driven by pandemic-related supply disruptions and increases in demand. Supply shortages and increased global demand also caused surges in these items' prices when their availability was brought into question.

These complications led to clinicians who were forced to work through and somehow around drug and medical equipment shortages. A prime example is the older sterile injectable medicines that have been in short supply frequently over the past several years despite their need and use as first-line and essential medicines to provide patient care. Clinicians and their patients were not

DOI: 10.4324/9781003668732-60

able to trust that they will have access to basic, quality medicines. Unfortunately, we live in an age where this is no longer guaranteed.

There are a number of other questions, besides the ethical ones, that need to be addressed by everyone involved in the global healthcare supply chain. Some of these questions are:

Why do supply chain disruptions happen?
Who should be responsible for their smooth operation when so many patients and clinicians rely on them?
How should the known present risks be mitigated? How should supply chain participants be positioned to better anticipate and respond to unknown future risks?

These are not idle or individualistic questions. They need answers in conjunction with the ethical questions. Responses to these questions must point to supply chains' vulnerabilities. Given the deep rooted issues, assigning responsibility to any single entity would be shortsighted and too simple a task. Believing this to be a simple task will almost certainly lead to failure.

Many groups involved in keeping the supply chain unbroken are presently "discovering" how to bolster medicines' supply chains in their respective countries, regions, and industries.

Each one of these groups has come up with ideas that focus on supply chains for medical products, including drugs, biologics, PPE, devices, and other equipment. The problem is: There is no interconnection. Some of these reports were written focusing on the consequences of significant and rare events, while other reports centered on the spikes in demand and prices and the stockpiling of medical supplies. But these reports were independent of each other as opposed to linking them together.

Reports and whitepapers are needed that show us solutions that are interconnected.

These reports are to be authored in conjunction by government agencies, academicians, think tanks, consulting companies, and other supply chain stakeholders to identify supply chain vulnerabilities and offer recommendations to improve domestic and global medical product supply chain resilience. The downfall of many of these reports is that they fall short in impressing upon all of us the need for better coordination and more effective creative solutions that fit together and meaningfully address any and all of the key gaps in the global medical supply chains.

FUTURE-LOOKING PERSPECTIVES ON THE HEALTHCARE SUPPLY CHAIN

IX

The healthcare supply chain stands at a critical juncture. The industry attempts to adapt to an era defined by uncertainty as the lessons of recent years have shed light on persistent vulnerabilities and surprising opportunities for change. From technological advancements like AI and BDA to the expansion of care outside of the hospital walls, there are other influences shaping the current healthcare supply chain.

The future of the healthcare supply chain is being formed by technology, from AI to value-based care to DEI to sustainability. Despite this progress, healthcare and its supply chain remain unstable. Preparedness is crucial to ensure the availability of safe medicines and medical supplies.

The healthcare industry supply chain system always runs out of sight and unknown to the casual observers or even the patient. It's not until there is a disruption to that flow that healthcare supply chain comes front and center. When clinicians do not have the critical medical/surgical supplies they need to deliver patient care, it will delay treatment.

There are a number of "educated" forecasts, based upon future technologies, which will shape and drive the progress of the healthcare industry and its supply chain. Some of these are the following:

1. Healthcare equity
2. Climate change in the healthcare supply chain
3. Healthcare supply chain and its fragility
4. Cybersecurity threats and new safeguards
5. Mergers, acquisitions, and divestiture will re-shape the healthcare supply chain
6. Innovative supply-chain models

DOI: 10.4324/9781003668732-61

Chapter 53

Equity and Supplier Mixture in the Healthcare Supply Chain

What does equity mean for healthcare supply chains? Understanding and exploring the challenges and benefits to incorporating equity into the healthcare supply chain can demonstrate how this might shape a socially responsive supply chain.

There has been growing conversation about supplier diversity as a quick to recover strategy since the pandemic drove healthcare systems, hospitals, and SCM leaders to rethink all pieces of the procurement process including logistics. This conversion includes greater attention to community public health of hospitals and has encouraged a new scrutiny of healthcare supply chain's role in social responsibility.

Has the healthcare industry made progress in its efforts to identify business relationships outside of their old and normal network of medical suppliers? Are there new sources of medical supplies? What challenges have healthcare systems had to overcome, and what benefits have they derived from their efforts? These are some of the questions I will attempt to answer.

Equity in healthcare supply chains involves integrating principles of equity into procurement processes, vendor relationships, and overall SCM to promote fairness, innovation, and community engagement. For the whole story of equity and social responsibility in hospital supply chain, it is the idea of inclusive operations that encompasses a greater diversity of individuals. Organizations aligned with the industry's efforts to engage in social responsibility better serve their communities, improve population health, and promote more sustainable supply chain practices.

Healthcare supply chain leaders that provide equal chances for local diverse-owned businesses to compete for medical supply and service contracts contribute to improved public health and well-being throughout the community. When medical facilities support local businesses, this can spur the generation of more jobs and provide employer-sponsored health plans to employees.

I have seen health systems recognize the link between health equity and the overall cost of healthcare in recent years, and how supply chain plays a significant role. More and more healthcare organizations are actively seeking to engage a diverse range of suppliers, partners, and stakeholders from previously unused or unknown sources. Some of these healthcare institutions that have implemented healthcare equity in their supply chains are some very well known institutions—the

DOI: 10.4324/9781003668732-62

Cleveland Clinic, NYC Health and Hospital Corporation, and Trinity Health. That does not mean there were no challenges to implement such programs.

There are a number of challenges confronting supply chain professionals when it comes to diversifying their supplier base and engaging with local businesses and communities to promote equity goals. They are the following:

1. Supplier capacity—some healthcare leaders say it is a challenge to find licensed suppliers with the capacity to meet their organization's needs. These obstacles can include a smaller labor force, limited delivery capabilities, lack of operational efficiency, inability to increase production to meet demand, and limited less access to raw materials.
2. Measurement—some health systems have inadequate data about their suppliers. They may know their total number of diverse suppliers, but no details on ownership description—women, minorities, veterans or LGBTQ, disabled. This lack of information puts unforeseen obstacles in front of equity programs.
3. Insurance requirements—large business in the healthcare supply chain is accustomed to complying with healthcare providers for insurance, requisitioning practices, payment terms. But smaller business involved in this industry might not have the resources to meet these requirements.
4. Perceived costs—if diversified healthcare suppliers have proven their ability to support sustainability, streamlined logistics, and supply management, and provided essential services to local communities, but if the costs of doing business with them are higher, it can be harder to ascertain buy-in from executive leadership.

Along with challenges comes benefits for implementing a healthcare equity program. Supplier diversity enhances the supply chain through innovation and driving greater value through cost reductions, competitive contract terms and conditions, and improved service.

Hospitals have spent close to $3.5 billion over the last few years in their communities. These funds have created jobs and supported economic stability in these communities. The healthcare institutions are making certain that our patients are physically and economically healthy. A perfect example would be Trinity Health's equity and supplier diversity programs that are having a measurable impact on their community, minority-owned suppliers, and further afield. In 2023, they spent $431 million with diverse vendors.

Whether the goal of a healthcare equity program is to impact public health or boost supply chain efficiency by sourcing locally, there are some essential strategies for an effective equity program management—conducting supply chain equity audit, set clear goals, leadership buy-in, change management, and continuous monitoring.

The most productive place to start is by performing an audit of the current operations through the eye of equity. One challenge that many providers face is the lack of data on their supplier base, including which suppliers fall into the equity category—operated and controlled by minority group members. By understanding where you currently stand, you can determine the best path forwards. It is called a road map.

It is particularly helpful to align supply chain equity efforts with organization-wide objectives such as sustainability and supplier diversity. If the organization has indeed prioritized sustainability, set the goals to connect with diverse suppliers that make use sustainable practices of their own.

It is critical to demonstrate potential ROI—whether it is the ability to reduce costs, contribute to the economic growth of communities, access better quality supplies, or support sustainability by shortening the length of supply chain and its impact on the environment—this is how one will get C-Level buy-in for the equity program.

Education and training are critical, not only for supply chain staff but also for clinicians and other stakeholders. Demonstrating the benefits of supplier diversity will help other employees and managers understand the reasons behind these equity programs. Change management does not necessarily mean a revolving door of managers.

Accurate data and achievable and measurable analytics are the keys to monitoring all equity initiatives in SCM and measuring improvement. Establish the minimum measurement level, the lowest level of accomplishment you would accept. What percentage of supply expenses does your organization want to align with equity and social responsibility goals?

What challenges might hospitals face in improving supply chain diversity and how can these be overcome? Hospitals may face challenges in gaining leadership and stakeholder buy-in, finding diverse suppliers with sufficient capacity and overcoming the existing vendor requirements that may exceed what equity businesses have in place. They can help overcome these challenges by presenting examples of equity initiative success from other healthcare organizations. Implementing effective change management strategies includes education and training, phasing in smaller suppliers with limited capacity, and streamlining procurement processes and requirements.

Chapter 54

After Climate Change, Should the Healthcare Supply Chain Change Now?

Climate change impacts on the healthcare supply chain are worldwide and greater than are widely acknowledged. Climate impacts are intensifying to become one of the most significant health crises in this century. From increasing and changing healthcare needs, such as increased injuries and infectious disease spread, climate change places undue strain on healthcare supply chain leaders through damaged facilities. Climate change exacerbates environmental, social and governance, or regulatory issues in healthcare supply chain.

There are three questions that need to be addressed to fully understand why climate change has increased in importance within the healthcare industry and its supply chain.

1. Why has climate change become the biggest threat to healthcare supply chain?
2. What is climate change doing to our health?
3. Does climate change expose future generations to life-long health supply chain harmful issues?

The healthcare system's reliance on the global supply chain and JIT delivery has been a boon for many healthcare institution's bottom line. Critical shortages of many medical supplies and equipment have raised the recognition of the weaknesses of supply chains around the world, while the current shortages can be traced to the COVID-19 pandemic causing an enormous surge in demand. At the same time that supply chains are becoming sporadic, similar disruptions can be expected in the coming decades as communities begin to experience the effects of climate change.

As the United States is a wealthy nation, we have been living under the belief that medical supplies are endless so wastefulness and disposability were the normal way of life. The last time our communities were challenged to obtain essential medical supplies and equipment was during World War II. But because of COVID-19, we are painfully reminded of being thoughtful of wasting resources. Now, we are trying to use only what is needed to reduce wastes. We're extending the use of supplies, sometimes past their proper use date.

DOI: 10.4324/9781003668732-63

A number of decades ago, we were not a disposable society. At present, a large proportion of medical supplies we use in healthcare are disposable. Most of these are manufactured clear across the other side of the globe which are far from the actual point of use. In addition, the products are delivered as they are needed to reduce the need for warehousing and to prevent expiration. This situation has left the healthcare supply chain in precarious circumstances and extremely open to supply chain interruptions.

Back in the 1980s, when all companies began to send manufacturing overseas, the medical device industry recognized the money-making potential of creating medical supplies that would become obsolete in a short period of time. The medical supply companies created a new label called "single-use disposables". The more stuff you throw away, the more you have to buy, so it's an advantageous business model for things not to be durable—disposability became the earmark for many medical and medical equipment companies. It may work for things that are difficult to clean which prevent infection. However, too many of our supplies have become disposable because of the availability of cheap materials and merely due to convenience.

The medical device industry then lobbied Congress to alter regulations to allow healthcare institutions to reuse equipment. This gave, to the public, a false impression and a dangerous one that these devices were brand new medical supplies. This was historically significant in driving our current throw-away culture in the healthcare supply chain. Many argue that this past history has left us vulnerable to the supply chain disruptions we are currently experiencing.

Many of our medical supplies are manufactured all over the world. Climate change related to all types of extreme weather events increases the risk of supply chain disruptions. Whether caused by severe storms or a global pandemic, the disruptions are similar—sudden decreases in manufacturing, interruption of transport services, and surges in demands for supplies.

A prime example of this disruption resulted from an extreme weather event—Hurricane Maria devastated Puerto Rico. A large proportion of our nation's drugs and intravenous fluids were manufactured in Puerto Rico, and the hurricane utterly halted production of these vital drugs. Some stocks of some of our most common local anesthetic drugs ran out. Many anesthesiologists proceeded to use substitutes of nonstandard drugs for anesthesia in the operating rooms. Naturally, these substitutions increased the risk of otherwise preventable adverse events.

The question is not whether we should attempt to mitigate these climate change disruptions, but can we? There are a few ways to take action that will start the process of mitigation.

There is a need to be much more aware of how embedded wastefulness is in healthcare and its supply chain. We must be aware of the fact that resources are limited, whether we feel the shortages or not. With this awareness must come ways to conserve materials.

We need to move away from our reliance on single-use disposal devices. We need to return to "old" manufacturing processes where medical products and supplies are reusable. Infection prevention is essential in healthcare. But is it realistic or even necessary for everything to be disposable? There are guidelines, such as the Spaulding Criteria, that guide levels of cleaning that are required for different types of medical devices based on their usefulness. Unfortunately, these guidelines have been ignored, or manipulated, to support disposability.

The medical supply manufacturers should have incentives to design those supplies to be durable and easier to disassemble, clean, and refurbish. The above are some of the principles of what is called the Circular Economy, a system that aims to design waste out and keep products and materials in use.

Finally, we need to re-shore the manufacturing of all medical supplies and equipment closer to where they are needed. This will reduce supply chain vulnerability and provide employment opportunities for members of local communities.

In response to this threat of climate change and increasing supply chain disruption, manufacturers have enlarged their inventories, developing twofold supply chains. These twofold supply chains deliver the same goods by means of two different routes. This is done to ensure at least one delivery of medical supplies. However, these solutions do increase production costs and cancel the "just in time" manufacturing approach. "Just-in-time" relies on vigorous supply chains to eliminate the need for companies to keep extensive parts inventories in stock. American companies could shorten their supply chains, shifting production facilities back to the United States or a nearby country.

In the healthcare supply chain, there's a built apathy in the management of the supply chain. Long-term strategy and logistics are opposite concepts. Logistic companies are trying to execute the strategy but not developing it. They're trying to figure out how to keep on delivering medical supplies while climate change has become a long-term problem.

Chapter 55

The Fragility Crisis in the Healthcare Supply Chain

Based upon the lack of healthcare equity and the continued crisis of climate change, the healthcare supply chain is in the midst of attempting to fix a broken supply chain system of delivering medical supplies to where they are needed and used. The healthcare supply chain has always been vulnerable to disruptions with patient care consequences. Shortages of medical supplies and equipment highlight the fragility of the healthcare supply chain.

These continuous shortages of medical supplies and equipment were further exposed by the COVID virus where every type of healthcare institution and its supply chain were affected. Lessons, insights, and experiences derived during the pandemic will thrust the supply chain industry to think of new directions and ways of operations.

1. Will global supply chains need to be re-configured, especially the healthcare supply chain?
2. How can any country protect against future disruptions and build stronger and less fragile supply chains?
3. Are integrated supply chains a myth?

The fragility of medical supply chains became a bleak reality for healthcare organizations during the COVID-19 pandemic. Life-saving products previously obtainable cheaply and readily suddenly were unavailable and without meaningful substitutions. One could dismiss these as unfortunate consequences of a once-in-a-lifetime event. However, medical supply chains have silently become vulnerable over the last few decades. The pandemic disruptions illuminated these existing vulnerabilities.

Medical supply chain events have become increasingly disruptive. These include global shortages of PPE, syringes, saline, cardiovascular and anti-infective drugs, and tourniquets. The increasing fragility of medical supply chain is multifactorial, interconnected, and complex. The underlying weaknesses of medical supply chains comprise five factors:

1. Economic incentives and regulatory pressure favoring offshore facilities of manufacturing
2. Increased logistics but with less transparency

DOI: 10.4324/9781003668732-64

3. Lack of standards in product sourcing
4. Razor-thin margins
5. Tremendous pressure to reduce supply costs

More than half of global hospitals are running with negative margins. Today's economic environment increases price sensitivity. Medical supply costs can reach 35% of total hospital supply expenses according to the Mayo Clinic. Suppliers react to customer price sensitivity by downsizing their operations. This reduces the cost of the product in the short term, but it increases the vulnerability of the product to disruption. The resultant fragility in product availability also forces individual healthcare organizations to accept the impacts on patients, pay the increased costs of product procurement during shortage, dedicate resources to urgently sourced meaningful alternatives, and expend resources to stockpile a product. These additional expenses can be avoided if medical supply chain resiliency are considered when purchasing the product in the first place. Having medical supply chains resilient will involve culture change and transparency from manufacturers, distributors, and healthcare organizations.

The value of medical products has traditionally been a function of quality and cost, but key factors are missing—resiliency, delivery, etc. Resiliency estimates the supplier's ability to deliver products during normal and abnormal times. Adding resiliency and delivery to this equation is to aid in critical and essential patient care. Incorporating resiliency into sourcing decisions will drive selection criteria that create stronger supply continuity. It is estimated that drug shortages alone cost hospitals nearly $360 million a year—hospitals often forced to secure alternative products at a 10% to 25% premium loss.

Reporting metrics for healthcare purchases need to account for medical supply chains outcomes. Outcomes include order fulfillment as well as the quality, cost, and performance of products. Metrics may include on-time-and-in-full fulfillment, quality, and the business continuity management assessment and resiliency scorecard. Historically, hospitals have failed to select for resiliency not because of a lack of virtue but because of the absence of a national standard.

Individual healthcare providers may seem powerless to improve global medical supply chains by themselves. Few clinicians are involved in strategic medical supply chain decisions or day-to-day operations decisions of the organizations. However, individual clinicians can and should share the influence of the selection of products used. Awareness of the roles of purchasers, the performance of suppliers, and manufacturers' assessed resiliency gives clinicians ability to make informed choices when presented with medical supply options. Clinicians can also influence strategic Mediterranean Shipping Company (MSC) decisions by inquiring about the durability of their critical products. Clinicians can partner with medical supply chains colleagues to reduce unwanted product variation, demand that their suppliers provide transparency, and work to identify critical supplies and alternative substitutes for them.

Medical supply fragility is the normal consequence of our day-to-day decisions in healthcare. Although we all bear responsibility for the problems we are facing, we can also collectively influence the solution.

Besides supply chain fragility, there are a number of other factors that will influence the future of the healthcare supply chain—cybersecurity threats; mergers, acquisitions, and divestitures; cloud-based platforms; and 3D printing.

Chapter 56

Cybersecurity Threats and New Safeguards

Is the healthcare supply chain in critical condition due to cybersecurity threats?

Cybersecurity threats in healthcare have declined considerably over the last decade, but they have not entirely faded away. Rather, these healthcare cyberattacks are expected to increase. Figure 56.1 shows that healthcare cyberattacks are of particular importance in the industry because they

Figure 56.1 Cybersecurity attacks are still with us.

DOI: 10.4324/9781003668732-65

directly affect the security of systems and information and the health and safety of people. The industry is beset by a slew of cybersecurity issues—from malware that jeopardizes system integrity and patient privacy to distributed denial of service attacks that impair healthcare institutions' competence to deliver patient care. While similar industry cyberattacks occur in other critical infrastructure sectors, the nature of the healthcare industry's attacks presents distinct obstacles. Cyberattacks on healthcare industry supply chain can have far-reaching consequences beyond financial loss and data leaks. For hospitals and their supply chain, ransomware is a particularly terrible kind of malware as the loss of medical data can endanger lives.

Healthcare businesses and institutions, large or small, are major targets for cybercrime. The growing incidence of healthcare-related hacks indicates that smaller health providers are becoming increasingly vulnerable to hackers. Large healthcare providers frequently have the resources required to develop an effective cyber defense plan. These large hospitals and healthcare systems can frequently afford to hire a chief information security officer, staff a security operations center, and subscribe to the most up-to-date threat intelligence services.

Healthcare organizations have been the targets of some of the most foremost healthcare cyberattacks in the recent decade. Community hospitals, independent doctors, and dentists may not always have the financial resources to invest in expensive cybersecurity protections. Regardless, they both face the same cyber hazards. According to the American Medical Association, approximately 57% of medical practices in the United States have ten or fewer physicians and approximately 10% being solo practitioners.

Due to these cyberattacks on healthcare industry and the supply chain, many small healthcare providers are unable to pay high payoffs, thus forced to close their doors. These supply chain professionals understand that paying a ransom demand will not ensure that the hacker would release data or equipment as well as won't assure that criminal would not sell patient's data on the web.

In the healthcare sector, the health and well-being of the patient are paramount. Communication between healthcare practitioners and patients and across various healthcare activities has been honed to an art form. Security issues that the healthcare supply chain is facing are as follows:

- Patient information is essential
- Medical gadgets lack security protections
- Remote access to medical data is required for medical employees
- Healthcare employees receive little or no cyber risk training
- Many healthcare institutions have out-of-date technologies to avert cyber risks

The growing digitalization of the supply chain and the increasing online part of our lives create chances for phishers, hackers, fraudsters, and extortionists. Unfortunately, there is currently no evidence of this abating. This is why healthcare companies and healthcare supply chain leaders must be aware of the ever-expanding conduits of recent healthcare cyberattacks and what can be done to limit the dangers. So, these are the most significant changes influencing our online security in the coming year.

- AI—may combat cyberattacks in healthcare industry by finding patterns of behavior that indicate something out of the usual is happening. AI enables this in systems that must deal with thousands of events per second. AI's predictive capabilities are what make it so beneficial for cybersecurity of healthcare supply chains that more businesses are investing in these solutions. Unfortunately, fraudsters are aware of the benefits of AI such as machine learning to thwart cybersecurity in healthcare safeguards. This makes AI even more critical, as it is the only way to combat AI-powered healthcare industry cyberattacks.

- Ransomware and phishing—the healthcare industry has been declared one of the top four targeted industries in 2024. The healthcare implications have been substantial forced closures of healthcare institutions. Ransomware is frequently disseminated via phishing attacks, in which employees are tricked into providing information onto a computer.
- IoT—has put nontraditional computer devices connected to the Internet within reach of malicious criminals. While baby monitors and other smart home gadgets are susceptible, so are countless pieces of technology used in physicians' offices and hospitals worldwide. Vulnerabilities linked to cybersecurity in healthcare supply chains have significant consequences for patient health. The supply chain must be monitored to ensure the newest software is maintained throughout the year.

The healthcare industry is losing its fight against healthcare industry cyberattacks. The healthcare industry is susceptible because of outdated computing systems and a scarcity of experienced cybersecurity personnel and a rise in modern medical equipment. Technological advancements in healthcare equipment, systems, and procedures have outpaced advancements in administrative support systems that store patient information. Cybersecurity in healthcare solutions should include safeguards of better quality than the hackers use and in financial institutions. For this to succeed, healthcare institutions must assess each new platform proposed in terms of the medical benefits provided to their patients as well as the risk of healthcare industry cyberattacks.

Cybersecurity in healthcare impacts every part of the sector, from the confidentiality of sensitive health information to insurance costs and patient treatment. According to healthcare industry, it falls behind in cybersecurity technology, standards, and practices. While some encourage more government regulation to safeguard patients and their data, many healthcare supply chain leaders recognize that compliance with standards is the only way to avoid onerous compliance laws.

The healthcare industry and its supply chain continue to face significant challenges to cybersecurity that are exclusive to that industry. When lives and not just profits are at stake, the finest and brightest in computer science, medical research, and supply chain business leaders must collaborate to create new responses and solutions to the challenges threatening medical care.

Chapter 57

Cloud-Based Systems Are Changing the Healthcare Supply Chain Landscape

Are cloud-based systems the answer to the healthcare supply chain data safety and integration issues? What are some common cloud integration challenges? And what benefits can they derive from cloud integration solution deployment? What steps must supply chain teams take to prepare for SCM cloud computing? We explore the answers to these questions below. But, first for those unfamiliar with cloud-based systems, an overview of these systems is necessary.

The healthcare industry has steadfastly evolved its supply chain technology in order for it to operate more efficiently and effectively to mitigate costs and waste. The healthcare supply chain technology started with a system for material management—procurement and inventory management—and now has grown into an ERP system that includes all areas of the healthcare industry.

The next phase of this information technology evolution is cloud-based healthcare SCM, with hospitals rapidly transitioning to cloud-based ERP systems. The change or upgrade comes alongside the shift to cloud-based technologies for EHR management, data management, and cybersecurity.

Unlike on-premises systems that require the healthcare institution to spend time and money into hosting, maintenance, upgrades, and other IT team support, the cloud ERP system provider assumes this responsibility by hosting the software in the cloud. The healthcare organization always has the latest software version available, with immediate updates and security protection, without the need for IT involvement.

A significant benefit of transitioning to cloud computing is the ability of cloud-based solutions to seamlessly integrate and share data with one another. This is sharply opposed to on-premises systems that are typically designed to be incapable of connecting and communicating with each other. Cloud integration enables greater process automation and less manual intervention, resulting in greater efficiency and accuracy.

Healthcare is an industry where Big Data and analytics have increasingly become an important component of decision-making. The move to a cloud system is allowing the healthcare supply chain teams to set up a comprehensive data platform.

 DOI: 10.4324/9781003668732-66

Healthcare system leaders and hospital supply chain leaders who have adopted cloud computing claim a number of clear advantages: streamlined operations, reduced costs, improved data analytics, improved decisions, improved security, and fewer manual tasks.

Cloud computing in healthcare supply chain operations supports efficiency through automation and standardization of processes. Data capture and integration through the cloud are limitless in their range. As opposed to on-premise systems that have a few specified designated users, the cloud systems are able to accommodate healthcare growth.

While supply chain teams and leaders with on-premises systems are challenged to perform their tasks when working remotely, those supply chain teams with cloud solutions can maintain operations to support patient care.

Unnecessary costs are plentiful in manual supply chain operations, including the cost of human intervention to procure pay transactions from either patients or health insurance companies, inventory management, and strategic planning activities. Cloud computing supports automation, which will minimize human involvement which in turn will lower labor costs.

A modern and robust inventory management software that is fully integrated into an ERP system can greatly enhance visibility, reduce expenditures, and help prevent waste. When hospital supply chain teams can flawlessly track and manage all inventory through automation and capture and store data in the ERP system, they also have the ability to generate clear and concise reports on daily operations.

Having all departments and functions within a healthcare setting on the same technology brings visibility, transparency, and control over supply-chain processes. This is critical to strengthening resilience in healthcare services. In a healthcare setting which relies on manual processes, unlike systems and separate silos, this will prevent supply chain leaders from gaining real-time visibility into the order process and inventory management, which in turn limits their ability to see the whole picture.

In a cloud-based supply chain environment that provides system integration and data sharing, supply chain leaders have immediate visibility into all processes and supply inventories throughout their organizations, which means they can make proactive decisions.

For example, if the supply chain team knows that a primary supplier's items are on backorder and one of its hospitals is running low on these items, due to visibility and transparency to inventory across all the other hospitals in the health system's network, this particular team can determine whether it can move medical supplies from one hospital to another to mitigate a shortage.

Of course, the selection of the right cloud partner—the right one for your particular needs—can help hospitals and other health institutions gain benefits from the move, especially the benefits discussed earlier. Organizations that are preparing for the transition should look for a cloud partner with supply chain expertise and solutions that support the full range of SCM capabilities. Some vital capabilities to consider when "entertaining" cloud-based systems are the following:

1. Process automation
2. Analytics and reporting
3. Supply chain risks tools
4. Demand forecasting tools
5. Value analysis
6. Fully integrated capabilities

Once a healthcare organization and the supply chain leaders have researched these six criteria or challenges and are satisfied with the results, the implementation can begin. There are five basic steps to prepare for the implementation.

1. Start planning early—create a cloud computing strategy that identifies reliable data sources, automates data management, and includes good data governance. Select a team to create this overall strategy.
2. Restructure existing processes—eliminate as many manual tasks as possible.
3. Secure a reliable data—a source of truth for every item and its attributes, avoiding GIGO: Garbage In, Garbage Out.
4. Drive collaboration—bring together the right people and processes, which includes the right vendors.
5. Set up the proper metrics—to *measure success* and identify ways to capture cost savings upfront.

In deciding to move data to a cloud-based technology, the main agenda on the minds of the healthcare supply chain leaders is cybersecurity and compliance. Digital cloud services for SCM can help safeguard operations, data, and patients by automating pay transactions, eliminating paper payments, and validating vendor compliance with local, state and national policies and requirements.

There are a number of ways a cloud-based supply chain can assist with cybersecurity and compliance, such as reducing fraud, ensuring regulatory standards from the FDA and/or OSHA, encryption, and compliance of the IT system.

There is continuous pressure from healthcare CEOs to healthcare supply chain leaders to reduce costs and improve efficiencies. Embracing cloud-based technologies for SCM can provide significant benefits. While the change does entail straightforward investment in costs and resources, the hospitals and health systems have made the move report positive outcomes.

As more and more healthcare organizations lean toward the implementation of cloud-based systems for their SCM, the industry's attention will shift from the cloud transition to cloud optimization. More hospitals and health systems will begin to explore advanced SCM capabilities to maximize the impact of cloud adoption.

More timely insights into supply chain optimization opportunities across the entire healthcare spectrum are driven by enhanced data integrity, analytics, and accessibility. Enhanced supply chain resiliency is supported by better processes and a more diverse and reliable supplier base. Improved strategic sourcing will uncover the best products and partners for the organization. This partnership will enhance resiliency and transparency throughout the supply chain.

Chapter 58

How 3D Printing Is Revolutionizing Healthcare Supply Chain

Before we can address the chapter question, we will explain what 3D printing is, how it works, what is a 3D printer, how a 3D printer works, and the advantages and disadvantages of 3D printing. Once we understand this, then it will be easier to understand how this technology is, indeed, revolutionizing the healthcare supply chain.

In conjunction with the printing industry and manufacturing industry, 3D printing also is known as additive manufacturing. 3D printing is a process that uses computer-aided design to create objects layer by layer. 3D printing is commonly used in manufacturing and automotive industries, where tools and parts are made using 3D printers. As the capabilities of 3D printing continue to grow, so does its value. This growth means we are certain to interact with products made with 3D printing.

3D printers use CAD to create 3D objects from a variety of materials like molten plastic or powders. 3D printers can come in a variety of shapes and sizes ranging from equipment that can fit on a desk to large construction models used in the making of 3D-printed houses. There are three main types of 3D printers, and each uses a slightly different method.

- Stereolithographic, or SLA printers, are equipped with a laser that forms liquid resin into plastic.
- Selective laser sintering has lasers that change particles of polymer powder into an already solid structure.
- Fused deposition modeling printers release thermoplastic filaments that are melted through a hot nozzle to form an object layer by layer.

As 3D printing is also known as additive manufacturing, it uses some of the similar methods as a traditional inkjet printer. Additive manufacturing describes the process of creating something in layers, adding material continuously until the final design is complete. This term most often refers to molding. It takes a combination of top-of-the-line software, powder-like materials, and precision tools to create a three-dimensional object from scratch.

DOI: 10.4324/9781003668732-67

If this was a work devoted to 3D printing, it would require much more technical language. As this is not the ultimate purpose of this chapter, we will not digress into the printing process, the construction of a 3D printing model nor examples of the industries that are using it—besides the healthcare supply chain. However, there is one aspect that we must consider—its advantages and disadvantages.

Advantages of 3D Printing

1. Printers are affordable—3D printing can use less expensive plastics and concrete that are easily accessible. There is no need for a mold in 3D printing, so that is another expenditure no longer needed.
2. 3D printers are faster—3D printing is ideal for fast trial product because it can be done in the same facility in small production batches. This allows manufacturers to work out bugs and make changes to products faster than a typical production process.
3. Works with specialty materials—the advantage means specialty parts and products can be made with specific materials like water-absorbing plastic, nitinol, gold, and carbon fiber. Specialty materials like this allow for properties such as high heat resistance, water repellency, and strength.

Disadvantages of 3D Printing

1. May not provide enough strength—a negative aspect to building an object up layer by layer is that this can affect the durability and strength of the object. Of course, the strength of 3D printing relies heavily on what materials are used.
2. Accuracy issues—although computer-aided design is often an accessible and accurate way to design, there can be errors. Accuracy with 3D printing is dependent on the techniques and printers use. Some smaller 3D printers, like desktop models, can wear out easily.
3. Requires post processing—a possible pitfall of 3D printing is that the work may require extra work to finish. This might include sanding, heat treatment, or removing support imperfections.

Now that we have covered the basics of 3D printing, I hope in a way that is understandable, we can tackle the main focus of the chapter—how 3D printing has revolutionized healthcare supply chain.

The 3D printing technology has shown success in improving surgical techniques through the development of organ models, bone and joint implants, and precision instruments. Research is also underway to use the technology to manufacture medications, skin tissue, and organs.

The number of hospitals with in-house 3D printing facilities also is growing. In 2019, 113 hospitals had centralized 3D facilities for point-of-care manufacturing, compared with just 3 in 2010, according to a Statista report. Meanwhile, the FDA has approved hundreds of medical products made with 3D technology, according to Pew Trust. The 3D printing healthcare market increased dramatically during the COVID-19 pandemic, when some hospitals relied on the technology for the rapid production of PPE and medical devices.

Medical device manufacturers are increasingly using 3D printing to reduce costs to meet growing demand, prompting a healthier organization. Yes, some questions remain about just how commonplace 3D printing will become in healthcare and how will reimbursement policies work regarding these products.

There is one area where 3D printing has affected the healthcare supply chain—clinical care.

These are some of the methods hospitals and health supply chains have used to benefit from the existing technology, and 3D printing might transform clinical care in the future, in the form of implants and prosthetics, medical equipment, and anatomical models.

Dental implants were one of the first medically approved uses of 3D technology. The FDA has approved 3D technology to develop other complex implants. A 2021 study in the *Journal of the American Academy of Orthopaedic Surgeons* concluded that 3D printing has "significantly impacted bone and cartilage restoration". Thus, 3D printing has the potential to completely transform how we treat patients with musculoskeletal injuries. 3D printing technology can improve how prosthetics fit and function.

3D printing technology has reached the capability to produce highly accurate and detailed anatomical models. These models aid surgeons in preparing for difficult procedures, improve patient outcomes, and reduce costs. One study, from 2022, showed researchers at Florida Atlantic University and the University of Virginia designing a robotic model of the human spine to help surgeons perform the surgery. This study also showed that the use of these 3D models as surgical guides reduces surgical hours from over 3 hours to 1.5 or 2 hours, thus reducing expenditures.

The manufacturing of medical devices, such as forceps, clamps, hemostats, and retractors, is among the most common medical uses for 3D printing. A key benefit is that precise design modifications can be made rapidly from the surgeon's feedback. This technology is playing an influential role in the need for the rapid deployment of medical equipment, helping to mitigate supply chain challenges.

3D printing does represent substantial opportunities for clinical innovation. However, many healthcare institutions and the healthcare supply chains remain challenged by reimbursement procedures and safety issues related for integrating this new and budding technology into the highly regulated healthcare supply chain. There are still many questions unanswered for this embryonic industry and the healthcare supply chain. These are some of those questions:

1. What will reimbursement models be for 3D printing services and products?
2. Do the benefits of establishing in-house 3D manufacturing facilities outweigh startup costs?
3. How will FDA regulatory scrutiny pivot to meet the demand for 3D products?
4. What products fall outside of FDA oversight, and what potential risks might they present for patient safety?

Chapter 59

Hospital Bankruptcies and the Healthcare Supply Chain

Hospital bankruptcies can significantly impact the healthcare supply chain in several ways. These factors collectively highlight the complex relationship between hospital bankruptcies and the healthcare supply chain. The following are those factors:

- **Financial Strain**: Bankrupt hospitals may struggle to meet their financial obligations, leading to disruptions in their operations and services
- **Operational Challenges**: The bankruptcy of hospitals can create operational challenges, such as reduced staffing and limited resources, which may affect the quality of care and the ability to provide services
- **Supply Chain Disruptions**: As hospitals file for bankruptcy, it can lead to disruptions in the supply chain, including delays in receiving necessary medical supplies and equipment
- **Reimbursement Issues**: Bankrupt hospitals may face reimbursement challenges, which can further strain their financial stability and impact their ability to provide care
- **Long-Term Effects**: The ongoing trend of hospital bankruptcies could lead to a more fragmented healthcare system, with potential implications for access to care and overall healthcare quality

We will delve into all of these with more detail.

The healthcare industry has experienced significant financial distress in recent years, with bankruptcy filings reaching unmatched occurrences in 2023. In 2024, there was a slight decline in the number of bankruptcies, but filings remained above any pre-pandemic numbers. This clearly indicates that financial pressures remain industry wide. The key drivers including rising labor costs, supply chain challenges, reimbursement issues, and the change in patient care models have contributed to this development. Understanding the primary factors influencing these bankruptcies is essential for healthcare leaders—both medical and supply chain, policymakers, and investors.

The number of healthcare bankruptcies in 2024 dropped to 57, down from 79 in 2023 but still exceeding the pre-pandemic annual average of 42 filings. Senior care, hospitals, and

 DOI: 10.4324/9781003668732-68

pharmaceutical bankruptcies described nearly half of all filings, displaying persistent financial pressures in these industries. Clinics and physician practices experienced their highest bankruptcy rate in six years, with ten filings in 2024 compared to an annual average of four from 2019 to 2023. Meanwhile, hospital bankruptcies declined from 12 in 2023 to 5 in 2024, though the collapse of the Steward Health Care System, involving 31 hospitals, marked the largest hospital sector bankruptcy in 3 decades.

Several factors have contributed to the financial hardships seen across the healthcare industry. One of the primary drivers has been labor and supply cost inflation. While hospital wage growth slowed to 4% in 2024, workforce shortages continued to strain operations, especially in rural areas. The introduction of new staffing regulations for long-term care facilities has further increased financial burdens on providers.

Another major factor in bankruptcy is reimbursement challenges. Many healthcare providers rely on government payers, yet rate increases have not always kept pace with inflation. Medicare Advantage plans have been a growing source of financial strain, with an increase in claim denials impacting cash flow. For 2026, Medicare Part B will be $185 and hospital impatient rates will rise to about 3.2%. The math doesn't work!

Regulatory changes and capital market limits have added to the financial pressures. Interest rate reductions in late 2024 provided some relief, but healthcare refinancing and investment remain vague. The changing regulatory landscape, particularly regarding Medicaid funding and anti-trust policies, has added another unwanted layer of complexity for healthcare providers.

Due to these challenges, the position for healthcare remains mixed. Operating margins have slightly improved in 2024, but doubt remains whether or not profits will return to pre-pandemic levels. The hospital supply chain is increasingly divided, as some stronger hospital organizations have steadied, while financially weaker facilities continue to struggle. The trend of shifting care away from hospitals to outpatient, community, and home-based settings is expected to continue, and these will continue to change the landscape of hospitals and their supply chain.

In order to plot a route or plan through these financial pressures, healthcare organizations must focus on strategic cost management, revenue cycle optimization, and operational efficiency. Reviewing service portfolios, improving vendor contracts, and leveraging technology for automation can improve financial resilience. In addition, early and frequent meetings with financial and legal advisors can help providers develop proactive restructuring plans and explore potential partnerships.

Although the number of healthcare bankruptcies declined in 2024, financial challenges remain significant. Increasing labor costs, reimbursement issues, and ever-changing regulatory pressures will continue to affect providers across senior care, pharmaceuticals, physician practices, and hospitals. The ongoing shift toward outpatient and community-based care is further reshaping the industry, creating both challenges and opportunities. As healthcare organizations navigate these financial pressures, a proactive approach on cost management, operating efficiencies, and strategic management will be essential for long-term sustainability for hospital supply chain.

Chapter 60

Will Mergers and Acquisitions Improve the Healthcare Supply Chain?

Mergers and acquisitions (M&As) have become one of the better tools that hospitals use to increase patient access, quality of care, and manage risk and financial pressures. Partnerships, mergers, and acquisitions enable hospitals to expand service offerings, expand networks and access to specialists, improve quality, and better serve patients where they live. They provide growth to help reduce costs associated with obtaining medical services and supplies or prescription drugs, and enable health systems to reduce other operational expenses.

Let's take a closer look at mergers, hospital consolidations, and similar healthcare business transactions; the benefits of operational, financial, and clinical integration of resources; healthcare acquisition challenges; and the role of technology in paving the way for successful partnerships.

Health systems and hospital mergers have increased in the United States over the past decade. Some of the main drivers of hospital mergers are economies of scale, higher revenue, competitive advantage, and the need to expand service lines in the same market or new geographic markets. The reasons for health systems and hospital mergers vary based on the organizations involved, their operational and financial situations, and their goals for hospital consolidation.

It is not uncommon for larger hospitals or health organizations to engage in M&A transactions with smaller hospitals and other smaller healthcare providers to meet challenging patient needs. With patient care increasingly shifting from acute care hospitals to outpatient settings to reduce healthcare costs, a health system might acquire a local hospital that has ambulatory surgery centers or an extensive network of clinics in its market.

For those merged or acquired hospitals who are struggling financially, ownership by a larger hospital or health institution is a way to keep the "lights on". At the same time, the larger entity gains new markets, access to more patients and physicians, and more specific medical expertise in certain medical areas.

Analyzing healthcare merger trends and any associated benefits—cost, quality, an edge in marketing—from the perspective of the acquired hospital provides critical insight for the company's strategy. The reasons that they engage this tool are the following:

DOI: 10.4324/9781003668732-69

1. Lower health costs: Hospital acquisitions and mergers are associated with a markedly significant 3.3% reduction in annual operating expenses per admission at acquired hospitals.
2. Improved quality: In most mergers and acquisitions, this approach leads to better mortality and re-admission rates, with significant reductions in deaths from several conditions.
3. Better access to care: Almost half of all hospitals acquired by an academic medical center added one or more services, and these institutions also obtained improved access to secondary services.

While the benefits of mergers have been listed earlier, there are negative consequences on hospitals, providers, patients, insurers, and other stakeholders. Consider the following negative aspects and results:

1. Costs: Combined hospitals' services cost 31% more compared with care delivered by independent hospitals. For instance, private nonmedical ownership is often associated with harmful impacts on patients.
2. Quality: Hospital acquisitions are tied to unexceptional patient care and experiences. It is documented by the AHA that M&As increased readmission rates for cardiac patients by 10–12%.
3. Care access: Healthcare mergers have been known to restrict care and access when partnerships drive up costs, result in the closure of hospitals in rural areas, and prevent physicians from working for other health systems and local hospitals.

The advantages and disadvantages of mergers are not the only obstacle facing hospitals and their supply chain. Another obstacle is the FTC and government regulations. The U.S. FTC has increased their efforts to oppose healthcare mergers that do not meet the antitrust laws in this country. In 2022, the FTC forbade the following four hospital mergers, arguing that they could negatively impact prices and quality of care for patients:

1. Lifespan and Care New England Health System in Rhode Island
2. Hackensack Meridian Health and Englewood Healthcare Foundation in New Jersey
3. RWJ Barnabas Health and St. Peter's Healthcare System in New Jersey
4. HCA Healthcare and five hospitals in Utah—Steward Health Care System

The second largest area of expense for hospitals after labor is supplies. Successful integration of supply chain systems is a critical component of success. When health systems attempt to integrate acquired hospitals' supply-chain processes into their own, they are often faced with disjointedness and redundancies.

When considering a merger or acquisition, here are some supply chain components and systems that require full integration:

1. ERP System
2. Item Master
3. EHR System
4. Group purchasing organization

Everything discussed earlier is vital to the understanding of M&As. However, there are a few other key considerations that healthcare administration and supply chain leaders need to review.

1. Do not assume the FTC will fully recognize the benefits of a potential merger. Conduct a careful antitrust analysis and risk calculation before pursuing transactions.
2. So, from my standpoint, culture is not just important. It's critical! It seeps into every single aspect of the process.
3. In addition to the CEO, other executives must devote an equal amount of time and energy to the project. When C-level executives are reported being involved in merger integrations, companies were much more likely to capture cost and revenue goals.

Chapter 61

Supply Chain Is the Key to Non-Acute Care Expansion

Over 2025, the University of Chicago Medical School in conjunction with Cardinal Health has attempted to expand locations for non-acute care facilities. In 2026, through combined efforts, they expect to add one to two more non-acute physician practice locations. When this program began, one of the growth challenges was to support the non-acute sites with an acute organization structure and strategy.

As non-acute care sites multiplied, supply chain issues quickly came into focus. Teams identified a need for standardization in the non-acute operational methods for supplies and equipment as well as for inventory supply room standards. As well, they realized the need for frequent performance reviews.

The combined team recognized the need for a playbook or a strategic plan to guide them in the expansion. The team needed to communicate standardized processes, supplier decisions, and its new metrics to measure success and growth. With no administrative staff at any of the non-acute locations, the need for new clinical structures and governance quickly became apparent.

The University selected and partnered with Cardinal Health for several reasons. Cardinal Health already had significant non-acute experience that was helpful to the University to cross-reference supply lists.

The combined team sought to create and promote consistency of brand, appearance, and experience across its sites and, most importantly, ensure the reliability of its supply chain. In its attempt to make certain of success, they implemented the Lean and Six Sigma methodology.

Through these two methodologies, a site progression metrics was instituted that indicated a location's system readiness in terms of patient access and level of supply chain success. Of course, a lower number indicates the lack of access to technology and related supply chain issues that would indicate a need for greater support.

They recognized the need for a qualified or supply chain expert to ensure success at the sites. A designated supply chain lead was employed at each location to steer its new growth strategy. An existing system resource was placed into the new role, and establishing a focused leader was a key element to both speed and success of non-acute growth.

Perhaps, the best way to understand how these non-acute care facilities were created and operated is with the diagram shown in Figure 61.1.

DOI: 10.4324/9781003668732-70

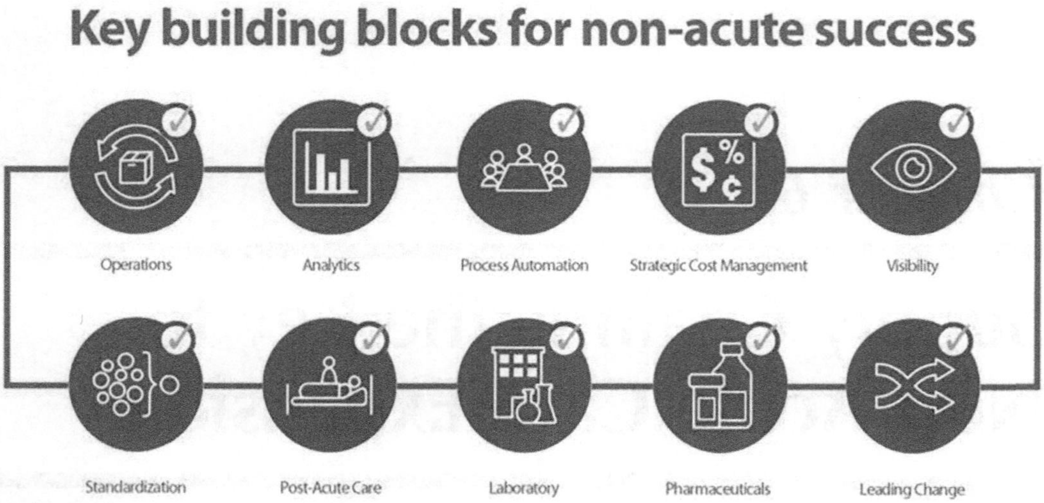

Figure 61.1 Non-acute care expansion.

This team realized the need for supply chain room standards, analytics, and supply chain support criteria. First, came the reorganization of the existing supply rooms and establishing an inventory system that was transferable and actionable at each location. Many existing locations had clinic cabinets with little supply organization, receiving rooms with no designated space for delivery placement and supply rooms where boxes were kept on the floor.

As sites were up and running, the team examined real-time analytics for maturing sites and performed routine supply room maintenance audits to provide complete visibility to off sites from a supply chain perspective.

The teams also created site-specific dashboards and began to evaluate fill rates weekly, analyzing lines by location to call out spikes and anomalies. This analysis demonstrated growth and its rate, helping the team to track trends in spend, line count, formulary compliance, and fill rate. With this information, the team was able to make adjustments in order levels to match care trends and tie orders to patient care.

The combined team has instituted four goals that all of its non-acute medical locations strive to support. They are quality of care, cost of care, delivery of care, and technology. The supply chain leader and team are seeking ways to be cost-efficient and at the same time deliver all medical supplies and equipment without any interruptions.

The team—University of Chicago Medical School and Cardinal Health—is leading the growth in this relatively new market. The combined number of employees of over 20,000 people support care at these non-acute facilities—four inpatient facilities, eight ambulatory care facilities, and more than 30 physician office locations. The system has come to manage 43,000 admissions and more than 1,000 outpatient encounters each year.

To support and grow this new market, the plan is to expand the established best practices and expand the model to additional ambulatory facilities. The team plans to implement standardized replenishment technology across all of its sites to streamline the supply ordering process.

Chapter 62

Workforce Strategies Transforming Healthcare Supply Chain

In an era marked by continuous innovation and an ever-changing health landscape due to the global economy, supply chains are confronting a triple threat: changing job expectations due to technologies like generative AI, variable consumer expectations, and global disruptions. As businesses continue to grapple with this situation, supply chains are swiftly transforming into autonomous and globally diverse networks to fortify their resilience in the face of these challenges. This transformation does not come without complications—the workforce must keep pace with this transformation for the future. This chapter will dive into the critical crossroads of supply chain adaptation and workforce evolution. It will showcase the need for upskilling the supply chain workforce with new leadership skills. Such an approach not only will allow the workforce to learn but will also ensure employees adapting to the ever-shifting demands of the supply chain.

Supply chain transformations will suffer without addressing the workforce implications. Organizations can maximize supply chain investments by advancing the supply chain talent.

New technologies, such as generative AI, will be key drivers in advancing automated supply chains. Integration of this technology into supply chains opens the door to different functions that can improve forecasting, resource allocation, risk management, and supply chain operational excellence.

This integration of AI into the workplace does not mean a wholesale replacement of humans. There is likely to be a percentage of tasks for every employee, which might be supported by AI tools—building an organization's capacity while better equipping employees. However, combining new technology with outdated processes often results in the maintenance of costly legacy systems that provide little benefit for both employees and customers. The enduring value of technology adoption is not solely derived from what the technology can accomplish, but rather from the enhanced capabilities it provides to the user.

All industries involved in healthcare will need to approach these advancements with humans at the center. Without training in emerging technologies, the talent gap will be further increased, and organizations will fail to realize the benefits of technology investments. Sustained success

DOI: 10.4324/9781003668732-71

requires organizations to shift their priorities from technology to people at the center of the technology strategy.

The global healthcare network will require upskilling or retraining in order to remain pertinent. Reskilling involves learning new skills outside of workers' existing skill sets which might lead to a different career path. To address skills gaps, both upskilling and reskilling will need to take place in the workforce. However, upskilling and reskilling cannot be a stagnant effort.

Digital technology is driving greater demand for workers who are comfortable and skilled using technology. Digital skills are becoming essential to every role, regardless of the industry or function. As organizations tackle reskilling and upskilling initiatives, creating a workforce with digital skills will be essential to remaining competitive in any industry. As a result, many organizations are investing in data and intelligence capabilities that provide real-time visibility into their organization's inventory or skills. Skills intelligence is empowering businesses by providing a centralized source of information about technology and business skills to identify areas that need to be revised and/or developed.

Supply chain leaders must be developed to help ensure a healthy leadership pipeline. With the shift to more independent and autonomous supply chains, it is paramount that leadership roles within supply chains change and have become even more complex. This new autonomy requires the new supply chain leaders to be experts in multiple areas of competency.

Today, supply chain leaders will be expected to develop their perspectives, maintain awareness, and possess a working knowledge of functions and technologies formerly outside of their purview. Digital automated supply chains will enable more intelligent and integrated data that provides visibility into all aspects of the supply chain. For leaders to exploit the power of this real-time data, it requires them to be competent in analytical and data-driven decision-making.

It is essential that healthcare organizations develop the skills of these emerging supply chain leaders as they are needed to fill critical supply chain roles. Training and promoting from within ensure there will be a pipeline and others are familiar with their way of working. Organizations with effective leadership development at all levels are more likely to rank higher for financial performance.

Today and in the future, supply chain workforces operate in a complex environment requiring diverse skill sets. Leading the healthcare institutions and or medical supply companies to future supply chain investments will require a cross-functional team of varied perspectives who can make team decisions.

As organizations upskill their supply chain workforce, adaptive skills will be important for all employee levels. Adaptive skills enable individuals to transform their abilities as their demands and environment change and unlock a competitive advantage.

New supply chain leaders should possess expertise in three major areas:

1. Domain knowledge: An end-to-end perspective encompassing the ability to understand how daily leadership decisions impact the broader supply chain, organization, and customer promise.
2. Strong leadership skills: Strategic thinking, effective communication, and team development with high trust.
3. Analytical decision ability: Employing data analysis and scenario-based decision engines to make informed strategic choices and solve problems effectively.

The best method to enhance and ensure success of the upskilling and reskilling of your employees is to create experience-based learning plans. The workforce will be engaged in achieving the skills necessary to operate the supply chain of the future.

Experience-based learning is not only important to driving business results but also widely valued among the workforce as a critical tool to drive and develop their own careers. The learners report valuing personalized course recommendations based on their own career goals and skills gaps, and it is a means to retain employees.

After establishing a dedicated employee development program, the next step is to create experience-based learning plans that cater to employees at all levels. It's crucial to collaborate with supply chain leaders to pinpoint proficiency and business-related needs within each step of the program and to develop usable templates based on the job level and function.

Crafting experience-based learning plans can empower employees at all levels to excel and adapt in the evolving supply chain landscape. Supply chain skills development must become a part of the DNA of your company. It should be deeply rooted as a requirement for future investments and, in addition, to ensure that the workforce is ready to implement and execute future supply chain strategies.

X

UNIVERSAL HEALTHCARE SUPPLY CHAIN VERSUS MARKET HEALTHCARE SUPPLY CHAIN

Healthcare reform, especially in the United States, has been a topic of debate for a number of decades. Recently, it has reached a zenith with the murder of a CEO from one of the largest market healthcare providers in the United States. Two terms often used to describe the discussion are "universal healthcare coverage" and "single-payer" system (for the purposes of this discussion, we'll call them "market system").

Sometimes, universal healthcare has been used to describe healthcare reform as "Medicare for All" plans or socialized medicine, but the reality is that there is no one-size-fits-all. Market systems can include universal coverage, but many countries have achieved universal coverage without a market system.

What follows in the next few chapters is the definitions of both systems with advantages and disadvantages of each. Following that will be discussions in detail as to how each system affects the healthcare supply chain.

DOI: 10.4324/9781003668732-72

Chapter 63

The Definition of Both Systems with Their Pros and Cons

Universal healthcare is a system that provides medical services to all people. The government offers it to everyone, regardless of their ability to pay, and it is largely funded through taxes. Universal healthcare offers free services, but participants may still pay premiums or copays.

In market healthcare systems, primarily in the United States, medical services are paid by the individual or by the patient's healthcare insurance company. Market healthcare is a system where there is minimal or no government interference aka regulation. In this minimal scenario, healthcare providers are free to provide services without needing to satisfy strict regulatory standards and requirements.

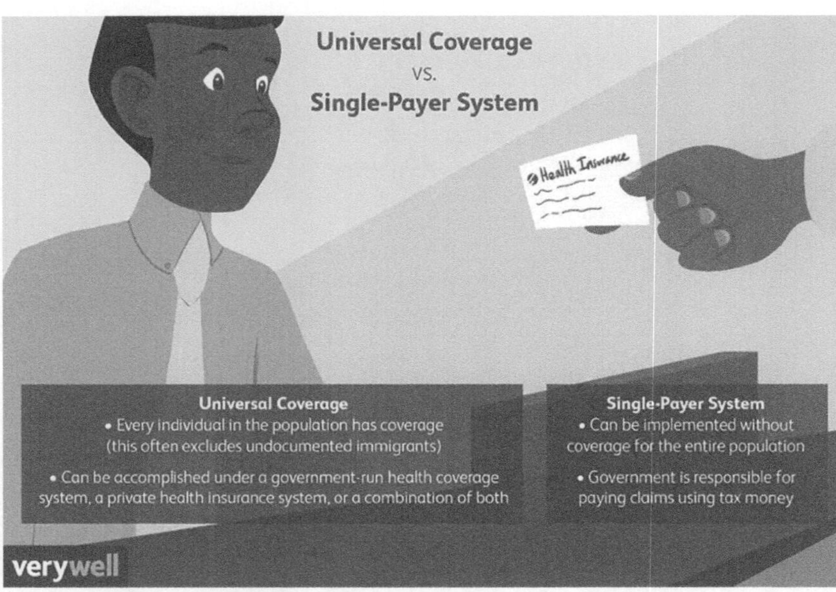

Figure 63.1 Healthcare system comparison.

DOI: 10.4324/9781003668732-73

Universal healthcare is undeniably expensive—the National Health System (England's version of universal health) is the largest single item of public spending by the UK government. Lack of coverage carries its own cost. In the United States, the uninsured are less likely to have a general practitioner and more likely to suffer from preventable diseases such as type 2 diabetes. Increasing preventative care results in better health outcomes on a society-wide level and increases productivity by lowering the number of workers forced out of the labor market due to illness.

Longer wait times for specialist care are common to government-run universal healthcare systems. However, there is no hard evidence that this problem of long waits is unique to countries with universal healthcare. The United States regularly ranks among the developed nations with the longest waiting times for medical care.

Ensuring everyone has access to medical care, regardless of their ability to pay, is the fundamental purpose of universal healthcare. This is not the case with market systems. In the United States, the healthcare industry is worth tens of billions and consistently breaks year-on-year profit records. However, in this scenario, there are thousands upon thousands who have put off healthcare due to cost.

Universal healthcare systems like the NHS in England gain huge benefits from using their collective purchasing sway to get better deals from drug manufacturers or medical suppliers. Market systems can easily become stuck in a cycle of mounting costs, where insurance firms, pharmaceutical companies, and healthcare providers all benefit from inflated pricing, at the expense of patients.

Finally, universal healthcare may have limited budgets dictated by the government. Due to those limited budgets, the state may not be able to offer treatments or medicines that are judged to be not effective or proven enough to justify the expense.

These are several of the key elements in a healthcare supply chain—inventory management, procurement, distribution and logistics, quality control, research and development, financing, and human resources (Figure 63.1). For each element, we shall attempt to gain an understanding of the differences in each healthcare model and their effect upon each.

Chapter 64

Quality of Care in a Universal Healthcare System versus a Market System

In either healthcare system—a market or universal—the quality of patient care has become tantamount. It is accomplished differently in each system due to the economics of each system. A short synopsis of how both operate financially will give a little better understanding.

Does the United States spending more on healthcare supply chain per person than other industrialized nations have a direct effect on the quality of patient care?

Using Figure 64.1, the question remains; does the United States healthcare spending per capita, more than other modern nations, have a direct impact on quality patient care?

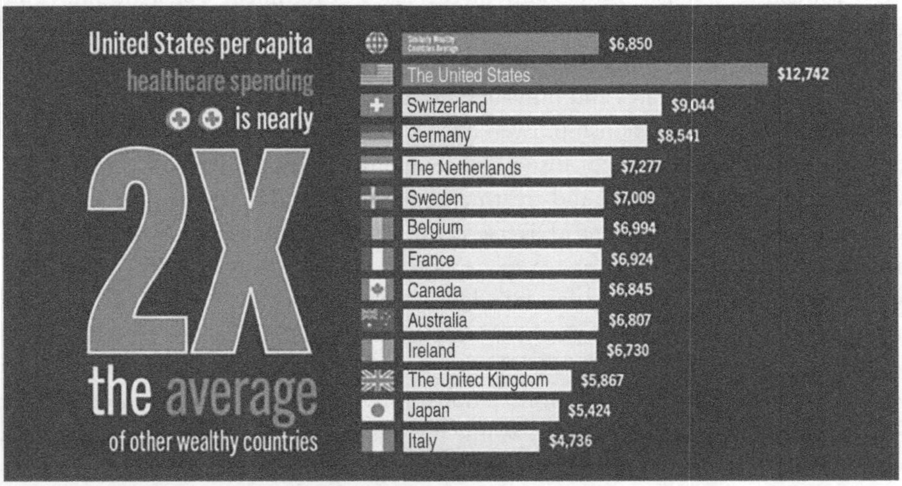

Figure 64.1 World in comparison to the U.S.

DOI: 10.4324/9781003668732-74

THE UNITED STATES SPENT $4.26 TRILLION ON HEALTHCARE IN 2021. WHERE DID IT GO?[20]

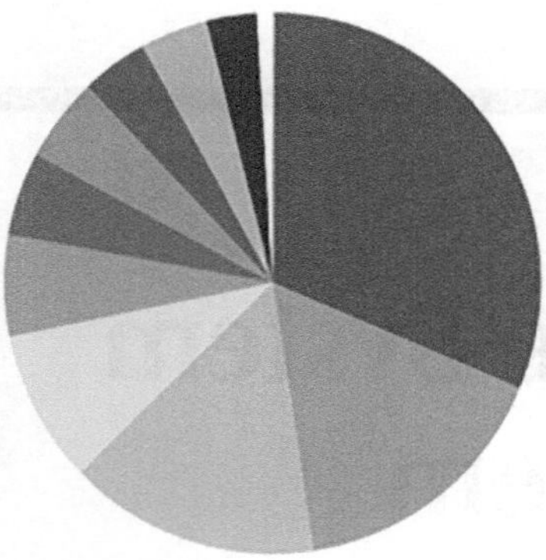

Hospital Care	31.1%	**$1.32 Trillion**
Other Personal Healthcare	16.0%	**$680 Billion**
Physician Services	14.9%	**$633 Billion**
Prescription Drugs	8.9%	**$378 Billion**
Net Cost of Health Insurance	6.0%	**$256 Billion**
Clinical Services	5.4%	**$231 Billion**
Investment	4.9%	**$207 Billion**
Government Public Health Activities	4.4%	**$188 Billion**
Nursing Care Facilities	4.3%	**$181 Billion**
Home Healthcare	2.9%	**$125 Billion**
Government Administration	1.2%	**$52 Billion**

Source: https://www.cms.gov/research-statistics-data-and-systems/statistics-trends-and-reports/nationalhealthexpenddata/nationalhealthaccountshistorical. Table 2, 9, and 10 in NHE Tables [ZIP].

Figure 64.2 U.S. breakdown of healthcare costs distribution.

Source: The U.S Department of Health and Human Services.

With the breakdown of healthcare costs (see Figure 64.2), in order to lower costs and achieve better outcomes for every patient, all healthcare stakeholders—supply chain leaders and those in the health professions—must be held accountable for the rising cost of care. Greedy practices such as unfair medical bills, exploitation of federal programs, and rampant exploitation by middlemen in the drug supply chain must end. Rising out-of-pocket costs and the lack of competition in healthcare markets—particularly the growing concentration between insurers, hospitals, and pharmaceutical companies—must find a solution. Increased government oversight and fundamental reforms are necessary to curb the existing waste, fraud, and abuse and lower costs for every patient.

Over the past few decades, the American healthcare system has evolved into a complex maze of large corporate conglomerates and bureaucratic processes, which has placed an increased pressure on the doctor-patient relationship. Even hospital mergers have failed to deliver the promised benefits. Thanks to the influence of insurance companies on doctors medical judgment, patient care has suffered with impersonal and treatments that are continually denied. Costs have risen, and the quality of care has declined. Diverse communities are at the most significant risk from these negative trends

The corporate healthcare model has failed. Why has it failed? It has left the most vulnerable parts of the population lacking the means to access and pay for ever more expensive services and treatments.

Over the last few presidential administrations, prescription drug prices have become a focal point for lawmakers and political leaders. While it is absolutely true that growing drug prices contribute to those costs, drug prices are not the only culprit of increased costs.

Can the U.S. government guarantee that adopting healthcare models from homogenous countries with smaller minority populations will hurt or help the underserved communities in the

United States? Is it possible that such legislation will diminish access and availability of medicines for our underserved communities? If we are committed to achieving more equitable health outcomes, such questions must be addressed.

Improving our healthcare supply chain system to deliver better quality care at lower cost is critically important to the U.S. long-term economic and fiscal well-being. The rising cost of healthcare with the lack of key improvements in the healthcare supply chain is one of the key drivers of our growing national debt.

Chapter 65

Human-Centric Healthcare Supply Chain

Whether in a market-based healthcare supply chain system or one revolving around a universal healthcare system, the idea of transforming both into a more human-centric system is the goal.

Human-centered design in healthcare supply chain is focused on developing an understanding of people and their needs and engaging all healthcare supply chain stakeholders in this pursuit.

Human-centered design is exactly what it sounds like: Putting humans at dead center of the design process. In healthcare supply chain world, this means bringing patients, clinicians, payers, and everyone else involved in any way into the conversation from the very beginning. This human-centered design operates with the principles of empathy and collaboration.

In human-centric design supply chains, the first step is to observe and speak to the actual users of the products. The goals are improved patient well-being, increased patient satisfaction, and reduced healthcare costs. A perfect example is a patient suffering from diabetes. These patients wear a device that frequently checks their insulin level. In order to design an effective medical instrument, there is a need to completely understand both the illness and the patient. A complete story of the patient's experience is required to design and produce such a technically sound device.

The healthcare supply chain is a complex system that makes product design and utilization not easy. There are many challenges to overcome, so now I will outline some of the leading issues that are holding back the design process.

Healthcare supply chain products are not just for physicians or patients. Others using these products are caregivers, hospital administrators, insurance companies, and healthcare workers. Each group or faction of the system has their own needs and perspectives on the system. A balance is needed when we are designing the human-centric processes. These balances include physiological outcomes, policies, how will they affect hospitals, and other healthcare enterprises.

Within healthcare supply chain, each stakeholder usually focuses on its own arena of expertise. This independent approach affects product design where companies are only thinking and concentrating on their little fiefdom as opposed to the entire picture. The result is technically remarkable products, but they are not universally adopted.

DOI: 10.4324/9781003668732-75

The human-centric design approach includes different points of views, backgrounds, and culture due to spending time with all participants in the system. After this participation, you can make any changes to ensure your human-centric design meets the needs of the entire population.

Human-centric design in any healthcare supply chain system—market or universal—develops direct connections between the many divisions and subdivisions of the healthcare supply chain. With the understanding of how products are used by all the stakeholders—patient, doctors, nurses, hospitals—the design can meet the needs of all the stakeholders.

Adoption and utilization are the primary concerns and objectives. The most modern technology is not useful if the stakeholders are not using it. Human-centric design in supply chain is supposed to tie together innovation and adoption. This embracing will create new possibilities and improve all facets of the healthcare supply chain.

Chapter 66

Challenges of Cost Management: Universal or a Market Healthcare Supply Chain

Healthcare supply chain costs are forecasted to rise globally for the third consecutive year. This persistent trend underscores the critical challenges faced by employers, insurers, healthcare providers, and healthcare medical manufacturers across the globe. The drivers of rising costs include increased utilization of services, rising pharmaceutical expenses, and innovations in medical technology. Addressing this issue requires a fine understanding of regional variations and targeted strategies to manage costs while maintaining quality care.

Several interrelated factors are driving the ever-increasing costs of the medical supply chain. Advances in medical technologies and pharmaceuticals play a dual role. On the one hand, they not only enhance patient outcomes but also contribute greatly to rising expenses. Breakthrough treatments often come at a premium, placing additional financial strain on healthcare systems and employers.

Another major factor is the increasing demand for healthcare services, which continues to outstrip supply—a combination of demographic shifts such as ageing populations and a growing emphasis on mental healthcare. Mental health services have seen particularly strong growth in utilization as societies are beginning to recognize the effects of not taking mental health seriously.

Public healthcare systems, already under pressure from rising demand, are often unable to keep pace due to resource constraints placed on them by their government. This pushes individuals toward private healthcare providers, which come with higher costs.

There are strategies that both systems are using to mitigate the increasing costs of healthcare supply chain—sourcing alternative providers, collaboration between public and private sectors, vendor partnerships, and digital health solutions. Controlling the costs that I mentioned above are worldwide issues.

DOI: 10.4324/9781003668732-76

The debate about which healthcare supply chain to choose—market or universal—is one of the most important and debatable subjects in the current political climate. It was ranked second in the list of important voting issues of the 2024 presidential election. Perhaps, the best way to understand the differences between a market system and a universal healthcare supply chain system is to compare the U.S. market system versus various other countries that have adopted the universal healthcare system and its supply chain.

The United States is one of only a very few countries that do not provide universal healthcare and the corresponding supply chain for their entire population. Only a very small fraction of the country's working population has public healthcare system—Medicare and Medicaid. American healthcare is too expensive for many as about 10% have no coverage and are not part of the supply chain. The U.S. multi-payer or market system has separate plans, separate providers, separate coverage, and separate deductibles, which have led to 8% of costs going toward administrative costs.

There are two plans being bandied about in Congress that, if either one is adopted, it would go a long way to universal healthcare. One is "Medicare for All", and the other is "Public Option". The former plan would create a single-payer or universal system that would allow a comprehensive coverage and do away with premiums, deductibles, and co-pays. It would also put a limit on price of drugs. The latter plan would allow Medicare to negotiate with pharmaceutical companies to reduce and hold the cost of drugs to ranges, with no penalties for preexisting conditions, and allow people to keep their private insurance, if so desired.

Now for comparison purposes, let's take some European countries—France, Germany, Switzerland—and one North American country, Canada. The one constant data throughout this comparison is that the populations of these other countries outlive the comparable U.S. population by two years.

France has a universal healthcare supply chain system and a compulsory one. In France, it is called Statutory Health Insurance and paid for through taxes such as payroll, income, and taxes on alcohol and tobacco.

Switzerland is a decentralized universal system. It is paid for by enrollment premiums, state taxes, social insurance contributions, and out-of-pocket payments. Swiss residents must buy basic coverage from private insurers covering doctor visits, hospital care, home care, and long-term care. Switzerland has lower government spending per capita than the United States.

Germany has a universal system with healthcare capped for those below a certain salary level, and those above that level have to purchase private insurance. This system is financed mostly by employees and employers. Employees donate 7.5% of the salaries into a healthcare pool which the employers match. All have access to the healthcare system, and there are strict limits on out-of-pocket costs.

Canada has free of charge and universal healthcare system. However, it is not under federal government restrictions. Each province creates their own healthcare system under guidelines of the Canadian Health Act.

Whether a nation's healthcare supply chain is a universal or a market one is not a "black and white" issue. There are many shades of gray such as government backing, public will, and basic financing structure, which must be extensively considered. There are clear advantages and disadvantages—as discussed—to a market-based or universal healthcare. In fact, there are some countries that have tried to adopt the best of both worlds.

Chapter 67

Is Innovation Suppressed in a Universal Healthcare Supply Chain?

One argument against universal health supply chain isn't so easy to dismiss—the argument about innovation and the cutting edge of medical care. In a universal healthcare supply chain system, the government seeks to limit spending through lower payments to pharmaceutical companies and other producers of medical supplies. This would lead to both less innovation and less access to the innovation that already exists.

If implementing universal healthcare supply chains could lead to less innovation and reduce the availability of high-tech care, that argument requires a leap of logic. The forces that produce innovation in medicine turn out to be a great deal more complicated than critics of universal coverage seem to understand. Whether innovation would continue to thrive under universal healthcare supply chain depends entirely on what kind of system we create and how well we run it. In fact, it's quite possible that universal coverage could lead to better innovation.

The single biggest source of medical research funding is the National Institutes of Health. Last year, this institute spent over $28 billion on research. This number accounted for almost one-third of the total dollars spent on medical research and development in this country. The majority of that money paid for the basic research might someday open cures for killer diseases like Alzheimer's, AIDS, and cancer.

National Institutes of Health has its own independent funding stream. During the late 1990s, President Clinton and the Republican Congress increased their funding substantially. This increase greatly enhanced their research ability. However, starting in 2003, President Bush and his congressional allies let their funding languish, even though the cost of medical research was increasing faster than inflation. The reason? They needed room in the budget for other priorities like tax cuts for the wealthy. The greatest threat to future medical supply chain breakthroughs may be the people who are trying so hard to fight it.

The best idea would be paying for innovation when it yields actual benefits to the supply chain. That is precisely what the leading proposals for universal healthcare seek to do. All of them would

DOI: 10.4324/9781003668732-77

establish independent advisory boards, staffed by leading medical experts, to help decide whether proposed new treatments or medicines can be put into the supply chain pipeline.

Of course, the idea of involving the government in these decisions is abhorrent to many in a market healthcare supply chain. The argument being the private sector is bound to make better decisions than bureaucrats in Washington. That may be true in economics, but healthcare supply chain is another matter. One feature of the market healthcare supply chain system is its relentless focus on short-term benefits. The for-profit healthcare medical industry—like the pharmaceutical and device industries—responds to Wall Street, which cares more about quarterly filings than long-term financial health. So there's relatively little incentive to spend money on the kinds of innovations that yield long-term, diffuse benefits.

Another advantage of a centralized healthcare is its ability to generate savings by reducing administrative waste. A universal coverage system significantly streamlines billing—either by creating one common form or by replacing basic insurance with one like Medicare. This one billing system will cut down on the need for so many insurance middlemen and would leave more resources for actual medical care and medical innovation.

Along with the issues we have discussed earlier, there has been an ongoing debate in the United States—whether universal healthcare is feasible and necessary in the United States. This debate circles around increased delivery time of medical services and lack of medical innovations. This debate is tied directly to the medical supply chain and those companies which supply the medical supplies and equipment.

The modern healthcare supply chain system is a maze of complex challenges. Innovation should be at the heart of medical progress. However, the present systems are supposed to support and nurture medical professionals. Instead, they often hold back their creativity and initiative. Financial incentives and systemic pressures in the medical field discourage innovation, favoring established, lucrative practices. This issue is particularly evident in certain specialties—oncology, cardiology, neurology, endocrinology, orthopedics, and radiology—where overdiagnosis and overtreatment for profit can occur.

Such is the case in dermatology. The overdiagnosis and overtreatment of common skin cancers such as basal cell carcinoma and squamous cell carcinoma have become prevalent. While being treatable, these conditions are sometimes handled to maximize financial gain rather than patient benefit. More profitable procedures are often favored over less-invasive, innovative treatments that might be just as effective.

As mentioned earlier, this is not an isolated to just one medical issue. Doctors are often pushed toward more lucrative procedures and treatments. This creates a cycle where the focus shifts from patient-centric care to profit-centric practices. As a result, innovative methods that could revolutionize patient care are sidelined because they don't align with healthcare institutions' financial goals.

This suppression goes beyond financial implications. There are organizational pressures, psychological dynamics, and costs of overdiagnosis.

With inflexible structures and protocols, the medical system tends to favor established practices over new and potentially disruptive ideas. Doctors who wish to introduce innovative treatments often face significant hurdles, including bureaucratic red tape, lack of funding, and resistance from colleagues accustomed to the status quo.

Supposedly, a doctor or a manufacturer of medical supplies wants to implement a new, less invasive technique for treating a common condition. Even if this new medical product has been proven effective in initial studies, getting it approved and adopted widely into the healthcare supply chain can be a daunting task. This discourages many doctors and medical manufacturers and pharmaceutical companies from pursuing innovative ideas.

The healthcare and medical community is not immune to the actions that influence society. Individuals and organizations naturally resist conformity and strive to bring innovative ideas to be accepted worldwide. Systemic structures within healthcare supply chain community aim to suppress innovation. Healthcare institutions which challenge the status quo may face professional isolation and outright hostility from their peers.

This resistance to change is deeply rooted in the healthcare culture. Healthcare supply chain is a field that values tradition and established knowledge. However, the emphasis on tradition can also create an environment where new ideas are viewed suspiciously.

The overdiagnosis and overtreatment of cancers serve as a harsh example of how financial incentives and organizational pressures can detract from patient care. While an early detection of any type of is crucial, the threshold for what makes up a positive diagnosis has been lowered to the point where benign lesions are often treated as malignant. This leads to unnecessary procedures and patient stress and diverts resources from innovative research and treatments.

Overdiagnosis can also have a flowing effect on healthcare costs. Unnecessary treatments drive up healthcare expenses, contributing to the overall financial burden on the system. This further reinforces the cycle of prioritizing profitable procedures over innovative care that could be more cost-effective and beneficial in the long run.

We need to break this cycle, but how to go about it? There are no simple answers, and it is not my intention to provide any. However, the current financial and systemic barriers need to be addressed to foster innovation. An important step is encouraging a culture that rewards creativity and new ideas as opposed to just profits. This includes funding and support for research into innovative treatments, streamlining the regulatory process for new medical technologies, and fostering an environment where doctors feel empowered to challenge the status quo without fear of retribution.

Medical institutions and policymakers must work together to create systems that prioritize patient well-being and support the introduction of new, effective treatments. This includes reevaluating how compensation and finances are structured to ensure they do not undermine innovative care.

Now, we will take a peek into the not-too-distant future and see what the future of the healthcare supply chain will look like and, by extension, the hospitals of the future.

Epilogue: The Optimistic Future of the Global Healthcare Supply Chain

There are numerous items to contemplate for the future of healthcare and its supply chain—financial pressures, digital transformation, workforce dynamics, counterfeit medical devices, and improving patient surgical readiness. Perhaps, the best approach is to limit our discussion to two to three of these issues. This will allow us to concentrate and zero in on how these issues will be addressed in the future.

The global healthcare supply chain is attempting to steer a course through a period of transformation fashioned by economic pressures, demographic shifts, and technological advancements. As shown in Figure 0.4, healthcare supply chains and systems throughout the world are facing increasing financial strain, workforce shortages, and changing patient needs. At the same time, digital innovation and regulatory reforms are redefining the care delivery. Leaders in healthcare supply chain must find a way to maintain equilibrium between efficiency and the goal of maintaining high-quality patient-centered care.

Figure 0.4 Balancing efficiency and cost of patient care.

DOI: 10.4324/9781003668732-78

This modern depiction of the world is the idea of how tenuous and unsure we are of what the future medical supply chain would look like. All we can do is use our best judgment to make an educated and objective decision.

The problems our healthcare supply chain and systems are facing now and in the future include poor quality of medical supplies, inadequate patient safety, and a misguided focus on acute care rather than on prevention and population health. The next decade will see considerable transformation in how health systems are designed, propelled by opportunities such as digital health, growing consumerism, and mounting financial constraints. This author discusses gaps and barriers in the current design of health and health systems and the needed escalation of transformation including transition from hospital-based systems to primary care, community, and social care-based systems.

Economic uncertainty and rising healthcare costs continue to lay significant pressure on global health systems. Ageing populations and the growing prevalence of chronic diseases are increasing demand for medical services and supplies, intensifying financial strain on governments, insurers, and healthcare providers. Many countries are grappling with how to fund their healthcare systems and supply chains while ensuring access to care for all.

To tackle these financial challenges, policymakers and supply chain leaders are implementing cost-containment strategies and alternative payment structures. These approaches prioritize patient outcomes over service volume and motivate for efficiency and effectiveness in healthcare delivery. Financial difficulties in many regions mean that necessary investments in healthcare infrastructure and workforce development may be difficult to prolong.

Yet, in spite of these financial pressures, health supply chains are expected to invest in new medical technologies, pharmaceuticals, and new care models to improve patient outcomes. Balancing cost control with the need for innovation remains a critical challenge. Collaboration between public and private stakeholders will be the driving force to ensure financial success, and that success does not come at the expense of high-quality care.

Digital transformation or automation of the global healthcare supply chain plays an increasingly principal role in global healthcare by offering solutions to challenges in economical, accessibility, and patient engagement. This digital age highlights the growing adoption of AI, remote monitoring, and predictive analytics to support clinical decision-making. These technologies have the potential to reduce costs, improve early diagnosis, and personalize treatments.

Telehealth has also gained momentum, in response to the COVID-19 pandemic, enabling patients to access care remotely. This shift has been particularly beneficial for those in rural and underserved regions, thus reducing geographical barriers to healthcare. However, this expansion of digital health solutions to those underserved has its drawbacks including disproportion in access to technology, data security risks, and concerns about the lack of integration between different healthcare systems.

Ensuring the success of digital transformation requires the synchronization of efforts between technology developers, healthcare providers, supply chain leaders, and regulators. Investment in secure and growth capability of the digital infrastructure is essential. This points to the cybersecurity risks and ethical concerns about AI-driven decision-making. Training healthcare professionals to effectively use digital tools will be crucial to maximizing the benefits of new technologies while maintaining the human touch in patient care.

Healthcare workforce shortages are a global issue made worse by the increasing patient demand, evolving care models, and an increasing aging population. Due to these three issues, burnout, high turnover rates, and skills gaps are becoming the major impacts to this industry.

In an attempt to stem this tide of challenges, many organizations are adopting workforce strategies focused on flexibility, well-being, and professional development. AI-driven automation

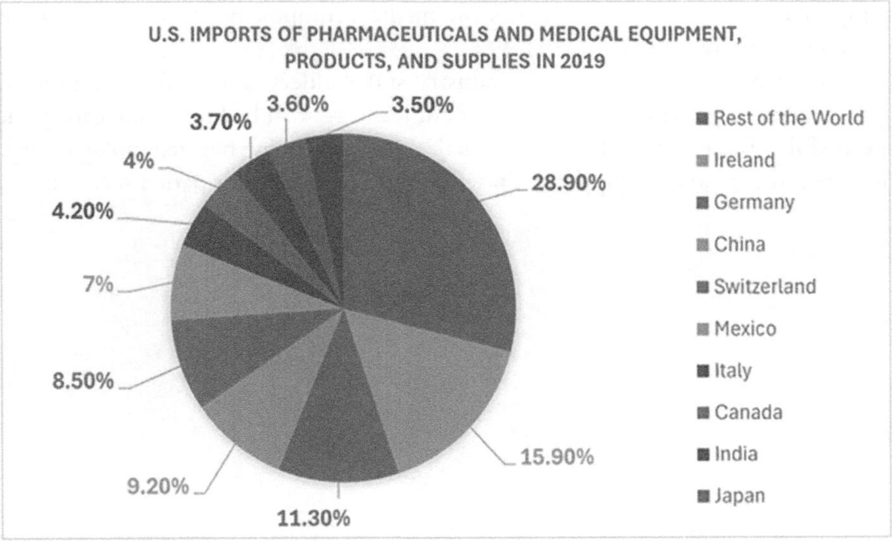

Figure 0.5 While this graph is from 2019, nothing much has changed, except for the percentages increasing.

is also being introduced to support healthcare professionals by reducing administrative burdens and streamlining workflows. AI-powered documentation tools and robotic process automation are helping to free up time for clinicians to focus on patient care. However, it cannot replace the need for a well-trained and motivated workforce.

Supportable workforce planning requires long-term investment in education and training. This investments will ensure that healthcare professionals and supply chain leaders are equipped with the skills to adapt to ever-changing care models. Policies that promote workforce retention, such as improved working conditions and mental health support, are vital to the success of this training. A resilient healthcare system depends on a workforce that is adequately supported, well-compensated, and empowered to deliver high-quality care.

Figure 0.5 depicts that the global healthcare supply chain is at a crossroads in facing these financial, technological, and workforce challenges. Healthcare leaders, whether medical or supply chain, need to embrace strategic innovations while maintaining a focus on patient well-being and equity. Digital transformation not only offers opportunities to improve efficiency and patient outcomes, but it also requires careful implementation and investment. Workforce transformation is a critical factor, and healthcare institutions needs to prioritize retention, training, and well-being.

Europe remains a key supplier of medical products, with Ireland emerging as a center for medical device manufacturing due to skilled labor and tax incentives. The leading European pharmaceutical firms like Roche, Merck KGaA, and Bayer dominate the global market. India is a major producer of generic drugs due to low labor costs. Indian manufacturers offer bulk drug production at significantly lower costs than U.S. manufacturers. China plays a crucial role in supplying active pharmaceutical ingredients and medical supplies. The United States imports billions of dollars in medical products from China, making it a key healthcare supply-chain partner.

The United States is utterly dependent on foreign production of essential healthcare products. Disruptions, weather related, geopolitical, or any international conflict, in the supply chain can severely impact access to essential medicines and medical equipment. The need for a more diversified approach is sorely required.

Collaboration between governments, industry stakeholders, and healthcare professionals—directly involved with patient care or supply chain leaders—will be key to navigating these challenges successfully. By attacking these inefficiencies and influencing new technologies successfully, the healthcare industry and its supply chain will build a future that is patient-centered.

Glossary

Additive Manufacturing: The construction of a three-dimensional object from a digital 3D model. It can be done in a variety of processes in which material is deposited, joined, or solidified under computer control, with the material being added together such as plastics, liquids, or powder grains being fused.

Anatomical Model: A three-dimensional representation of human or animal anatomy, used for medical and biological education.

Antimicrobial Resistance: Occurs when microbes evolve mechanisms that protect them from antimicrobials, which are drugs used to treat infections.

Artificial Intelligence: Capability of computational systems to perform tasks typically associated with human intelligence, such as learning, reasoning, problem-solving, perception, and decision-making. It is a field of research in computer science that develops and studies methods and software that enable machines to perceive their environment and use learning and intelligence to take actions that maximize their chances of achieving defined goals.

Autonomous Mobile Robots: A robot that acts without recourse to human control. Historic examples include space probes, self-driving vacuums, and cars. Industrial robot arms that work on assembly lines inside factories may also be considered autonomous robots, though their autonomy is restricted due to a highly structured environment and their inability to locomote.

Bar Codes: A method of representing data in a visual, machine-readable form. Initially, barcodes represented data by varying the widths, spacings, and sizes of parallel lines. These barcodes, now commonly referred to as linear or one-dimensional, can be scanned by special optical scanners, called barcode readers, of which there are several types.

Benchmarking: Used to measure performance using a specific indicator (cost per unit of measure, productivity per unit of measure, cycle time of # per unit of measure or defects per unit of measure) resulting in a metric of performance that is then compared to others.

Biopharmaceuticals: Any pharmaceutical drug product manufactured in, extracted from, or semi-synthesized from biological sources. Different from totally synthesized pharmaceuticals, they include vaccines, whole blood, blood components, allergenics, somatic cells, gene therapies, tissues, recombinant therapeutic protein, and living medicines used in cell therapy. Biopharmaceuticals can be composed of sugars, proteins, nucleic acids, or complex combinations of these substances or may be living cells or tissues. They are isolated from living sources—human, animal, plant, fungal, or microbial.

Blockchain: A distributed ledger with growing lists of records that are securely linked together via cryptographic hashes. Each block contains a cryptographic hash of the previous block, a timestamp, and transaction data. As each block contains information about the previous block, they effectively form a chain with each additional block linking to the ones before it. Consequently, Blockchain transactions are resistant to alteration because, once recorded, the data in any given block cannot be changed retroactively without altering all subsequent blocks and obtaining network consensus to accept these changes.

Bottlenecks: In production and project management, a bottleneck is a process in a chain of processes, such that its limited capacity reduces the capacity of the whole chain. The result of having a bottleneck are stalls in production, supply overstock, pressure from customers, and low employee morale. There are both short- and long-term bottlenecks. Short-term bottlenecks are temporary and are not normally a significant problem. Long-term bottlenecks occur all the time and can cumulatively significantly slow down production. An example of a long-term bottleneck is when a machine is not efficient and constantly breaks down.

Catheter Ablation: A procedure that uses radio-frequency energy or other sources to terminate or modify a faulty electrical pathway from sections of the heart of those who are prone to developing cardiac arrhythmias.

Center for Medicare and Medicaid Innovation: An organization of the U.S. government under the Centers for Medicare & Medicaid Services. It was created by the Patient Protection and Affordable Care Act. CMS provides healthcare coverage to more than 100 million Americans through Medicare, Medicaid, Children's Health Insurance Program, and the Health Insurance marketplace. The center is to test innovative payment and delivery system models that show important promise for maintaining or improving the quality of care.

Cold Chain: A supply chain technique that uses refrigeration to maintain perishable goods, such as pharmaceuticals, produce, or other goods that are temperature-sensitive. Common goods include fresh agricultural produce, seafood, frozen food, photographic film, chemicals, and pharmaceutical products. The objective of a cold chain is to preserve the integrity and quality of goods such as pharmaceutical products or perishable goods from production to consumption.

Demand Sensing: A forecasting method that uses artificial intelligence and real-time data capture to create a forecast of demand based on the current realities of the supply chain. Traditionally, forecasting accuracy was based on time series techniques which create a forecast based on prior sales history and draws on several years of data to provide insights into predictable seasonal patterns. Demand sensing uses a broader range of demand signals (including current data from the supply chain) and different mathematics to create a forecast that responds to real-world events such as market shifts, weather changes, natural disasters, and changes in consumer buying behavior.

Enterprise Resource Planning: The integrated management of main business processes, often in real time and mediated by software and technology. ERP is usually referred to as a category of business management software—typically a suite of integrated applications—that an organization can use to collect, store, manage, and interpret data from many business activities. ERP systems can be local-based or cloud-based. Cloud-based applications have grown in recent years due to the increased efficiencies arising from information being readily available from any location with Internet access.

Environmental, Social, and Governance: Investing principle that prioritizes environmental issues, social issues, and corporate governance. Investing with ESG considerations is sometimes referred to as responsible investing or, in more proactive cases, impact investing.

Epizootic Disease: An epizootic disease occurs in a specific locale more generally or becomes widespread. High population density is a major contributing factor to epizootics. The aquaculture industry is sometimes plagued by diseases because of the large number of fish confined to a small area.

European Medicines Agency: An agency of the European Union in charge of the evaluation and supervision of pharmaceutical products. Prior to 2004, it was known as the European Agency for the Evaluation of Medicinal Products or European Medicines Evaluation Agency.

Food and Drug Administration: A federal agency of the Department of Health and Human Services. The FDA is responsible for protecting and promoting public health through the control and supervision of food safety, tobacco products, caffeine products, dietary supplements, prescription and over-the-counter pharmaceutical drugs, vaccines, biopharmaceuticals, blood transfusions, medical devices, electromagnetic radiation emitting devices, cosmetics, animal foods and feed, and veterinary products.

Group Purchasing Organizations: Entities that are created to leverage the purchasing power of a group of businesses to obtain discounts from vendors based on the collective buying power of the GPO members. Many GPOs are funded by administrative fees which are paid by the vendors that GPOs oversee. Some GPOs are funded by fees paid by the buying members. Some GPOs are funded by a combination of both of these methods. These fees can be set as a percentage of the purchase or set as an annual flat rate. Some GPOs set mandatory participation levels for their members, while others are completely voluntary. Members participate based on their purchasing needs and their level of confidence in what should be competitive pricing negotiated by their GPOs.

Health Equity: Arises from access to the social determinants of health, specifically from wealth, power, and prestige. Individuals who have consistently been deprived of these three determinants are significantly disadvantaged from health inequities and face worse health outcomes than those who are able to access certain resources. It is not equity to simply provide every individual with the same resources; that would be equality. In order to achieve health equity, resources must be allocated on the basis of an individual need-based principle.

International Organization for Standardization: The organization develops and publishes international standards in technical and nontechnical fields, including everything from manufactured products and technology to food safety, transport, IT, agriculture, and healthcare.

Just in Case: A term sometimes applied to traditional manufacturing systems used before the influence of modern technologies and newer transportation infrastructures. It is the contrary in many ways to the recently evolved Just In Time manufacturing system.

Just in Time: This manufacturing approach tries to match production to demand by only supplying goods that have been ordered and focusing on efficiency, productivity, continuous improvement, and reduction of "wastes" for the producer and supplier of goods.

Kanban: A scheduling system for Lean manufacturing. Taiichi Ohno, an industrial engineer at Toyota, developed kanban to improve manufacturing efficiency. The system takes its name from the cards that track production within a factory. Kanban is also known as the Toyota nameplate system in the automotive industry. A goal of the kanban system is to limit the buildup of excess inventory at any point in production.

Lean: A method of manufacturing goods aimed primarily at reducing times within the production system as well as response times from suppliers and customers. It is closely related to another concept called just-in-time manufacturing (JIT manufacturing in short).

Machine Learning: A field of study in artificial intelligence concerned with the development and study of statistical algorithms that can learn from data and generalize to unseen data, and thus perform tasks without explicit instructions. Within a subdiscipline in machine learning, advances in the field of deep learning have allowed neural networks, a class of statistical algorithms, to surpass many previous machine learning approaches in performance.

Malware: Any software intentionally designed to cause disruption to a computer, server, client, or computer network; leak private information; gain unauthorized access to information or systems; and deprive access to information or which unknowingly interferes with the user's computer security and privacy. Researchers tend to classify malware into one or more subtypes (i.e., computer viruses, worms, Trojan horses, logic bombs, ransomware, spyware, adware, rogue software, wipers).

Material Safety Data Sheets: A document that lists information relating to occupational safety and health for the use of various substances and products. Safety data sheets (SDSs) are a widely used type of fact sheets used to catalog information on chemical species including chemical compounds and chemical mixtures. SDS information may include instructions for the safe use and potential hazards associated with a particular material or product, along with spill-handling procedures. The older MSDS formats could vary from source to source within a country depending on national requirements; however, the newer SDS format is internationally standardized.

Medical Science Liaisons: A healthcare consulting professional who is employed by pharmaceutical, biotechnology, medical device, and managed care companies. Other job titles for medical science liaisons may include medical liaisons, clinical science liaisons, medical science managers, regional medical scientists, and regional medical directors. The term "MSL" was originally trademarked by Upjohn as "Education services—namely, initiation of drug studies in laboratory and clinical settings and development of workshops, symposia, and seminars for physicians, medical societies, specialty organizations, academicians, in concert, concerned with drug related medical topics" in 1967 and with first use in commerce in 1967.

Medicines and Healthcare Products Regulatory Agency: An executive agency of the Department of Health and Social Care in the UK, which is responsible for ensuring that medicines and medical devices work and are acceptably safe.

One Health Joint Plan: The collaborative efforts of multiple disciplines and nations working locally, nationally, and globally to attain optimal health for people, animals, and our environment. It developed in response to the evidence of the spreading of zoonotic diseases between species and increasing awareness of the interdependence of human and animal health and ecological change.

Overstock: Excess inventory when there is more than the "right quantity" of goods available for sale, or when "the potential sales value of excess stock, less the expected storage costs, does not match the salvage value". It arises as a result of poor management of stock demand or of material flow in process management. Excessive stock is also associated with loss of revenue owing to additional capital bound with the purchase or simply storage space taken. Excessive stock can result from over delivery from a supplier or from poor ordering and management of stock by a buyer for the stock.

Predictive Analytics: In business, predictive models exploit patterns found in historical and transactional data to identify risks and opportunities. Models capture relationships among many factors to allow the assessment of risk or potential associated with a particular set of conditions, guiding decision-making for candidate transactions.

Radio Frequency Identification: This technology uses electromagnetic fields to automatically identify and track tags attached to objects. An RFID system consists of a tiny radio transponder called a tag, a radio receiver, and a transmitter. When triggered by an electromagnetic interrogation pulse from a nearby RFID reader device, the tag transmits digital data, usually an identifying inventory number, back to the reader. This number can be used to track inventory goods. RFID tags are used in many industries. For example, an RFID tag attached to an automobile during production can be used to track its progress through the assembly line, RFID-tagged pharmaceuticals can be tracked through warehouses, and implanting RFID microchips in livestock and pets enables positive identification of animals. Tags can also be used in shops to expedite checkout and to prevent theft by customers and employees.

Reshoring: The act of reversing an offshoring change—moving a business process that was offshored, back to the original country.

Robotics: Within mechanical engineering, robotics is the design and construction of the physical structures of robots, while in computer science, robotics focuses on robotic automation algorithms. Other disciplines contributing to robotics include electrical, control, software, information, electronic, telecommunication, computer, mechatronic, and materials engineering. The goal of most robotics is to design machines that can help and assist humans. Many robots are built to do jobs that are hazardous to people, such as finding survivors in unstable ruins and exploring space, mines, and shipwrecks. Others replace people in jobs that are boring, repetitive, or unpleasant, such as cleaning, monitoring, transporting, and assembling. Today, robotics is a rapidly growing field, as technological advances continue; researching, designing, and building new robots serve various practical purposes.

Saline: A mixture of sodium chloride (salt) and water. It has a number of uses in medicine including cleaning wounds, removal and storage of contact lenses, and help with dry eyes.

Standard Operating Procedures: A set of step-by-step instructions compiled by an organization to help workers carry out routine operations. SOPs aim to achieve efficiency, quality output, and uniformity of performance, while reducing miscommunication and failure to comply with industry regulations.

Statutory Health Insurance: A system of health insurance that insures a national population against the costs of healthcare. It may be administered by the public sector, the private sector, or a combination of both. Funding mechanisms vary with the particular program and country. National or statutory health insurance does not equate to government-run or government-financed healthcare but is usually established by national legislation. In some countries, such as Australia's Medicare system, the UK's National Health Service, and South Korea's National Health Insurance (NHI) Service, contributions to the system are made via general taxation and therefore are not optional even though use of the health system is. In practice, most people paying for NHI will join it. Where an NHI involves a choice of multiple insurance funds, the rates of contributions may vary, and the person has to choose which insurance fund to belong to.

Stock-Keeping Units: An inventory term. It is the unit of measure in which the stocks of a material are managed. It is a distinct type of item for sale, purchase, or tracking in inventory, such as a product or service, and all attributes associated with the item type that distinguish it from other item types. For a product, these attributes can include manufacturer, description, material, size, color, packaging, and warranty terms. When a business records the inventory of its stock, it counts the quantity it has of each unit or SKU.

Telehealth/Telemedicine: The distribution of health-related services and information via electronic information and telecommunication technologies. It allows long-distance patient and clinician contact, care, advice, reminders, education, intervention, monitoring, and remote admissions. Telemedicine is sometimes used as a synonym or is used in a more limited sense to describe remote clinical services such as diagnosis and monitoring. When rural settings, lack of transport, a lack of mobility, conditions due to outbreaks, epidemics or pandemics, decreased funding, or a lack of staff restrict access to care, telehealth may bridge the gap as well as provide distance-learning; meetings, supervision, and presentations between practitioners; online information and health data management and healthcare system integration. Telehealth could include two clinicians discussing a case over video conference; a robotic surgery occurring through remote access; physical therapy done via digital monitoring instruments and live feed and application combinations; tests being forwarded between facilities for interpretation by a higher specialist; home monitoring through continuous sending of patient health data; client to practitioner online conference; or even videophone interpretation during a consult.

U.S. Customs and Border Protection: The largest federal law enforcement agency of the United States Department of Homeland Security. It is the country's primary border control organization, charged with regulating and facilitating international trade, collecting import duties, as well as enforcing U.S. regulations, including trade, customs, and immigration. CBP is one of the largest law enforcement agencies in the United States. It has a workforce of more than 45,600 federal agents and officers. It is headquartered in Washington, D.C.

The U.S. Securities and Exchange Commission: An independent agency of the United States federal government, created in the aftermath of the Wall Street crash of 1929. Its primary purpose is to enforce laws against market manipulation.

Value Stream Mapping: A Lean management tool or method for analyzing the current state and designing a future state for the series of events that take a product or service from the beginning of the specific process until it reaches the customer. A value stream map is a visual tool that displays all critical steps in a specific process and easily quantifies the time and volume taken at each stage. Value stream maps show the flow of both materials and information as they progress through the process.

World Organization for Animal Health: An intergovernmental organization founded in 1924, coordinating, supporting, and promoting animal disease control. The primary objective of WOAH is to control epizootic diseases and prevent their spread. Further objectives include the sharing of transparent, scientific information; international solidarity; sanitary safety; and the promotion of veterinary services, food safety, and animal welfare.

Zoonotic Diseases: An infectious disease of humans caused by a pathogen (an infectious agent such as a virus, bacterium, parasite, fungi, or prion) that can jump from a non-human vertebrate to a human. When humans infect non-humans, it is called reverse zoonosis.

Bibliography

AHA Trustee Services, "List of Cost Factors That Understate Affordability", American Hospital Association, Washington, DC, 2021.
American Hospital Association, "Robotic Model of Human Spine", University of Virginia, Virginia, 2022.
Cardinal Health, "Save 25 Billion Annually through Proper Inventory Management", United States, 2014.
Counterfeits, "10% to 30% of Drugs Are Counterfeit", The Health Research Funding Organization, https://healthresearchfunding.org/
Gates, Geoffrey, Dr., "The Cleveland Clinic, Awarded the Number 1 Slot on Gartner's Healthcare Supply Chain Top 25 Companies", Self-Driving Vehicles for Moving Medical Materials, 2021.
Gibbins Advisors, "Hospital Bankruptcies: Full Year Report", Bankruptcies Declined, 2024.
Grand View Research, "Global Distribution for Healthcare", San Francisco, United States, 2024.
Harvieux, Tom, Supply Chain Officer, "5 Year Initiative to Drive Resiliency", BJC Healthcare of Missouri, St. Louis, 2023.
Jacobson, Nora, "The Dignity of Health", Science Direct, Ontario, Canada, 2013.
The Joint Commission, "Sustainable Healthcare Certification Program", U.S. Hospitals, Overland Park, Kansas, 2023.
Lang, Jim, CEO of Eversana, "Increased Cold Chain Capacity & Expenditures", North America, 2025.
Merrill, Patrick, MD, "3D Printing for Bone and Cartilage Restoration", The Journal of American Academy of Orthopedic Surgeons, California, 2, 30–35, 2021.
Milligan, Colin, "M & A's to Stop Financial Pressures", American Hospital Association, Washington, DC, 2025.
The NORC Center Poll, "The Public's Priorities and Expectations", The Associated Press & Center for Public Affairs, NORC Health at The University of Chicago, IL, 2023.
Radcliff, Bruce, Senior VP of Supply Chain, "On-Going Transportation Issues & Disruptions", Premier: Healthcare Performance Improvement, Charlotte, NC, 2024.
Schlosser, Michael, Dr., Chief Medical Officer at HealthTrust, "The Clinically Integrated Supply Chain", AHRMM, Chicago, IL, 2022.
Sinclair, Shane, "The Healthcare Compassion Model", BMJ Open, Canada, 1, 50–56, 2018.
The U.S. Secretary of Health & Human Services, "Healthy People 2030", The Office of Disease Prevention and Health Promotion, Washington, DC, 2022.
World Health Organization, "Definition of Health", World Health Summit, 2022.
Yancopoulous, Luka, CEO of Grapevine Technologies, "20% to 30% of Medical Supply Costs Are Mired in Warehouse Costs", Fairfield, CT, 2023.

Index

Note: Page numbers in *italics* indicate figures, and page numbers in **bold** indicate tables on the corresponding page.

I

J

K

L

M

N

O